SHELL GUIDES
edited by JOHN BETJEMAN *and* JOHN PIPER

CORNWALL
John Betjeman
DERBYSHIRE
Henry Thorold
DEVON
Ann Jellicoe and Roger Mayne
DORSET
Michael Pitt-Rivers
ESSEX
Norman Scarfe
GLOUCESTERSHIRE
Anthony West and David Verey
THE ISLE OF WIGHT
James Pennethorne-Hughes
KENT
James Pennethorne-Hughes
LEICESTERSHIRE
W. G. Hoskins
LINCOLNSHIRE
Henry Thorold and Jack Yates
MID WESTERN WALES
Vyvyan Rees
NORFOLK
Wilhelmine Harrod and C. L. S. Linnell
NORTH WALES
Elisabeth Beazley and John Brett
NORTHAMPTONSHIRE
Lady Juliet Smith
NORTHUMBERLAND
Thomas Sharp
SHROPSHIRE
John Piper and John Betjeman
SOUTH-WEST WALES
Vyvyan Rees
SUFFOLK
Norman Scarfe
WILTSHIRE
J. H. Cheetham and John Piper
WORCESTERSHIRE
James Lees-Milne
THE SHELL PILOT TO THE SOUTH COAST HARBOURS
K. Adlard Coles
edited by JOHN PIPER

*Michael Moriarty
part of a present from
the Justices' Clerks' Society
Sept. 1978*

WILTSHIRE

A SHELL GUIDE

A SHELL GUIDE
WILTSHIRE

by J. H. CHEETHAM & JOHN PIPER

Faber & Faber   3 Queen Square   London

First published in 1935
Second edition 1956
Third edition 1968
Reprinted 1975
by Faber and Faber Limited
3 Queen Square London WC1
Printed in Great Britain
by R. MacLehose & Company Limited
Printers to the University of Glasgow
All rights reserved

ISBN 0 571 04633 9

Shell-Mex and B.P. Limited are
not responsible for any expressions
of opinion by the authors of this guide

© 1968 by J. H. Cheetham and John Piper

ILLUSTRATIONS

Front endpaper
    Stonehenge
    John Piper

Frontispiece
    Stourhead: The Grotto, 1740
    Peter Burton

Title page
    Keystone of the northern gateway at Fonthill
    John Piper

Page		
8	Marlborough Downs	
	Barnaby	
	Marlborough Downs	
	Barnaby	
	Compton Down	
	A. F. Kersting	
9	Near Orcheston	
	Edward Piper	
10	Bulford	
	Edward Piper	
	Bulford	
	Edward Piper	
	Winterbourne Down	
	John Piper	
12	Steeple Langford	
	John Piper	
13	Middle Woodford	
	John Piper	
14–15	Overton Down	
	Barnaby	
16	Codford St Peter	
	John Piper	
17	Bradford-on-Avon	
	John Piper	
18	Malmesbury	
	Edward Piper	
19	Knook	
	John Piper	
21	Salisbury Cathedral	
	Mustograph	
22	Bromham	
	John Piper	
23	Lydiard Tregoze	
	John Piper	
25	Winterslow	
	John Piper	
26	Great Chalfield	
	Edward Piper	
	Westwood	
	John Piper	
27	South Wraxall	
	John Piper	
28–9	Longleat	
	John Piper	
30	Longford Castle	
	John Piper	
31	Wilton	
	John Piper	

Page
32 Stourhead
    John Piper
33 Wilton
    John Piper
35 Bradford-on-Avon
    John Piper
36 Limpley Stoke
    Edward Piper
37 Box
    Edward Piper
38–9 Westbury
40 Avebury
    John Piper
43 Winterbourne Stoke
    Ashmolean Museum
44 Avebury and Silbury Hill
    Ashmolean Museum
46 Bishopstone
    Ashmolean Museum
48 Wandsdyke
    Ashmolean Museum
51 Near Devizes
    Edward Piper
52 Cherhill
    Edward Piper
    Westbury
    Edward Piper
53 Alton Barnes
    John Piper
55 Alderbury
    John Piper
57 Alvediston
    John Piper
59 Avebury
    Barnaby
60–1 Avebury
    John Piper
63 Biddesden
    John Piper
65 Bishop's Cannings
    John Piper
66 Bishopstone
    John Piper
69 Bowood
    Edward Piper
70 Bradford-on-Avon
    John Piper
71 Bradford-on-Avon
    John Piper
73 Broad Chalke
    Reece Winstone
75 Bromham
    John Piper
76 Broughton Gifford
    Edward Piper

Page
77 Castle Combe
    A. F. Kersting
79 Charlton
    John Piper
80 Cholderton Church
    John Piper
81 Chitterne House
    John Piper
82 Colerne
    Edward Piper
83 Corsham Court
    Edward Piper
84 Corsham
    Peter Burton
85 Corsham
    Edward Piper
86 Corsham Court
    Edward Piper
87 Cricklade Tower
    John Piper
88–9 Devizes
    Edward Piper
90 Devizes, Long Street
    Edward Piper
    Devizes, Brownston House
    Edward Piper
91 Devizes, Market Place
    Edward Piper
92 Old Dilton Church
    John Piper
93 Dinton
    John Piper
95 East Grafton
    John Piper
96 Easton Knoyle
    John Piper
97 Easton Grey
    John Piper
98 Edington
    John Piper
99 Monument at Edington
    Edward Piper
101 Farley
    John Piper
102 Fonthill
    John Piper
103 Great Bedwyn
    John Piper
105 Hardenhurst
    John Piper
107 Above Heddington
    Edward Piper
108 Kingston Deveril
    John Piper
109 Kellaways
    Edward Piper

Page		Page		Page	
110	Lacock *John Piper*	135	Newton *John Piper*	163	Stonehenge *A. F. Kersting*
111	Lacock Abbey *Edward Piper*	136	Nunton *John Piper*	165	Stourhead *Reece Winstone*
112	Landford Church *John Piper*	137	Orcheston *John Piper*	166–7	Teffont Evias *Anthony West*
113	Littlecote *John Piper*	139	Quidhampton *John Piper*	168	Steeple Langford *John Piper*
115	Little Langford *John Piper*	141	Rodbourne *John Piper*	169	Tilshead *John Piper*
116–17	Longford Castle *John Piper*	142	Salisbury *John Piper*	171	Tisbury *John Piper*
118–19	Longleat House *John Piper*	144	Salisbury *Reece Winstone*	172	Bradford-on-Avon *John Piper*
120	Longleat House *John Piper*	145	Salisbury *Barnaby* Salisbury *Barnaby*	173	Tisbury
121	Longleat House *John Piper*			174	Westbury *Barnaby*
122	Longleat Stables *John Piper*	146	Salisbury Cathedral *Reece Winstone*	175	Wardour Castle *W. Henderson*
123	Lydiard Tregoze *John Piper*	147	Salisbury Cathedral *Mustograph*	176	West Dean Church *John Piper*
124	Monument at Lydiard Tregoze *A. F. Kersting*	148	Salisbury Cathedral *Peter Burton*	177	West Dean Church *John Piper*
125	Triptych at Lydiard Tregoze *John Piper*	149	Salisbury Cathedral *Edward Piper*	178	Westwood Church *John Piper*
		150	Old Sarum *Edward Piper*	179	Westwood Tower *John Piper*
126	Malmesbury *Edward Piper*	151	Savernake *Edward Piper*	180	Wilcot, Ladies Bridge *John Piper*
127	Malmesbury Abbey *Edward Piper*	152	Shaw Church *John Piper*	181	Wilcot, Ladies Bridge *John Piper*
128–9	Malmesbury Abbey *Edward Piper*	153	Sherston *John Piper*	182–3	Wilton House
130	Marlborough *Barnaby*	154	Sherston Tower *John Piper*	185	Winterbourne Stoke *John Piper*
132	Mildenhall Church *Oliver Frost*	157	Steeple Ashton *John Piper*	186–7	Wooton Basset *A. F. Kersting*
133	Netherhampton *John Piper*	158	Steeple Ashton Church *John Piper*	189	Yatton Keynell *Edward Piper*
134	Dinton *John Piper*	160–1	Stonehenge *Reece Winstone* *A. F. Kersting*	*Back Endpaper*	Silbury Hill and the Bath Road

FOREWORD

The first edition of this book was published over thirty years ago, in April 1935, edited by Robert Byron who was drowned at sea during the last war. The late Edith Oliver wrote most of the original gazetteer, which was revised and enlarged in 1956 by David Verey. In the present edition, the gazetteer has again been re-written and much expanded.

Robert Byron's original introduction is retained where still appropriate. He was an original observer and ahead of his time as a writer; but changes in landscape and townscape, revisions of principles by archaeologists, and other causes have clearly dated his work here and there.

Many incumbents and owners of country houses have been kind and helpful. So too have librarians, local councils, booksellers and other Wiltshire residents. The Rev. B. F. L. Clarke has provided information about 19th-century churches and stained glass. The description of Stonehenge in the gazetteer is by Myfanwy Piper. J. P. Gaudin and David Bland kindly read the proofs and both made useful suggestions. Julia Cheetham and others acted as uncomplaining drivers and companions in all weathers.

The *Victoria County History* volumes and the Proceedings of the *Wiltshire Archaeological and Natural History Society* have been of much service, as have the *Little Guide*, Geoffrey Grigson's *Wiltshire* (1957) and, of course, *Wiltshire* in the *Penguin Buildings of England* Series by Professor Pevsner.

A record of any mistakes of fact will be gladly received by the editor through the publishers.

J. H. CHEETHAM
JOHN PIPER

For further reading on Wiltshire archaeology the following are recommended, besides the above general reading:

Atkinson, R. J. C., *Stonehenge*, 1956.
Beresford, M., *The Lost Villages of England*, 1954.
Fowler, P. J., *Wessex*, 1967 (Regional Archaeologies).
Grinsell, L. V., *The Archaeology of Wessex*, 1958.
Hudson, K., *The Industrial Archaeology of Southern England*, 1965.

INTRODUCTION

"WILSHIRE", says Camden, writing at the end of the sixteenth century, "which also pertained to the Belgae... is altogether a mediterranean or mid land county. For enclosed it is with Somersetshire on the West, Berkshire and Hampshire on the East; on the North with Glocestershire; and on the South, with Dorsetshire, and a part of Hamshire. A region which... is exceeding fertile, and plentifull of all things, yea, and for the varietie thereof, passing pleasant and delightsome."

Today the county enjoys a various reputation. The old, recalling what their fathers said, term it a rich country, referring thereby to the splendour of its country seats and the then prosperity of agriculture. The middle-aged, on the other hand, regard it as a poor county, sunk in apathy and sloth. The young, or the young in mind, disdain these material categories. To them, it is a new discovery, a beauty-spot fragrant to the soul, which fulfils the twin conditions of such a title: convenient access from London, and an appearance of reposeful good taste unblemished by mountains, cliffs, lakes, moors, or any other dramatic natural features. This discovery, though still only in its early stages, threatens to overwhelm the eastern part of the county with the fate of Sussex and the Cotswolds.

To those who inhabit Wiltshire, its geography is not so prosaic as must appear to the passing

The Wiltshire Landscape
opposite, 1 and 2: *Marlborough Downs*
3: *Compton Down, south-east of Devizes*
below: *Near Orcheston*

The Plain Landscape developed: *By the Army at BULFORD Camp*

motorist. The county is roughly oblong in shape, and stands vertically on the map, being 54 miles long by 37 broad. But for the north-west and south-east corners, where the landscape is less distinctive there occurs a succession of grass uplands, cleft by narrow valleys and the larger vales. These uplands occupy three-fifths of the county's total area. They fall into four groups, of which Salisbury plain is the chief. To the north of the plain, separated from it by the Pewsey vale, are the Marlborough downs, which extend into Berkshire as far as Wantage. These boast, in Tan Hill, the highest point in the county, 958 feet. The two other groups lie to the south-west of the plain, one divided from it by the Wylye valley, the other following the course of the river Ebble.

The chief rivers are the Thames, which forms the northern boundary of the county; the Kennet, which flows into the Thames, and thus into the North Sea; the Somersetshire Avon, which rises in the north-west of the county and flows into the Bristol Channel; and the Salisbury Avon, of which the Ebble, Nadder and Wylye are tributaries, and which flows into the English Channel.

The distribution of population is based on the rivers and the low ground beside them. The uplands are deserted, save by sheep, racehorses, and tanks – seasonal occupants. Thus there is an air of mystery about them. Their outline is always visible, provoking a perpetual curiosity as to what goes on up there atop these harmonious, domestic Pamirs. Across Salisbury Plain, which measures roughly 20 miles by 12, there has never been a railway.

The outstanding beauty of the county is the landscape of the uplands, an ocean of rolling grass, over which the cloud-shadows play like a cinematograph – an ocean suddenly frozen, as it were, into green cliffs, whose pastoral escarpments guard the valleys and vales like giant fortifications. These are nature's contribution. Among the works of man the county is unrivalled in the monuments of two widely separated epochs: those of pre-history, such as Stonehenge; and those of the 16th and 17th centuries, the golden age of English taste and invention. Sporting amenities, agriculture, and a few industries, complete the scene. The latter are chiefly at Swindon, a place whose existence is regretted by those who seek the beautiful without reference to human development. This sentiment may be shared by the tourist; to the resident it is unacceptable.

Since this was written (in 1935) the landscape of Salisbury Plain has changed a good deal. It had always been said, until the war, that tillage was not a proposition on the Plain; that the chalk would at once absorb the tilled top-soil. This has proved to be untrue, and thousands of acres are now under cultivation which had been grass uplands from time immemorial. The landscape has been changed also by the addition of many a silo, dutch barn, broiler house and shed in iron or concrete placed (because they are agricultural) without planning permission, and not by any means always in positions undamaging to views. Large scale farming has removed hedges and hedgerow trees. There is development on the outskirts of most villages, and by "infill" in the centre of many; double-decker buses are visible far and near on the long roads of the Plain. Wiltshire is a traditional resting place of the Army and the Royal Air Force and was more scarred by all the appurtenances of war – except bombing – than any other county between 1939–45. Many scars, along with derelict huts, broken runways, overgrown dumps, remain. But Wiltshire remains also. It keeps the relationship, quite personal to it, of bare downs falling into shallow fertile valleys, where trees, churches, barns, houses, streams with many bridges over them to cottage

and otherwise, at WINTERBOURNE DOWN, north-east of Salisbury

The Wiltshire landscape: river-valleys. above: *STEEPLE LANGFORD*. opposite: *MIDDLE WOODFORD*

gardens, streams that wander in water-meadows and often widen into watercress beds: a relationship immediately recognizable as characteristic and local to the native, or the noticing visitor. The nearest parallels are probably with parts of southern Yorkshire, or the chalklands near the Normandy coast or in the Pas de Calais; but in fact Wiltshire is indelibly, unforgettably Wiltshire. In the north and the west where Gloucestershire and Somerset impinge, where the bottoms are deeper and more wooded, the slopes steeper, and the buildings of stone – the landscape of Castle Combe or Slaughterford – the county still has a character of its own, somewhat less cosy and West-country in feeling than its neighbours. The influences of neighbouring counties that spread into Wiltshire, in fact,

make the only marked deviations from the norm. There is the Bath, Badminton, Cotswold invasion – the Wiltshire of golden lichened stone, wooded bottoms, primrose dells and, in terms of the horse, the hunter rather than the courser. There is the Hampshire–Wiltshire of yew woods and beechwoods on the downs and of hanging woods above many-hedged flinty fields and brick and stucco Georgian and Victorian houses, south-facing, in small parks – the landscape of Tidcombe, West Dean and Chute. It is non-military country, and unspoiled. Then there is Somerset-and-Dorset Wiltshire; long, largely-wooded undulations that roll towards Cranborne Chase and beyond Stourhead Park to Alfred's tower – one of the true outposts of the West Country. And of course there is Wiltshire of the main roads, the anonymous roads of the long journey, speed, the lorry and the traffic jam.

The Wiltshire downs, particularly in the Marlborough district, are dotted with large stones, called Sarsen stones or Grey Wethers. They lie incongruously about the turf and have been described as "startling reminders of the marvellous aqueous action whose denuding force has been so active hereabouts". Some have been artificially arranged in circles; though with what object, how, and by whom, several centuries of speculation have failed to determine. The chief of these circles are those of Avebury and Stonehenge. Others, of lesser interest, are found at Hackpen and Winterbourne Bassett. They change the "feel" of the landscape by their presence, and they have become part of the scenery, along with the great earthworks, Whitesheet, Yarnbury and the rest, and even the barrows on the skyline. These are Wiltshire's earliest architecture.

The church of St Lawrence at Bradford-on-Avon is a complete Saxon church founded by St Aldhelm, who died in 709, and whose "churchlet" is mentioned by William of

Sarsen stones on OVERTON DOWN

Malmesbury. It was heightened and otherwise altered in the 10th century. By degrees its ecclesiastical functions lapsed in favour of the parish church adjoining; it became known as the Skull House; and it was not until 1856 that it was rescued from various secular uses and disentangled from the surrounding buildings. In appearance it resembles a double dog-kennel, the height of the chancel being greater than its length. Inside are sculpted two angels. The chancel was originally cruciform. One transept remains on the north. In place of the other are now two buttresses. But the roof-line of the missing transept can be plainly seen.

The churches of Britford and Burcombe contain Saxon work. And at Ramsbury, created a West Saxon bishopric in the year 909, the church contains a series of stones carved with interlacing patterns, which were exhumed from the foundations of a Saxon church. A few other churches contain Saxon fragments and sculptured stones – those at Colerne, Codford St Peter, Inglesham and Knook pretty grand ones (though Knook, say the archaeologists, may belong to the years just after the Conquest).

The finest Norman work in the county is at Malmesbury, and the carvings on the porch constitute a great work of art. The church whose porch they adorn is only the fragment of a larger edifice erected in the 12th century. It is the end of the Romanesque; already the round arches are soaring heavenward, and soon they will point as well. But the apostles, who occupy two lunettes on either side of the present vestibule, betray no such transition of artistic purpose. They follow the formulas current in Eastern Europe since the 9th century, even to the text-scrolls upheld by the angels above them. But within the limits of these formulas there is a life and characterization peculiar to the artist – and, we

Saxon sculpture at CODFORD ST PETER

BRADFORD-ON-AVON Saxon church, the east end

might say, to English art in general. These robust old men, whose stately attitudes are portrayed in sumptuous relief, have little in common with the wilting asceticism and angular carving of their Gothic successors. We detect, in fact, a tendency exactly opposed to the artistic canons of the later Middle Ages: a reversion to Hellenic naturalism.

The inner and outer doorways of the Malmesbury porch also have carving, including biblical scenes in decoratively arranged circles that have elongated figures of surpassing elegance and beauty, though they are badly weathered.

Wiltshire otherwise has not a great deal of showy 12th-century work, but St John's, Devizes, is a good restored Norman church and so is Manningford Bruce, though it speaks as strongly of Victorian J. L. Pearson as it does of its Norman architect; and there are about the usual number of carved doors

Romanesque carvings on the outer door of the porch at MALMESBURY Tympanum at KNOOK

and fonts in the county. Also there is some splendid early stained glass at Wilton, which came from abroad – one panel at least from Abbot Suger's cathedral at St Denis.

Salisbury Cathedral was begun in the year 1220 and the main structure was finished about thirty years later. Twenty years afterwards the cloisters and chapter-house were added. The spire, though undoubtedly part of the original conception, was not added until 1330.

A Frenchman once described English cathedral architecture as mere plumbing. This phrase, if somewhat inappropriate to the interior of Salisbury cathedral, is certainly explained by it: the whole expression of the building lies in its clustered pillarettes and pipe-mouldings. But of all Gothic interiors, this and that of Seville rank first in their particular kind of expression – an affirmation of classic order and harmony, of a design completely realized, unromantic, and at once apprehensible. This affirmation, in Salisbury, is accented by the glistening dark green of the Purbeck marble pillarettes, capitals and bases that enclose the main columns. Nor is it obscured by the colour-play of Victorian stained glass. Cold, precise and pure, the inside of Salisbury cathedral stands as a monument to the mastery of the senses by the intellect – but by an intellect of the highest aesthetic perception.

There used to be rich-coloured medieval stained glass, but it was removed and largely destroyed. Certain fragments have been disinterred and reinstated piecemeal. Only grisaille glass remains of the original, and this is magnificent, but lacking in needful colour.

The roof of the chapter-house is supported on a single, central pillar of Purbeck marble, whence rises a great spout of tracery. The base is carved with delicious small animals. Round the walls are other carvings which depict the remoter events of the Old Testament and are mainly modern. The stained glass, by Ward, is Victorian, but a worthy effort in "restoration".

The cathedral is best seen, if permission can be obtained, from the Palace lawn. There it sits, surrounded entirely by grass, like a crown on velvet, impeccable in its general mass and in the tapering lift of its spire.

Potterne and Bishop's Cannings have remarkable Early English churches, though the architecture of the latter has to be read internally through the obscuring light of a tremendous late 19th-century restoration. Amesbury also belongs to the 13th century. Among 14th-century works the tower and spire of the cathedral and the church of Bishopstone are the prime examples, but it is not otherwise much of a 14th-century county, for though fine building stone was available (the cathedral and many of the churches are of Chilmark stone) sheep farming and promoting did not become popular and profitable on the Plain until the 15th century, when grand churches began to appear of a kind to vie with those of the Cotswolds – Edington, Bromham, Lacock, Steeple Ashton, Colerne, the lesser churches in Salisbury, and many others. Of these Edington is the most satisfying, but it stands somewhat apart, having been founded by the Bishop of Winchester as a collegiate church, and was not dependent on local prosperity. Bromham and Steeple Ashton are the showiest. At Bromham the Baynton chapel has a mass of complex heraldic and other carving, inside and out, and at Steeple Ashton the whole fantastic composition (which had a spire until the 17th century) is a wedding cake of pinnacles, battlements and other trickings. Inglesham in the flat meadows of the upper Thames is a remote and "unimportant" church (though it is now visited by archaeologists for its early carving of the

opposite: SALISBURY Cathedral: the nave looking east, before the recent removal of the Victorian screen

p. 22: A detail of the perpendicular south chapel at BROMHAM

p. 23: The 17th-century screen and east window at LYDIARD TREGOZE

Virgin and Child) where, more than in any other Wiltshire church, it is possible to recall and "feel" medieval atmosphere. For this we have to thank William Morris, who lived at Kelmscott nearby, and looked after it through the perilous period of the late 19th century. "Ten years ago", says Byron in our first edition (that is, 1925) "a fiddle still accompanied the evening service."

Lydiard Tregoze evokes the 17th century better than any other church in Wiltshire, though the fabric is Perpendicular. The furnishings and monuments are the thing here, together forming one of the great aesthetic experiences of southern England. At Farley, on the Hampshire border, was born Sir Stephen Fox, the paymaster, and grandfather of Charles James Fox. In 1688 he enriched his now tiny hamlet with a red-brick church whose character resembles that of Wren's churches in the City of London. He knew Wren, because he had to do with the building of Chelsea Hospital, and he may well have asked him to provide the design for the church. At West Dean are extraordinary baroque monuments.

The county is thin in 18th-century churches. The chapel at Wardour, by Paine and Soane, and John Wood's church at Hardenhuish are the most complete. Georgian furnishings, with or without box pews, are rather more frequent. See Mildenhall for a complete and well-carpentered Gothick interior, and Old Dilton for unrestored-village-church atmosphere. For early 19th-century flavour Orcheston St Mary can be recommended, and for High Church, Tractarian, there is nothing to beat Cholderton, where Newman's brother-in-law was incumbent, and the passionate builder. Though Leigh Delamere vies with it.

The Byzantine grandeur of the town church at Wilton (by Wyatt and Brandon) apart, Pearson's Sutton Veny is the most impressive Victorian church. His churches at Chute and Chute Forest are also memorable – the latter in a sorry condition at present. There are several Butterfield churches, and a few by G. E. Street. But T. H. Wyatt was the great Wiltshire Victorian builder and restorer. He was much less drastic than is commonly supposed, and was more sensitive to atmosphere and feeling than many of his active contemporaries. C. E. Ponting, with his mannered churches in a Perpendicular Arts and Crafts style ushers in the 20th century, which up to now has not produced anything remarkable in the way of churches.

Unexpected churches disclose the best monuments (some of them unconnected with great houses). For Elizabethan richness of detail Lacock and Ludgershall are to be recommended; for 17th-century imagination and fantasy Lydiard Tregoze and West Dean are unmatchable. The one-legged, praying, Baroque figure at West Dean, comforted and encouraged by a fluttering cherub, all in a dark niche behind brass doors, is unforgettable. Clyffe Pypard has a big marble tomb of 1786 to a carpenter who made money, and his tools of trade are carved below the figure.

Among early houses, King John's House at Tollard Royal is remarkable – partly 13th century. At Clarendon, excavations terminated by the Hitler war had begun to reveal the foundations of a palace of Henry III, which was one of the largest buildings of the 11th century in Western Europe; but after some interesting finds had been made the site went back to nature. The list of late medieval domestic buildings includes Lacock Abbey and Wardour Castle (the first added to, the second a ruin), the enormous thatched stone barns at Tisbury and Bradford-on-Avon, and the story-book picturesque manor houses of South Wraxhall, Great Chalfield and Westwood.

The Tudor and later big houses are, more than

opposite: "Wyatt was here". T. H. Wyatt, diocesan architect, restored many churches in the county in the 19th century, such as this one at WINTERSLOW

Three Medieval Manor Houses
p. 26, 1: GREAT CHALFIELD; 2: WESTWOOD
p. 27: SOUTH WRAXALL

usually, inseparable from their landscape – they belong not only to their own parkland but to their whole surrounding countryside. Littlecote is a quiet assemblage of brick and tiled Elizabethan gables, rising among the surrounding trees, that tells a tale of long continuity. In its chalk valley, flanked by beech copses near the Berkshire border, haunted, maybe, by ghosts and legends but also by its own human story, it resembles Stonor Park not far away in a Chiltern fastness. Longleat, an Italianate palace in a vast wooded countryside, executed in a stone of whitish buff which age has suffused with gold, and set on a plateau of park rolling away from wooded hills, presents a supreme picture of that domestic environment, that combination of splendour, repose, and unadvertised resources which is peculiar to our island and which has nourished so many of the islanders' most individual characteristics. Longford, in a wide river valley near Salisbury, is a triangular house built by John Thorpe for Sir Thomas Gorges, whose tomb in Salisbury Cathedral has astrological symbols. It was built, maybe, in honour of the Trinity, as was the triangular lodge at Rushton in Northamptonshire. It is a fascinating house in its flat Avon-side park, and Spenser may have been thinking of it when he described the Castle of Temperance in the *Faerie Queene*.

Inigo Jones may have designed the grand entrance to Fonthill from Fonthill Gifford. Rutter, an early 19th-century topographer, says he did so, and it looks like his work.

Another remarkable work of the early 17th century is the Hall, Bradford-on-Avon, "the ornate residence of a lesser squire". Corsham Court keeps only the centre of its south front from the original building of 1582. When the Methuens bought it in 1745 it was greatly enlarged and altered, partly to accommodate a large art collection. Also of the 16th, or

LONGLEAT

earliest years of the 17th century, are Charlton Park near Malmesbury, Keevil and Lake House near Amesbury – the latter largely destroyed by fire and rebuilt by Detmar Blow.

Wilton, seat of the Herberts, remains the glory of the 17th century. Already, in the preceding age, it had acquired literary associations (as the home of Sir Philip Sidney's sister, that great patron of the poets, Mary Countess of Pembroke), with Ben Jonson, Massinger, Spenser and Sir Philip Sidney, to whom Queen Elizabeth, visiting the place, presented a lock of her hair; and possibly even with Shakespeare. Aubrey says it was Charles I who suggested the rebuilding of part of the old house in classical form. Inigo Jones was approached, and his son-in-law Webb supervised the work. When it was finished Charles II observed that the Double Cube room was the best proportioned room he knew.

To turn from Wilton to Ramsbury Manor, which was designed by Webb, Inigo Jones' son-in-law, is to exchange the great in art for

WILTON: The Inigo Jones façade, from the south

LONGFORD CASTLE:
A photograph that shows its triangular plan

the pleasant. Yet how pleasant, how beautiful it is, this unobtrusive red-brick dwelling, with its perfect symmetry and its windows spaced, if more domestically, yet with something of the genius that characterizes the greater house. Comparable to Ramsbury, though on a smaller scale, is Mompesson House in the Close at Salisbury, the town house of a local squire without the pretensions of a nobleman's seat. Biddesden was built at the beginning of the 18th century in the reign of Queen Anne. But its spirit is typical of the preceding age.

Wiltshire is also rich in houses and gardens of the 18th century. The chief house of the period, Bowood, has been so interfered with since its original erection by Robert Adam that only the Mausoleum retains any general coherence. This is considered by some to be the Adams' finest exterior work, and cer-

WILTON: The Palladian Bridge

STOURHEAD

tainly has a strength and severity unusual in his designs. The gardens here still have much splendour.

Those at Stourhead provide magnificent landscape and water effects, enhanced by classical temples, urns, and "other adjuncts of the pastoral environment under strict control". Another garden ornament of renown is the Palladian bridge at Wilton, a covered bridge of exquisite design and entrancing frivolity.

Other first class examples of Georgian architecture are the houses at Stourhead, Trafalgar and Wardour, the saloon at Corsham Court and the many fine town houses in Salisbury, Devizes, Trowbridge, Warminster and Bradford-on-Avon, besides many smaller country houses, good examples being Belcombe Court near Bradford-on-Avon by the elder Wood of Bath, and Iford Manor, also near Bradford.

The remarkable creations of the 19th and 20th centuries in the county are not great houses or churches but the industrial developments that came in the service, and the wake, of the canals and the railways. But Wiltshire had a long industrial history, anyway, even if it was "cottage" industry. When Edward III invited Flemish weavers to England a number of them settled in Wiltshire, at Bradford-on-Avon, Corsham, Trowbridge and Westbury, Marlborough and Salisbury. At this time the mill at Eliot, near Marlborough, was in use as a fulling mill. Some contemporary stone houses with weaving lofts exist at Corsham and Bradford and elsewhere. The weaving of broadcloth, which received a fresh impetus from Paul Methuen's second importation of Flemings in the 17th century, continued until the middle of the last century. Records and tombs preserve the memory of many benefactions by wealthy clothiers. The late 18th century saw the end of weaving in the cottage home. To the early years of the 19th century belong factories which then took over, comparable with those of Derbyshire, Yorkshire and the Stroud Valley. The Frome valley had many mills. Tellisford and Stowford are worth visiting for their mills, workers' cottages and clothiers' houses. Dryden's antique warehouse at Malmesbury is a grand 18th-century silk mill.

Bemerton was an active centre for paper making for three hundred years from the mid-16th century. At Slaughterford, near Chippenham, the rag mill, which produced the "stuff" to be made into paper, was first established as a weaving mill in medieval times. At the end of the 18th century came the canals. The Thames and Severn Canal, with its long tunnel, was finished ten years before the 18th century ended, and crosses the north eastern corner of the county. It joins (or joined, for the tunnel has had a collapse) the Thames near Inglesham with the Severn below the Stroud valley. The Kennet and Avon Canal was being made when the next century was born. John Rennie designed it, and built some fine aqueducts and bridges on its course between Newbury and Bath – especially near Bath. The best of these is the Dundas aqueduct, which crosses the Avon below Bradford. This canal bisects Wiltshire from east to west. It has the spectacular flight of twenty-nine locks outside Devizes. The Wilts and Berks Canal (Abingdon to Trowbridge) and the North Wiltshire (only 9 miles from Swindon) are shorter and dimmer; tracing the course of them would provide some wonderfully remote walks. The best canal buildings, at Honey Street, near Alton Barnes, on the Kennet and Avon, have lately been pulled down (1967), but there is still a big Victorian boatmen's inn there. Cuttings for the Salisbury Canal, which was to link Salisbury with Andover, can be seen at East Grimstead. The cuttings only got as far as Alderbury when the promoters ran out of cash in 1798.

Brunel's Great Western Railway to Bristol came in the early forties. J. C. Bourne's *History and description of the Great Western Railway* (1846) with its large lithographs,

BRADFORD-ON-AVON, 19th-century Gothic factory

shows the romance, the grandeur, the skill, the ingenuity and the attention to detail of the enterprise. The Victorians saw it all as new empire building, and Bourne pictured it as a Piranesi of the Industrial Dawn. The countryside might be in the process of being ravished; but mankind was being benefitted, if not saved.

The railway blew Swindon up from a small town to a near city, being mid-way between Bristol and Paddington. Its mid-19th-century architecture and planning is still impressive. (There is an industrial estate of 300 houses in the Tudor style built from the stone excavated from Box tunnel.) Millions of bricks were made in a field outside Chippenham to line Box tunnel; the western end of the tunnel is self-supporting, being hewn through the rock. The entrance is triumphal.

Life in modern Wiltshire might be said to be chiefly governed by the horse, the pig, the railway and the motor tyre. Training, stud-farming and hunting constitute an industry, and one that has influenced the landscape as well as the life of the county. The pig created modern Calne. Mr Harris started curing bacon here in 1770, on premises which may still be seen. For all but two whole centuries his name, attached to every product of the pig, has been carried into every corner of the world. The railway made Swindon, and has deeply affected Chippenham, where the Westinghouse brake works were established in 1932. Motor tyres are made in vast quantities at Melksham and at Bradford-on-Avon. Wilton, as all the world knows, makes carpets, Devizes makes snuff and tobacco, Melksham and other places now deal in a big way with milk. These industries, as well as modern building, the increase in population and the commuting habit have caused changes in the face of the landscape; but it remains still recognizable, and full of character.

pp. 38/39: *Looking north-west from Bratton Camp, WESTBURY*

ROBERT BYRON
JOHN PIPER

Rennie's Dundas Aqueduct at LIMPLEY STOKE

BOX: One of Brunel's triumphal tunnel entrances on the G.W.R.

ARCHÆOLOGY by ANNA BACHELIER

No OTHER county is so rich in archaeological sites. Ploughing has taken a big toll, but a great many remain. Most of them are accessible, and to visit them means walking over some of the grandest grasslands in England: though some are on War Department land and can be visited only when the flags are down.

The potential of Wiltshire for the study of man's early history has been recognized by antiquarians since the 16th century; indeed, the development of archaeology itself is bound up closely with the discovery and interpretation of Wiltshire field monuments. This early interest was also a disadvantage, for it caused the destruction without record of many sites, especially round barrows or tumuli. The opening of barrows was a popular amusement for sunny afternoons during the 18th and 19th centuries.

Traces of the very earliest periods of settlement, Palaeolithic and Mesolithic, are rare. Apart from a few scattered finds from the chalk uplands, objects attributable to the Palaeolithic period (Old Stone Age) occur in river valleys. Several flint hand axes of the lower or earlier Palaeolithic period have been found in the gravels of the river Avon near Salisbury and at Knowle Farm near Savernake. These tools represent the traces of nomadic peoples dependent for survival on hunting along forested river valleys. There is no certain upper, or later Palaeolithic, material. During the following period, the Mesolithic, beginning about 7500 B.C., Wiltshire seems still to have been sparsely populated; traces of flint working have been found near Chippenham, near Fovant and on Windmill Hill near Avebury.

The geological formation of Wiltshire is a predominant factor in explaining the concentration of settlement in the county. After the Mesolithic period the geographical distribution of settlements depended on natural environment, for early communities were restricted by the limitations of their tools to areas where the soil was easily worked. Chalk was good, since it carries light and well-drained soil. These chalklands have rivers and streams, and water is not a problem except in areas over 650 feet above sea level and then only during dry summers. On the lower chalklands are many dry valleys carrying seasonal streams or bournes (hence the "winterbourne" of many place-names). On the chalk, too, after the final retreat of the ice about 8000 B.C., the climate became warmer and drier, and forests gave way to open grasslands. By the end of the Mesolithic period, the chalklands must have looked much as they do now, though with more woodlands in river valleys and on downs where a capping of heavy clay-with-flints covers the chalk.

The arrival in Britain about 3200 B.C. of Neolithic colonists from the continent, who practised agriculture, marked the beginning of the area's intensive settlement. Communities were no longer entirely dependent on hunting, fishing and gathering wild crops, and were, therefore, no longer migratory. They settled in chosen areas, cleared the land, cultivated barley and wheat and raised cattle, sheep and pigs. Increased food production and food storage meant a bigger population; this created a surplus of labour available for the construction of monuments. For the first time, elaborate funerary and ritual structures were raised.

Scattered over the downs are many barrows, circular and oblong. Long barrows are Neolithic graves. One end of the mound is normally wider than the other and covers the burials; the chalk rubble for the mound was dug out on either side, forming ditches, now silted up. Excavation has shown that the bones of more than one person were buried beneath the mound, and that they were protected by a low timber hut until the time

AVEBURY: The Avenue

came to pile up the chalk mound. The total number of long barrows and the labour required to build them indicate that they must represent the family vaults of chieftains. Well preserved examples are those just south of Tilshead (e.g. SV 022476; 11), the Beckhampton barrow (SV 087693; 8), the Corton barrow south of Heytesbury (ST 932404; 14) and those near Stonehenge on Winterbourne Stoke, Lake and Normanton Downs (e.g. SV 100415, 108402, 115417; 14).

Instead of timber mortuary houses, some of these long barrows cover stone-built chambers in which successive burials could be made after the construction of the surrounding mound. These stone structures are carefully built with large slabs and dry stone walling. At West Kennet (SU 105677; 8) an excavated example has been reconstructed by the Ministry of Works. There are five chambers opening off an entrance passage, and the semi-circular forecourt in front of the entrance is lined and sealed by large upright slabs of sarsen stones. These sarsens occur naturally on the surface hereabouts, and it is worth walking over the Marlborough Downs to see them. Other stone-chambered barrows (with fewer visible traces of stonework) are at East Kennet (SU 116668; 8), Adam's Grave on Walker's Hill above Alton Barnes (SU 113635; 8), Lanhill near Chippenham (ST 8875; 4) and Lugbury near Castle Combe (ST 8379; 4).

Not far from West Kennet are three earthwork enclosures known as causeway camps, of the same period as the long barrows. They are enclosed by one or more circular or oval banks and ditches interrupted by causeways. The best, Windmill Hill, near Avebury, (SU 0871; 8), has three enclosing lines of discontinuous banks and ditches. The one on Knap Hill (SU 122637; 8) has a single bank and ditch, and there is another under the later hill-fort on Rybury Hill (SU 084640; 8). These camps were neither domestic nor defensive but seem rather to have been social meeting places, perhaps for festivals.

Windmill Hill has been extensively excavated and showed traces of temporary occupation, including deposits of animal bones, perhaps the remains of feasts. Pottery and stone axes from as far afield as Devon indicate how far people travelled to these festivals. Other causeway camps are Robin Hood's Ball on Salisbury Plain (SU 103460; 14), and Whitesheet Hill (ST 804346; 13).

There is little structural trace of domestic life at this time, but Wiltshire must have been a great centre of spiritual life for more than a thousand years, for it is extraordinarily rich in ritual monuments. The focal areas are Avebury in the north and Stonehenge in the south. Avebury is the older, and may have been the scene of ceremonies connected with the construction of Stonehenge, since the big sarsens at Stonehenge came from the area. The stone circles and surrounding ditch and bank at Avebury were linked by an avenue of standing stones to the site of another, smaller, sanctuary on Overton Hill. This was destroyed at the beginning of the 18th century. It consisted of two concentric rings of standing stones four circles of timber posts within them. Evidence suggests that it had a ritual connection with the burials in the West Kennet long barrow. Traces remain of three other stone circles at Day House Farm near Coate (SU 182824; 6), at Winterbourne Bassett (SU 095755; 5) and below Thorn Hill south of East Kennet (SU 118658; 8). The last has an avenue of stones leading from it a short way to the east.

Stonehenge must have become more important than Avebury after about 1800 B.C. The earliest structure was a circular bank and ditch with an inner ring of small pits, and to this were later added an earthwork avenue leading up to the entrance, and, inside, circular and horseshoe settings of standing stones. Apart from the erection of the stones (the heaviest weighs fifty tons), their transport to the site presented formidable problems. The biggest, of sarsen, came from the Marlborough Downs, but many of the smaller,

WINTERBOURNE STOKE: *Barrow group*

igneous, stones came from the Prescelly Mountains in Pembrokeshire.

Avebury and Stonehenge are "henge" monuments, earthen banks and ditches, with or without an inner stone circle. There is another henge site two miles north-east of Stonehenge at Durrington Walls (SU 150437; 12), a circular bank and ditch, and there is a similar one at Marden in the Vale of Pewsey (SU 091584; 8/11). Immediately south of Durrington Walls is Woodhenge (SU 151434; 12). Excavation here revealed six concentric inner rings of holes which had held wooden posts, probably meant to support a roof; the circles have been reconstructed with small concrete posts marking the position of the timbers.

About half a mile north of Stonehenge is the Stonehenge cursus (SU 120430). The name was first given by the 18th-century antiquary William Stukeley, who thought such enclosures must have been racecourses. It is a hundred yards wide and $1\frac{3}{4}$ miles long, and it is likely to have been a ceremonial processional way. It was probably earlier than Stonehenge, and the presence of ten long barrows nearby supports the idea.

Building and alterations at Stonehenge continued for five hundred years until about 1400 B.C. During that time customs changed. The knowledge of copper and gold working was brought to Britain by settlers from the continent about 1800 B.C.; copper-working led to the use of bronze, and a new economic era of widespread trade and advanced tool and weapon manufacture began. Stonehenge apart, the visible traces of these early bronze-using people are abundant in the many hundreds of round barrows. These are now grass grown and the ditches have silted up, but one can often see the position of the ditch as a slight depression or as a band of darker, more lush, grass. The mound contained the body of one person, with pottery food containers, bronze tools or weapons, or jewelry of gold, amber or blue glass *faience*. 1600–1400 B.C. was a wealthy period in Wiltshire and north Dorset, the Wessex Culture period; burials have produced objects from the east Mediterranean and central Europe, and traces of trade contact with Scandinavia and Brittany. One of the best known of these rich burials came from a round barrow in the group on Normanton Down: Bush Barrow (SU 118413; 14). A man had been buried with possessions including two large bronze daggers, one of which has an elaborately decorated gold haft, the bone mounts and stone head of a sceptre similar to one found in a contemporary royal grave at Mycenae in Greece, and decorated gold ornaments.

The most spectacular monument of this period is the huge mound of Silbury Hill between Marlborough and Calne (SU 100686; 8). This mound, 130 ft. high, has a surrounding ditch and looks like an enormous barrow. It has been suggested that it may be the burial place of the chieftain responsible for the final building of Stonehenge and for the wealth of Wessex at that period. If this is so, the grave-goods accompanying the burial may be outstanding in richness, but full-scale excavations have yet to be done.

About 1500 B.C., in the middle of this wealthy

AVEBURY and SILBURY HILL

period, the burial rite changed gradually from inhumation to cremation, but burials continued in round barrows (or were inserted into older barrows) for at least the next four hundred years. These were the graves of important men and women, not of the entire population. Scattered among groups of barrows are some of a more unusual form, sunken instead of raised; large circular hollows surrounded by low banks, they seem to have played a special part in the ritual attached to these barrow cemeteries. This type is known as a pond barrow; there are several fine examples on Lake Down near Amesbury (SU 1040; 14), and another closer to the road among the group at Winterbourne Stoke cross-roads (SU 1041; 14) just over a mile to the west of Stonehenge.

We know a good deal about burial customs in the early Bronze Age, but it is not until about 1400 B.C. that we find traces of domestic life apart from bronze tools. Despite the material wealth in the graves of their chieftains, Wiltshire people in the Early Bronze Age must have lived in unpretentious settlements, probably clusters of small timber houses. After 1400 B.C., however, the outlines of domestic life become increasingly clear. People lived in enclosed farmsteads as family units, reared cattle, sheep and pigs, and ploughed fields for grain. Itinerant craftsmen kept them in touch with the developments in bronze tools and weapons, and pottery was produced locally. In the course of stock-raising, these people constructed small earthwork enclosures as animal pens, of which there are examples on the Marlborough Downs to the north of the road from Marlborough to Broad Hinton. To prevent animals from wandering over cultivated areas, ditches were dug over the downs, separating pasture from arable fields. One such system may be traced, in the triangle of downland between Everleigh, Ludgershall and Amesbury. Linear ditches with banks were also made at this period as boundaries between communities; the longest runs from the downs above Warminster eastwards for twelve miles until it joins another at right angles on West Down, east of Tilshead. This ditch is visible south and east of Tilshead and on Knook Down (ST 9544) between Chitterne and Heytesbury. A longer walk would trace the two ditches along the slopes on either side of Water Dean Bottom, south of Charlton (SU 0953; 11).

On the tops and slopes of downs one can often see squares and rectangles, like patchwork, formed by low banks. They stand out well in the evening when the sun is low, and are visible from a distance, especially from the air, as lighter or darker bands in the landscape or crop, even when ploughed flat by modern cultivation. These are the divisions between small fields cultivated in prehistoric and Roman periods. A simple form of light plough was used at least as early as 1700 B.C., but there is no reason yet to date any of the Wiltshire field-systems earlier than about 1300 B.C. This method of agriculture was used until the end of the Roman period, between A.D. 400 and 450. The banks between the fields were formed by clearing stones from the area to be ploughed and by the ploughing itself, which loosened the soil so that it was washed downhill by rain and wind. The level of the top end of a field gradually dropped and that of the lower end gradually rose, creating steps between the fields down the slope and banks between them along the slope.

Many of these ancient fields have been ploughed out in modern times, and air photography has been used to trace lost systems. There are well-preserved field-systems on Fifield Down near Marlborough (SU 1471; 9) and Pertwood Down near Kingston Deverill (ST 8737; 13). Discoveries of burnt grain on settlement sites have indicated the type of crop grown in these fields: during the Bronze Age it was mostly barley, but wheat increased in importance into the Iron Age.

Between 600 and 500 B.C. iron working

BISHOPSTONE: *Cultivation terraces*

came to Britain with the arrival of small groups of settlers from the mainland of Europe.

There are many of these, on hill-tops or spurs; though Yarnbury and Ogbury are on the gently-sloping plain. They vary greatly in size. Ogbury (SU 1438; 15) covers 62 acres; Olivers Castle (SU 001648; 8) $3\frac{1}{2}$ acres. The ramparts were often strengthened with timbers set upright at the front as a retaining wall to prevent the chalk of the rampart from sliding back into the ditch. Sometimes the rampart was also laced internally with timbers. The top of the rampart provided a patrol platform and the entrances were often quite elaborate, with wooden towers and gateways. Inside were circular wooden houses, small sheds for storage, pits in the ground for storing grain. Their defences were so effective as to prohibit assault with any weapons until the Roman siege batteries, and it is more likely that inter-tribal quarrels were settled by open pitched battles away from the forts.

There are about forty hill-forts in Wiltshire. Yarnbury, near Winterbourne Stoke (SU 0340; 14), has three well-preserved rings of rampart and ditch, enclosing twenty-eight acres; the innermost ring represents the earliest fortification on the site, built probably in the fifth century B.C., and this was later strengthened with extra defences. The innermost rampart was damaged on its eastern side when low banks forming a series of small rectangular enclosures were laid out for the sheep fairs that used to be held here. The Fair at Yarnbury is mentioned by Thomas Hardy, in "The Return of the Native". It was famous for centuries, and drovers came to it from as far as Pembrokeshire. On the west side of Yarnbury is an irregular triangular enclosure of uncertain date. The large forts crowning the hills of Battlesbury and Scratchbury near Warminster (ST 8945, 9144; 10) are more obviously striking. There was settlement outside the double defences of Battlesbury, either preceding or contemporary with the erection and occupation of it. Middle Hill, between Battlesbury and the univallate (single rampart) fort on Scratchbury, looks deceptively like another hill-fort, but the banks on its slopes are in fact the result of cultivation. To the north, at Bratton (ST 9051; 10), there is a fine bivallate fort of 25 acres. One of the several chalk-cut "White Horses" of Wiltshire lies on the western slope of this hill. It may have been cut in the Early Iron Age, but it was re-cut and modified in the eighteenth century.

The fort on Winkelbury Hill (ST 952218; 17) lies on a spur of the downs overlooking the village of Berwick St John, and has a fine view across the Ebble valley to the ridge of downs to the north. The area enclosed by the original rampart was extended by another line of defence probably not long before the Roman conquest. Several centuries later, Saxons buried their dead in a cemetery outside the hill-fort, but it is unlikely that they used the fort itself.

Oldbury Castle, near Cherhill (SU 049693; 8), had the same long period of occupation throughout the Iron Age; the fort overlooks a wide expanse of downland to the south which is rich in archaeological remains, including barrows, enclosures, a Roman road and Wansdyke. Better preserved, however, is the fine bivallate hill-fort of Barbury Castle (SU 149764; 6), which, although unexcavated, has yielded tools of the 3rd and 2nd centuries B.C.

The hill-fort of Old Sarum outside Salisbury (SU 1332; 15) was probably constructed in the early part of the Iron Age and occupied until the arrival of the Romans. Its appearance has been much altered by building, in Norman times and later.

These fortified camps represent a remarkable degree of social organization. More people must have been involved in building them than lived in them at any one time. This implies that tribal chieftains could command service from the farming communities.

There is more evidence for the nature of domestic settlements in the Early Iron Age in the preceding period. This is partly because there are more sites to be found as a result of an increased population at that time, and partly because the settlements were more elaborate in form and are therefore more easily detectable. Even when they have been filled in they may show as hollows. Still, most of them (hill-forts apart) are visible only during excavation or in air photographs. They varied in form from unenclosed villages of circular timber houses to small family farmsteads enclosed by an earthen bank and ditch. Hill-fort communities must also be considered as villages, together with those large enclosures which have banks too slight to have been effective defences. One of these has been excavated recently near Longbridge Deverill. The best-known Early Iron Age village was discovered near All Cannings, and, like a similar site on Boscombe Down, seems to have lacked any enclosing bank.

Settlement sites readily visible on the ground are small earthwork enclosures, circular, oval or rectilinear. On Mancombe Down near Warminster (ST 895471; 10) is an oval earthwork enclosing one acre, which was probably the farmstead of a single family. Some of these enclosures were used almost certainly for cattle rather than for houses: for instance Church End Ring, south of Wylye (SU 012357; 14). This is linked by a sunken, embanked, trackway to the large and complex settlement of Hanging Langford Camp, which is of the latter part of the pre-Roman Iron Age. Half a mile to the north, the hill-fort of Bilbury Rings seems to have been occupied into the Romano–British period.

Houses were normally circular, 30 to 50 feet in diameter, with timber posts supporting thatched roofs. Weaving, leather-making and pottery, both freehand and on the wheel, were practised. Iron working was also a local craft, and bronze was now used mainly for jewelry. Trade with the continent brought imported brooches and some fine pottery. Grain (barley and wheat) grown in the fields was ground into coarse flour in the settlements. Manure for the fields came from domestic rubbish heaps; so consequently

fragments of pottery are scattered over "Celtic" fields: a useful indication of the period over which the fields were in use.

In the Early Iron Age, the ditch systems were supplemented by another type of linear earthwork; the cross-ridge and cross-spur dykes which run from escarpment to escarpment across chalk ridges and spurs. These are strikingly present on the two ridges running westwards south of Salisbury, one between the Nadder and Ebble, the other between the Ebble and Cranbourne Chase. Cross-ridge dykes vary in size; a few are very large, like their contemporary hill-forts. The bank and ditch of a small one is on Middle Down, above Alvediston (ST 965253; 17), well seen from the road climbing the north escarpment from Ansty. Further west along the same ridge, is a big one on White Sheet Hill (ST 947244; 17), with a bank on each side of the ditch. The most impressive of all is on Win Green (ST 925205; 16), crossed by the road leading from Donhead St Mary to Ashmore. These dykes seem to have fulfilled a dual purpose: they were land boundaries, dividing up the valuable land on the ridge-top, and barriers against traffic passing along the ridge-top trackway. Such big dykes must have had a defensive value. In some places, these earthworks are associated with hill-forts. Chiselbury (SU 018281; 14/7) on the ridge south of Compton Chamberlayne has a length of dyke on either side so that dyke and fort together block the ridge-top. Northwest of Mere, the fine hill-fort on Whitesheet Hill is flanked by two cross-ridge dykes.

There is a fine group of cross-spur dykes on Cold Kitchen Hill, Brixton Deverill (ST 8438; 13), where they seem to have acted as land boundaries enclosing the top of this miniature ridge, perhaps to prevent cattle from straying. There was a large Early Iron Age settlement on the north slope of the hill, which kept its importance into the Roman period, when a temple was built, though there are now no remains of it.

Wansdyke

The trackways along ridge-tops provided the main means of communication throughout prehistoric times, and were undoubtedly still used by the native population under the Romans in preference to the new roads. The main trackways, or ridgeways, traverse Wiltshire and the bordering counties. The Great Ridgeway runs from Streatley in Berkshire to Seaton on the Dorset coast, passing Liddington and Barbury hill-forts, Wilsford, Battlesbury and Win Green on its way. Other trackways cross Salisbury Plain and North Wiltshire, and local ridgeways serve smaller areas: the Ox Drove ridgeway runs along the chalk downs from Win Green to Clearbury Ring, south of Salisbury.

There is also a network of carefully constructed Roman roads. There were two major cross-roads within the county at Old Sarum, outside Salisbury, and at Mildenhall near Marlborough. Roads led from Old Sarum to Mildenhall, Silchester, Winchester, Badbury Rings in Dorset and the Mendips, and had a junction with the Bath to Badbury Rings road. From Mildenhall, roads led to Bath, Cirencester, Silchester and Winchester as well as to Old Sarum. In several places, these roads lie under modern roads. There is a short stretch between Old Sarum and Winterbourne Gunner where the modern lane is superimposed upon the old Roman Portway, and another stretch between Ogbourne St George and Wanborough in the north. To the west of Salisbury, a length of the original Roman road is visible as a wide flat bank in the undergrowth in Grovely Wood. Part of the Old Sarum–Winchester road can be seen on the downs a quarter of a mile south of the A.30 on Winterbourne Down (SU 190331).

There must have been a settlement of some size at Old Sarum in the Roman period, but little trace of it has been found. If it lay inside the old hill-fort, all remains of it would have been destroyed by the building activities of the Normans. At Mildenhall, however, part of an important town has been excavated in Black Field, near the modern village. There is no trace of the town (Cunetio) above ground, but it had a strong enclosing wall with bastions and a large paved main gateway. Just within the town wall, houses have been excavated, which had painted wall plaster in some rooms, and a well has also been found. The Romans reached Wiltshire in A.D. 43, soon after they landed, when the Second Augustan Legion under the command of Vespasian advanced across southern England, building main roads as they went. The rest of the network followed as soon as the economic life of the new agriculturally rich province became settled. Villas of retired Roman officers and prosperous Britons were naturally built close to the new roads.

Several have been found near Box and near Calne on the road from Mildenhall to Bath. A large villa at Box had forty rooms, many with mosaic floors, built round a courtyard, (two small areas of mosaic are still visible in a garden in the village). There was a small settlement south of Calne at Sandy Lane (Verlucio). Others have been found at West Dean, East Grimstead, Norton Bavant and elsewhere, but only at North Wraxall is there any trace of stonework. There were early Roman period pottery kilns in Savernake.

The natives continued to live in farmsteads and villages. One village, formed by adjoining ditched compounds, was excavated at Rotherley near Tollard Royal.

Towards the end of the 4th century A.D. a massive earthwork boundary was thrown up across Cranborne Chase: Bokerly Dyke. Though it is in Dorset and Hampshire it is part of the archaeology of the Chase. It has a large bank and ditch and blocked entry into Cranborne Chase from the Salisbury direction. It is four miles long, and ended originally in heavy woodland on both sides. It was built when Roman authority was weakening and local people needed to fend for themselves and their economy: here the pastures and arable fields of the Chase. The most impressive stretch is between Bokerly Junction and Blagdon Hill (SU 057180; 17).

There is another huge earthwork barrier, built some two hundred years later: Wansdyke (Woden's Dyke), visible on the downs south of Avebury, between Morgan's Hill (SU 025672; 8) and Gore Copse (SU 172665; 9). The bank and ditch were constructed against some threat of invasion from a northerly direction in the latter part of the 6th century A.D. It is not known by whom. Wansdyke is well preserved and stretches for eleven miles. On Tan Hill it cuts through several earlier ditches. It was certainly defensive.

By this time, the pagan Saxon period, the "Celtic" field method of agriculture had in some places been replaced by strip lynchets. Long narrow strips of ploughed land which appear usually as terraces following the contours of slopes, though sometimes the strips run at right angles or obliquely to the contours. A fine group, covering about two hundred acres at Mere (ST 8233; 13), can be seen to overlie the squarer fields of the earlier "Celtic" system. They seem to be of medieval date, as are those at Calstone Wellington (SU 045690; 8). There are also some fine ones on Middle Hill near Warminster (ST 910452; 10).

There are very few traces of pagan Saxon domestic settlement, but there are a number of burials: in round barrows or in cemeteries. In a barrow near Coombe Bissett rich grave-goods had been placed beneath the mound, including an iron sword with a bronze-studded hilt, but the body, presumably that of a warrior, had never been buried – the barrow was a cenotaph. The finds dated to about A.D. 650. The Saxons seem to have used existing barrows, rather than building new. Saxon burials have been found inserted into the sides of Neolithic long barrows and Bronze Age round barrows. One such intrusive burial in a round barrow on Roundway Down, Devizes, belonged to a wealthy woman, buried in a wooden coffin together with gold jewelry set with garnets and a wooden bucket bound with bronze.

Roundway Down, near DEVIZES

Inhumation burials were also made in cemeteries. Those at Harnham Hill and Petersfinger, revealed each about seventy burials, some of which were accompanied by fine grave-goods, including swords and brooches.

The county suffered little from the depopulation of villages in the Middle Ages as a result of economic pressures and epidemics of plague. The earthworks at Bupton (SU 057764; 5) near Clyffe Pypard, south of Wootton Bassett, are clearly visible as the remains of a deserted medieval village. The main village street is sunken, as are the gardens or yards of the houses adjoining the street, so that low banks survive to indicate the form of the village. The probable site of another medieval village is in the combe just south of Barbury hill-fort (SU 152758; 6); earthworks here are associated with a ditch running between two banks up the slope and over the ridge on which the hill-fort stands. Most villages have been greatly modified over the centuries as a result of continuous settlement on the same site; the deserted villages are therefore good sources of information about ordinary domestic life, which is absent from contemporary historical records.

There are plenty of traces of medieval roadways and tracks. Deep cuttings were made (for instance) in the steeply-sloping escarpment south of Shalbourne, to make the descent easier. Earthworks on Rivar Hill (SU 316615; 9) and on Ham Hill (SU 333617; 9) carve an oblique course down the escarpment alongside the modern roads, curving out into a broad entrance at the foot of the slope. These tracks were constructed deliberately, but elsewhere traffic was left to find its own way on slopes. The result may be seen on Beacon Hill (SU 2044; 12), near Bulford, where divergent tracks thread the slope, one succeeding another as the last became impassable.

White Horses
p. 52, 1: *CHERHILL, 1780*
2: *WESTBURY, 18th century (originally)*
p. 53: *ALTON BARNES, 1812*

GAZETTEER

The number at the end of each entry indicates the square on the map where the place is to be found.

Aldbourne. A pretty, twisting place. There is a village green with an old cross and a duck pond, encompassed by a variety of small houses and cottages in brick and colourwash and thatch. A stuccoed Gothick house, symmetrical, at the beginning of the road to Hungerford, is worth looking at (c. 1800). But the local council has carried out a heavy-handed programme of urban tidying-up. The pond is now primly cased round with municipal concrete curbs and there is a proliferation of notices and traffic signs. There is untidy modern development to the north and east. But the overall impression is still pleasing. The church, lifting a fine stepped tower above the green, is mostly Perpendicular, although it shows a continuous building history from Norman times through Early English to the present day. Chevron-ornamented south arcade. A not-too-drastic restoration was carried out by Butterfield in 1868; he also did the red-tiled school close by in a much gentler manner than usual. There is a large and lofty nave with much lower aisles, and chancel aisles. Attractive old wooden roofs throughout, and pleasant, irregularly tiled and stone flagged floor. Jacobean pulpit, Victorian furnishings and a number of good monuments. The cleanly incised alabaster tomb chest of John Stone, rector here at the start of the 16th century, is beautifully done. So, too, is the richly carved and coloured memorial to William and Edward Walrond. Dying at a great age in 1614 and 1617, the two old gentlemen kneel piously together in brotherly affection, their virtues extolled in three languages. In the elaborate Goddard monument, the same unknown sculptor portrays father, mother and six children. The boys have flowing moustaches and small goatee beards, and there is well-carved Elizabethan decoration in deep relief. Clayton and Bell glass in chancel: otherwise clear glazing. In the nave are two eighteenth-century fire engines. The remains of a motte-and-bailey, south of the village, are *Lewisham Castle*, occupied by troops of Louis the Dauphin in 1215. Aldbourne had a bell foundry, which closed in 1824 after two centuries of casting. It was also noted for the plaiting of straw and willow. The local pronunciation of the place name is "Auburn" – not the "Sweet Auburn" of Goldsmith, but certainly one of the pleasantest villages in these parts. 6

Aldborne Chase. Once a royal hunting ground is now favoured as galloping country by trainers. King John is said to have come here often and John of Gaunt built himself a hunting lodge nearby. At *Upper Upham* near the middle of the Chase and not easy of access is *Upham House*, a silver-grey stone house of the late 16th century, the home of many of the Goddards who are buried in Aldbourne church. It has mullioned windows, gables and topiary gardens. 6

Alderbury. Looks over the Avon valley and the wooded park of Longford Castle. *The Green Dragon* here is described in *Martin Chuzzlewit* as "The Blue Dragon" – the inn used by Mark Tapley. The second inn of Alderbury has historic, rather than literary, associations: *The Three Crowns* may refer to the fact that Edward III hunted in nearby Clarendon Forest with his two prisoner kings, John of France and David of Scotland. St Mary's church was built by S. S. Teulon in 1858 with a tall four-gabled tower and a very sharp little broach spire. It has one good window by Clayton and Bell. Across the road is the driveway to *Alderbury House*, a simple late 18th-century stone mansion whose fabric incorporates material salvaged from Salisbury Cathedral after James Wyatt's destructive restoration of 1789. Along the main road into Salisbury is *St Marie's Grange*, a Gothic Revival fantasy by Pugin. He built this house in 1835 (altered later) for himself and his young bride, but lived here for only two years before returning to London where he helped Charles Barry with the new Houses of Parliament. A few ruined walls and stone fragments in a little farmhouse mark the site of *Ivychurch*, a one-time Augustinian priory founded in the 12th century by King Stephen to provide services for his Clarendon Foresters. It was let to Lord Pembroke in the 16th century, converted into a Georgian house and finally demolished in 1888. Most of the stonework has provided a ready-made quarry for buildings round about, but there are still a couple of Norman columns and big capitals. Other carved work has found its way into Salisbury Museum and the parish church at Pewsey. Some of the double columns of the cloisters have been built into a modern fountain structure on the main road near to the church. *Clarendon House* (not to be confused with the historically more famous *Clarendon Palace*) is a big classical mansion in fine parkland to the north-east of the village. On a high ridge to the south is *Eyre's Folly* (National Trust) known from its shape as the Pepper Box. This look-out dates from 1606. 18

Alderton. A hamlet with a straggling collection of early Victorian estate houses and cottages. There is a school house of 1845 with an Italianate

ALDERBURY

tower. The entrance doorway and a triple Gothic window were taken from the old village church when it was rebuilt. *St Giles* was completed in the same year as the school and is all imitation Norman and Early English work, built for that misguided millionaire, Joseph Neeld of Grittleton. The chancel is a fine example of 1845 melodrama, with an east window of the Crucifixion and side lancets in the same style: perhaps early O'Connor work. There are late brasses and well carved floor slabs. There are one or two older houses in the neighbourhood: *Manor Farmhouse* with its gables and mullioned windows is 17th-century. 4

All Cannings. Thatch and half-timber, brick and tile and a pleasing medley of styles and periods in houses and cottages among a network of little lanes. The church is very big for so small a village; cruciform with a tall tower over the crossing. There are bits of Norman work, and the nave arcades are Early English, but most is Perpendicular or Victorian restoration. Clear glass in some windows gives glimpses of trees and hills. The elaborate chancel is Victorian and was built as a family memorial by the Methuen family "as a testimony to a happy home". The Rev. Anthony Methuen, rector here for 60 years, was a friend of Samuel Taylor Coleridge, who stayed at the rectory in 1817. The chancel with its carved alabaster reproduction of Leonardo's *Last Supper* as a reredos, and glass by Lavers and Barraud, was dedicated in 1867, the 50th anniversary of the poet's visit. There are some good monuments, including a large and intricately carved memorial in stone of 1581 to William Ernle, full of foliage and fierce eagles. In the north aisle, another massive monument to 18th-century members of the same family is crowned by relief bust in profile of a saucy and décolletée young woman wearing a sort of carnival hat. This is an item in the Ernle armorial bearings. The same hat in the guise of a Tartar's head-gear crops up in other churches hereabouts, notably at Bishop's Cannings. 8

Allington (near Chippenham). The smallest of hamlets on the fringes of Chippenham. A little to the north is *Bolehyde* (or *Bulidge*) *Manor*, a large, 17th-century stone house with mullioned windows and gables standing by the roadside, its entrance on one side flanked by two 18th-century pavilions. On the road towards Chippenham is what appears to be a fine tall stone barn, with mullioned windows. In fact the "barn" is all that remains of a great house built in 1612 for Sir Gilbert Prynne. The original back-door knocker still bears this date and inside are two stone fireplaces of the period. In the farmyard close by is the little church, converted from a stable in the 1860's. 4

Allington (near Devizes). A collection of small houses and cottages contained within a loop of lanes. The area is rich in prehistoric remains and ancient burial places and the one-inch Ordnance Map shows it thick with barrows and tumuli. *Rybury Camp*, about a mile to the north-east, is an Iron Age hill fort, so far unexcavated. At the farm of *All Cannings Cross* the remains of an Iron Age settlement were discovered in the 1920's, when more than seventy-five dwelling and storage pits were excavated and produced a vast quantity of pottery, brooches, pins and working implements, all of the Hallstatt period (600 B.C.). 8

Allington (near Salisbury). A few old houses of no special note stand about a small village green which is fitted out with swings and see-saws as a children's playground, uglified with a protective fence of chain link wire. The path to the church runs between cob walls once thatched but now coped with corrugated iron. The shallow Bourne flows by, with a ford crossing. The church was rebuilt in 1851, of flint and stone, with a pyramid roof on a low south tower, and records indicate that the previous crumbling structure was quite faithfully copied: welcome though unusual in a Victorian restoration. The vicar of a neighbouring parish criticized the curate of Allington who undertook the rebuilding for reconstructing St John's "as dark and dull and cheerless as before". "The curate was William Grey . . . Grey was a thorough ecclesiologist at a time when I was beginning to pass out of that vein. I think he allowed himself to be the victim of an excessive reaction against my own rather extravagent work at Cholderton. Collecting some twelve or fifteen hundred pounds, he took down his church, already crumbling to pieces, and rebuilt it with scarcely the slightest deviation from the original structure only good masonry instead of bad. It certainly was as dark, and dull, and cheerless as before." (T. Mozley, *Reminiscences of Towns, Villages and Schools*, Vol II.) In fact, the church is more pleasant than many a Victorian "improvement". The delightful chancel is in a William Morris manner, no doubt by Morris & Co, with east window, tiled floor and wall and ceiling painting well done; all a memorial of 1875. 15

Alton Barnes, like its close neighbour, Alton Priors, stands in the Vale of Pewsey with the clean sweeping shapes of Marlborough Downs in the background. There is not much more than a straggle of cottages and, at the end of a short lane, the tiny church of St Mary. A simple and ancient building; the long-and-short work of quoin stones outside and the tall narrow proportions of the interior of the little nave are a clear indication of Saxon origins. The plain plastered walls are an excellent setting for some good 18th-century panelling, and for the three-decker pulpit and Georgian gallery, put in when the chancel was rebuilt in 1748. There is a memorial gallery of wall tablets. Next to the churchyard is the Rectory, early Georgian and nicely proportioned. Half-a-mile down the road towards Woodborough, *Honey Street* was once a busy wharf and depot on the Kennet and Avon Canal. A former group of canalside buildings has disappeared except for some cottages and a handsome early 19th-century inn, *The Barge*. From the hump bridge here is a view of the White Horse cut into the chalk of Walker's Hill in 1812. 8

Alton Priors. There are thatched cottages and a scattering of old farms with some thatched barns. One little Georgian house by the roadside has an impressive shell porch that seems too big for the rest of the facade. The church is old and simple and stands in the middle of a field and is a stone's-throw from St Mary's at Alton Barnes. The interior, whitewashed and barn-like with big country-made roof trusses and open timbering, escaped major Victorian restoration. Norman chancel arch, Perpendicular west tower with the entrance beneath and a panelled arch of the same period looking towards the nave. Box pews, 18th-century communion rails and other woodwork. Tomb of 1590 with a brass. A mile to the north can be seen *Adams Grave*, a prehistoric long barrow with part of the burial chamber exposed to view. Not far away is *Knap Hill*, a fortified camp of the New Stone Age. 8

Alvediston. The name means "Alfgeat's farm" and has nothing to do with the local corruption of " 'Ellofadistance". A pretty place, among leafy lanes and green meadows. Along the road at the south end of the village is the *Manor House* with shell porch; a well-proportioned building in brick, an unusual material among the older structures in this predominantly stone area. St Mary's church, with a big Victorian parsonage behind, is on a beautiful south facing slope, looking across undulating meadows. It was mostly rebuilt by T. H. Wyatt in 1866. Old features remain, including the charming Perpendicular tower. There are four finely wrought wall monuments and a west window of 1881, dark but rich-coloured and worthy, of Christ preaching under a spreading tree. Evidently artist-designed. Hidden behind heating pipes in one of the transepts is a fine effigy of a knight in armour, Sir John Gawen, who died in the 14th century. There are also classical wall tablets to members of the Wyndham family. That to John Wyndham, dated 1724, is an impressive piece by Rysbrack. The Wyndhams lived at *Norrington Manor*, part-medieval, part-Elizabethan, about a mile from the village. They bought the estate from the ancient Gawen family in 1658, the same Sir John Gawen who lies in the church having made the original purchase of the property in 1377. The great hall and porch of the medieval house survive. 17

Amesbury. A brash and bustling town on the Avon at the intersection of the main north-south, and east-west roads crossing Salisbury Plain. An ancient settlement whose old character is being eroded by traffic, by the constant movement of military material and personnel, by commercial pressures and "developments" and by all those modern trends and activities that change villages into towns, and towns of an urban sameness. The army camps at Bulford and Larkhill have had much to do with the process. The uniformed population is permanently "in camp" on the Plain but makes of Amesbury an off-duty locale – "now mostly a sort of Aldershot, strung with wire, roaring with lorries and humming with aeroplanes . . ." A handful of good buildings have survived into the 1960's, to stand like rocks in this restless sea. The present *Amesbury Abbey* is the

ALVEDISTON

last descendant of the great Priory "to which Queen Guinevere fled and from which Lancelot led her sombre funeral procession over the downs to Glastonbury...". Of the old religious buildings, not a stone remains. After the Dissolution of the Monasteries, the property was granted in 1541 to Edward Seymour who later became Duke of Somerset and Lord Protector of England. He and his son, the Earl of Hertford, built and completed the first house on the site; of this, two strange gatehouses still exist along the Pewsey road. The one dated 1600 is called "Diana's House" because of the inscription still to be seen, "Diana her hous". The other, "Kent House", dates from 1607 and was considerably enlarged in the 18th century. In 1661, the second mansion to be built on the site was completed to the designs of John Webb, son-in-law of Inigo Jones. It was a noble classical building, to which the architect James Paine added big wings during the 18th century. John Gay is reputed to have written *The Beggars' Opera* at Amesbury Abbey, using as his study "The Diamond", a curious grotto in the grounds. Gay's patron was "Kitty, beautiful and young" – the sparkling and eccentric Duchess of Queensberry, wife of the third Duke and friend of the literary men of the age. This second house fell into disrepair and was pulled down at the very beginning of the Victorian era. The third Abbey, built in 1840, is in the general tradition of Webb's house. Close to the park are ancient earthworks known as *Vespasian's Camp*, so named quite wrongly by the antiquarian Stukeley in 1743. These ramparts, in fact, pre-date the Roman occupation by many centuries. The other great structure to be seen in Amesbury is the parish church St Mary and St Melor. It is nicely set at the edge of the town and a little removed from the central noise and busyness. The great size and splendid proportions point to it as the priory church. A big and noble building; cruciform, with a tower over the crossing. Of Norman origin, the interior is mainly Early English. The wagon roofs are gradually being re-painted. Butterfield did some restoration work here in the 1850's. The harsh tiling in the chancel and the rather coarse vigour of the Victorian turret at the crossing are typical of the man. In the town the *George*, a coaching inn, is long and rambling, and the *Queensberry Bridge* over the Avon, close to the main gates of the Abbey, is a five-arched classical design of 1775. In *Antrobus House* is a museum endowed by the family of that name who took over the Abbey from the Queensberrys. Outside the town, *West Amesbury House* is a flint-and-stone chequerwork manor, with medieval bits and pieces hiding behind a symmetrical 17th-century facade. 15

Ansty. The name comes from the Old English word "anstig" – meaning steep path – and the way down from the main Salisbury–Shaftesbury road into this pretty little place is steep indeed. Houses and cottages strung along a wooded valley lead to a big village pond where ducks, moorhens and swans share possession. St James's church is simple, cruciform and charming, with a bellcote. Basically Early English with the transepts added as part of a Victorian restoration. Inside, the subdued colours of new carpeting and damask hangings to the reredos are commendable. There is a Norman font and the elaborate bench ends are said to have been throw-outs from an early restoration at Salisbury Cathedral. Ansty has the distinction of being the very last parish to which a Church of England clergyman was "donated". Following legal adjustments, Quartus Bacon, M.A., incumbent from 1898 to 1936, was the first *legally* appointed Vicar of Ansty since the Reformation. There was once a Preceptory of the order of Knights Hospitallers here. The dilapidated old workshop building on the roadside near the church was their hospice and dates from the very early 16th century. Other traces survive in *Manor Farmhouse*, across the pond, a half-Jacobean, half-Georgian building. 17

Ashton Keynes. A watery place of many bridges, in the flat meadows of the upper Thames. New housing on the outskirts is raw, but this village varies from the pleasant to the delightful. It is easy to drive through without stopping: a mistake, since there is more to be seen than the main street, where the shallow stream runs alongside and every house has its own small bridge. At the end of Church Walk is a charming collection of old stone houses, mostly 18th-century, with *Ashton Mill* and *Brook House* forming the climax of an eye-stopping group where the stream becomes a little river running wide and clear and wavy. The church (Holy Cross), in the field beyond, is of stone, stone-tiled, Early English and Decorated, but with a fine wide Norman chancel arch. It is only a small let-down to find that until 1877 this was much smaller and narrower. In this year Butterfield did a remarkably good enlargement job. Late Norman or Transitional font. Perpendicular reredos and one or two good wall monuments, including one to Charlotte Nicholas by Flaxman, of the lady on her death-bed. Original wagon roof, but the interior rather spoiled by some inappropriate painted Victorian decoration in the chancel and "commercial" lighting fittings. Also by dull though well-intentioned Victorian and modern glass in several windows. A table-tomb opposite the south porch is well carved with cherubim. Near the church, the *Manor House* and its barns form another good group. There are the stumps of no less than four village crosses. Here is the home of the *Cotswold Bruderhof*, a farming community of European peoples driven from their own countries. 2

Atworth. The newer parts along the main road consist mostly of messy development of various periods during the last sixty years. The older and original Atworth is found down a side road leading to the church, where there is a group of 17th-century and Georgian houses and the *Foresters Arms*, a pleasant inn. The church is unusual: a cheap Gothick building of 1832 was erected close to a Perpendicular tower, all that remains of the original St Michael's. The two parts are connected by a passageway and the outlines of the former chancel arch and nave roof can be clearly seen. The 19th-century church is wide and chapel-like and has to be entered in lowly fashion beneath the gallery, the squatness of which tends to make tall men stoop. A gallantly modern colour scheme in blues and greys, reds and greens has recently been carried out (1966) and is not unattractive (by Campbell Smith of London). There is an unfortunate east window of 1935. *Manor Farmhouse* and *Poplar Farmhouse* (which does have big poplar trees in front!) are two attractive Georgian buildings. So, too, the *White Hart Inn* back on the main road. A big Roman villa of the 3rd century A.D. was excavated in the neighbourhood in 1938. 7

Avebury. The building of prehistoric Avebury was contemporary with the earlier phases of the building of Stonehenge. It is possible that the sarsen stones for Stonehenge III were actually removed from it and certainly in the end Stonehenge superseded it in ritual importance. Today this is understandable. Compared with the gaunt self-sufficiency of Stonehenge Avebury has an inconsequent domesticity; the great ditch embraces the cottages of the modern village, stones that were once in precise and ritual positions stick up amongst village elms, or, smashed to a suitable size, are embedded in the cottage walls themselves. Concrete posts mark the places of old stones and make up the Kennet avenue, one and a half miles long, that once approached the site from the south. They look like a vast game of archaeological chess. It consisted originally of a large bank and ditch and a stone circle within it all, surrounding two smaller stone circles. It is possible that it cut an earlier, uncompleted circle on its northern side. Though much silted up, the ditch is still impressive because of the height of the bank. It is entered by four modern roads on the sites of the old entrances, (the fourth has not yet been checked by excavation). The sarsen stones are from the neighbouring down and, though not shaped and worked like those at Stonehenge, were clearly chosen for their natural shapes: two alternating ones, tall and straight or broad and diamond shaped, symbolizing perhaps male and female. The whole site may have been used for fertility rites. The

AVEBURY

inner circles were quite small, only containing thirty and thirty-two stones respectively. In the middle of the smaller, centre circle three large stones were arranged on three sides of a square (two are still there). It is called a "cove" and its purpose is not known. In the middle of the southern circle a large upright, twenty-one feet long was still standing the 18th century. To its west was an arrangement of smaller stones in a straight line. Very few stones remain upright and complete in the avenue and circles because they were removed to make ploughing easier, or broken up for local building on an even larger scale than at Stonehenge. Much less is known about Avebury than Stonehenge. It was not mentioned in the earlier histories, or until 1648, when John Aubrey came across it one fine winter morning and reported, with great excitement that "it did as much excell Stonehenge as a cathedral does a parish church". Very little excavation has been done there since Alexander Keiller's work of reconstruction and exploration was interrupted in 1939.

Silbury Hill. About a mile to the south of Avebury and sixteen miles from Stonehenge, this enormous mound never fails to surprise. The largest man-made mound in Europe, it is a hundred and thirty feet high and over two hundred yards in diameter. Only the top three quarters is artificial, being the chalk rubble from the ditch on the north and west piled onto a natural chalk ridge. The chalk ridge was shaped for conical symmetry. It looks as if it must be an outsize barrow and it has, romantically, been thought of as the grave of the master-architect of Stonehenge (if such a single person existed). Nothing has ever been found or proved. Though only two shafts have been sunk in it, one in 1877 from the top to the chalk and one in 1849 from the south to the bottom of the first shaft. B.B.C. excavations began in the summer of 1967.

The village is attractive in itself, of stone and brick, and enhanced by its site. *Avebury Manor* is among fine trees. The stone gabled Elizabethan house is National Trust property. There is elaborate topiary work, and a big circular dovecote. The classical stable block houses a small museum. *St James's church* stands just outside the main circle. It was restored in 1879, when the present chancel was built. Much original work remains. Parts of the nave are Anglo-Saxon, including two windows and the tall, stately proportions are Saxon too. The Normans added its north and south aisles and chopped arcades out of the Saxon walls. The font of this date is a fine geometrically carved one, with abstract symbols. The tower was added in the late 14th century and in 1812 Mr Button, a builder of Calne, replaced the Norman arches of the nave with Renaissance arcading of the Tuscan order. The fine 13th-century chancel arch is hidden almost completely behind a big modern screen, although the rood loft above is genuine 15th-century work. The stained glass is poor, and there is a feeling of over-furnishing. Next to the church the thatched *Great Barn* still stands. At one time (and that not so long ago) there was talk of allowing it to fall into ruin. A little to the west of the village is *Trusloe Manor*, a stone-faced house of the late 17th century, approached from the churchyard by the tiny New Bridge and a footpath. In Bray Street, close at hand, *Bannings* is a Georgian house of chequered brickwork. *Westbrook Farmhouse*, further along the lane, is a thatched building of the same period as Trusloe. 8

Avoncliff. From Westwood, a very steep hill leads down to the woody gorge of the Avon. Near the bottom is *Old Court*, a group of buildings that has had an interesting career. The main block, ranged barrack-like round three sides of a square courtyard is said to have been built as a weavers' hostel towards the end of the 17th century. A chapel was built on in the late Georgian era, together with the domed Drying House. With the addition of a Master's Lodge, the whole group later became Bradford Workhouse. Nearby is the pleasing *Cross Guns Inn*, Jacobean with dormers and mullioned windows. Along the valley, one of John

Rennie's big Kennet and Avon Canal aqueducts strides majestically across the gorge. Avoncliff is well worth a visit. The approach by the motorist needs care. 7

Axford. On the Kennet east of Marlborough is a place that one tends to drive through with little more than a passing glance. It has thatched barns and other farm buildings. The church of St Michael is a slated shed lit by lancet windows at each end with domestic-style sashes along each side. It is plain and simple and was built in 1856 of flint and, brick, inside and out. At *Priory Farm*, on the banks of the river to the east, in a beautiful situation, in a collection of farm buildings, is a 14th-century chapel, plastered outside, attached to the brick and flint farmhouse. 9

Barbury Camp. Prehistoric hill fort on the Downs south of Swindon with views to the north and west. Also called Barbury Castle, its present name may be derived from the Battle of Beran Byrig (or Beranburh) fought on the slopes of Burderop Down. Below the ramparts of Barbury the West Saxons decisively defeated the Britons in A.D. 556. The ridgeway from Hackpen Hill passes through the fort, whose inner area of 12 acres is enclosed by a double ditch and earth wall. Many objects of occupation have been excavated: iron tools, jewellery, coins and arrowheads are part of a collection in Marlborough Museum. This was a favourite walking place of Richard Jefferies, who was born at Coate, an hour's tramp from here. A big sarsen stone brought to Barbury from Overton Down bears inscriptions to his memory. A second memorial plate on the same stone recalls the life of Alfred Williams, Swindon railwayman and local poet. 6

Barford St Martin. A pleasing village with 17th- and 18th-century cottages, a few well thatched. The *Green Dragon* is a Georgian pub with a delicate

AVEBURY

porch. The church is cruciform. Not over-restored (though without original furniture or interesting glass), it has an Early English chancel and the crossing with its tierceron stone vaulting and tower above is Perpendicular, like most of the rest. But the stepped gable of the west front was not built until some time in the 1600s and belongs to the tail-end of Gothic. The altar has been adapted from a Spanish chest and some of the older monuments are curious. In the chancel is a late-Elizabethan tomb chest on which lies the painted near-naked figure of a young woman. There is a brass of a woman with eleven children. Near to the church is a village cross. Over the river in a woodland setting is *Hurdcott House*, a 17th-century structure hidden behind a classical stone front of 1809. 14

Baverstock. A hamlet in the valley of the Nadder, beneath the slopes of Grovely Wood with stone and whitewash cottages and a *Manor House* with mullioned windows, and summer aubretia. The church, with uncommon dedication to St Edith, is nearer the main road, outside the village, with a big 19th-century *Rectory* opposite, yellow washed. The small west tower is Perpendicular but the rest is by Butterfield, who did a thorough re-build job in 1883. Elaborate reredos and coloured tiling. Green glass. Castellated timbering across the tower arch and chancel screen which goes right up to roof level. In the churchyard, the graves of a number of Australian soldiers are marked by the neat War Graves Commission headstones. 14

Baydon is more than 750 feet above sea level: the highest village in Wiltshire. Village green encircled by brick-and-flint thatched cottages, the *Red Lion* inn to one side. The brick bus shelter helps to hide a garage. The church has a late 14th-century tower in stone and flint, like the rest of the exterior walls. The arcades inside are much earlier; Norman on the south side, Early English on the north. East window by Kempe. The poor Victorian pulpit is to be replaced by a modern one in stone (1966). Oil-fired heaters. *Finche's Farm*, not far away, was once in the ownership of Sir Isaac Newton. 6

Beanacre. A village straggling along the A350 a couple of miles north of Melksham with St Barnabas, the plainest of late-Victorian churches, newly built in 1886. The font is Norman and came from Melksham. There are two manor-houses here: the *Old Manor* is the L-shaped late-medieval building whose 15th-century hall retains its original roof. The neighbouring *Beanacre Manor*, the New Manor, is 350 years old, gabled with a good two-storey entrance porch. 7

Beckhampton, now possesses as its chief feature a vast roundabout on the Marlborough-Chippenham road, close to Silbury Hill and the turn-off for Avebury. The Downs rise grandly about in every direction. Racing stables, cottages and a brick Georgian house facing the main road. 8

Beechingstoke. Hamlet in the Vale of Pewsey, close to the railway, but not spoiled. St Stephen's church was heavily Victorianized in 1860. The interior is orthodox, with stained glass and tiles in period. It shares a driveway and carriage sweep with the pink-washed late-Georgian rectory. *Beechingstoke Manor* has formal 18th-century facade of brick, with two bows and elaborate iron porch and a thatched roof. 8

Bemerton. A suburban extension of Salisbury reaches out a long finger and touches the parish where George Herbert was rector from 1630 until his death in 1633. There are two churches; the big one, built by T. H. Wyatt in 1860, is well done, with big two-aisled nave, tower to north of chancel, and well-carved capitals. The Pembrokes of Wilton built it. A great restorer himself, had Wyatt lived longer he might have had the doubtful satisfaction of seeing his new church "restored" by C. E. Ponting, in 1896. Then, or a bit later, the elaborate and colourful reredos and frieze below it were executed by a rector's daughter. Good-coloured, vivid glass in east and west windows. St Andrew's, George Herbert's own church, is one of the smallest in Wiltshire, and is literally in the shadow of Herbert's rectory. Nave and chancel in one, much restored but retaining a 17th-century atmosphere. A blocked doorway in the north wall is Norman, and there is some Decorated work. A double memorial window shows the poet with his friend Nicholas Ferrar, organiser of the community at Little Gidding, Huntingdonshire. *Little Gidding*, one of T. S. Eliot's *Four Quartets*, is influenced by the work of Ferrar. Across the street, the old Rectory still stands, a flint and stone gabled house. He died from consumption in this house, aged 40. It has been added to later. 14

Berwick Bassett. Hamlet below the Marlborough Downs in the shadow of Hackpen Hill. The 15th-century *Old Manor* is partly stone and partly half-timbering filled with herringbone brickwork. The church of St Nicholas has a plain interior, was restored in 1857 by T. H. Wyatt and is now in need of renovation (1966). Tower and nave are of sarsen, chancel of brick, early 19th century. Oil lamps and a great iron stove. Priest's brass of 1427. Pulpit and reading desk are fitted with Georgian candle glasses. A sad little building. *New Manor House* (new only by comparison with the old one) stands by a stretch of grass with a weed-laden stream, and dates from the second half of the 17th century. 5

Berwick St James is miles away from Berwick Bassett, in the valley of the Till on the southern edge of Salisbury Plain. The main road curves past stone houses and thatched cottages with a softening of trees and gardens. The church, a charming composition, is entered by a large north porch, Perpendicular, with beam-corbels inside showing the position of a one-time priest's room above. A Norman doorway with the

BIDDESDEN House

favourite green and white stone patterning leads to a fine original interior, with chancel and side chapels of the early 13th century. A big arch of the same period spans the full width of the chancel: a dramatic feature. Towards the altar, deep-set lancets give a concealed lighting effect. The 17th-century communion rails have enormous knobs. There are few signs of drastic Victorian restoration. Crude heating pipes and lighting fittings at present (1968). 14

Berwick St John is an attractive village with a cluster of stone houses, thick with trees and well-kept gardens. The church is behind pantiled walls in a large graveyard. Fully restored in 1861 by Henry Woodyer, it almost counts as a church *by* him, except for the central tower, which is a pretty grand one of the 15th century. There are well-painted hatchments, clear coloured and attractive glass of 1850 by Hardman, two effigies of knights and, in the churchyard, some striking table tombs. From the church there are views southwards of bare downland; northwards of copsed undulations. The *Old Rectory* of 1795 was built by the parson partly out of his own pocket and with the aid of funds from New College, Oxford. The Georgian house a few yards away, with its shell porch, is a few years older. The triple-arched classical bus shelter in the village is a pleasing modern feature. In 1735 the Rev. John Gane left a legacy for the ringing of the church bell at eight o'clock every winter night as a guide to uncertain travellers on the downs. *Ferne House*, a mile west, is a big early 19th-century mansion in the classical manner on a hill above fine parkland. It is now used as the Ferne Animal Sanctuary. On *Winklebury Hill*, behind the village, are a prehistoric fortified camp and a series of earthworks. Splendid view. Although the site dates from the Iron Age, a Saxon cemetery was excavated here by General Pitt-Rivers towards the end of the last century. 17

Berwick St Leonard. A handful of cottages and farm buildings with a small church looking like one of them. It was almost completely rebuilt in 1860: nave and chancel with little of the old work except a Norman doorway, now blocked, and a few monuments. Patterned glass. The big tablet to George Howe (d. 1647) shows man and wife each caressing a skull. Their old home, the Manor in which William of Orange later passed the night on his way to Salisbury, was pulled down at the turn of the century. It was subsequently re-erected for the late Hugh Morrison M.P. at Fonthill, where it forms the centre section of a mansion designed by Detmar Blow. The big house of the village is now *Berwick House*, with a porch and Georgian front in blue and red brick. 13

Biddesden. *Biddesden House* was built in 1712 for General Webb. It is easy to see: the road from Chute to Ludgershall runs past the entrance gates. The architect's name is unknown. Set against the symmetry of its facades is a castellated turret, built to house a bell trophy carried back from Lille by the General, who fought under Marlborough and appears as a character in Thackeray's *Henry Esmond*. There is a modern temple and gazebo nearby. 12

Biddestone, west of Chippenham, now has depressing grey concrete-block housing on the outskirts, but the centre of the village has old stone houses grouped around a green. The gabled *Manor House*, with silver-grey stone and mullioned windows, is 17th century, with good stables, and a pretty little gazebo perched on its garden wall. *Pool Farmhouse*, of the same period, also has its gazebo and was built about the same time as the *White Lion* inn (1672). There are some Georgian houses, including *Willow House* with a pedimented front. The church, St Nicholas, has a Norman doorway with a Maltese cross above and Norman windows in the chancel. Long and aisle-less, without tower or spire, it has a most unusual 13th-century bell turret on its roof. Inside there is a fine tunnel-like recession through the arches of nave and sanctuary. Not over-restored. The 18th-century gallery and box pews and many rustic wall monuments have been left undisturbed. A very pleasing interior. St Peter's was demolished many years ago. The bell turret survives as a garden feature in the grounds of the Manor House at Castle Combe. Many good churchyard monuments, including table tombs. 4

Bishop's Cannings is small and quiet, in spite of its proximity to the Devizes–Swindon road. A pub and thatched cottages, all overshadowed by the large and splendid church. St Mary's looks so original and unaltered that from a small distance it might be a fine example of Gothic Revival architecture. In fact it is pure Early English, only the soaring spire, the top section of the tower and the aisle and clerestory windows being later (15th century). The nave is tall and cool; to stand beneath the fine triple lancet of the west window and look at the altar is to see it framed at the end of a dramatic receding vista of arches and vaulting. But this interior has been badly treated: the walls scraped of their plaster and the windows nearly all filled with a greenish ripple glass that sheds a bad light on the not very good Victorian furnishings. The east window – mid-Victorian – has some welcome clear colour. The church is cruciform and aisled; the nave has clerestories, an unusual pedestal poor box, and a penitential seat of the early 1600s – a chair painted on the back with a huge hand and various pious and gloomy admonitions to the sinner, in Latin. The Gothick organ, 1809, came to the church through a legacy from William Bayley, who voyaged round the world with Captain Cook. In the Ernle Chapel is an elaborate monument to John of that family who died in 1571, the date being expressed as "The yeare of Our Lorde God – A thousand five hundred three score and eleven." Standing on the tomb chest is the painted wooden head of a thoughtful and not very terrible Tartar, or Turk, or Saracen. There is also an iron helm; both head and helmet are part of the Ernle arms. Bishop's Cannings has been noted for strange and interesting people: from here came the original Wiltshire Moonrakers "who fooled an Exciseman by pretending they were raking for the moon when he caught them retrieving smuggled brandy from a pond". Then the whole population "once walked to Devizes to see a comet which they heard was to be seen from the Market Place there". Aubrey claimed that this place could beat all of England "for musique, football and the ringing". King James I and his Queen were entertained here by masque composed by Parson Ferraby, acted and sung in costume by priest and parishioners. 8

Bishop's Fonthill, also known as Fonthill Bishop, is in the Beckford country. Stone houses and cottages stand around triangular greens among many big trees. Nearby is the triumphal-arch entrance to Fonthill Park erected by Lord Cottingham in the reign of Charles I, the design being quite possibly by Inigo Jones. The village school is pretty, Victorian; the *Old Rectory*, many times altered, but basically Tudor, is near the church. All Saints is a complete little Early English building gently restored by T. H. Wyatt in 1879. Tiled floors, and general Victorian atmosphere. Dr Wren, father of Sir Christopher, was rector here in 1620.

BISHOPS CANNINGS

BISHOPSTONE (near Salisbury)

During his incumbency he married the daughter of one of his churchwardens and moved to East Knoyle, where the architect was born. 13

Bishopstone (near Salisbury). The Ebble runs through the village under many little bridges, feeding big watercress beds as it goes. New housing developments in progress. The church is a mile away, among big trees. St John Baptist is a splendid cruciform building decorated with a fine tower over the crossing. The mouldings are elaborate and the design of details skilled. There is a shrine, or tomb-housing, against the south wall of the south transept outside, low, vaulted and buttressed. The chancel is stone-vaulted with a highly elaborate 14th-century triple sedilia, canopied over. In the north transept is a wall tomb under an ornate arch. In a similar position in the south transept, the even more elaborate tomb chest and canopy in fact is the tomb of a one-time rector of Bishopstone, the Rev. George Augustus Montgomery who was killed by a fall of new vaulting in East Grafton church in 1842. The monument was designed by Pugin for a fee of 50 guineas; he was also responsible for the stained glass in the window above. There is fine Victorian glass – especially the pretty grisaille in the chancel. (The modern east window is purplish brown, and a sad affair.) There is also some original 14th-century glass in traceries. English and foreign woodwork of various dates has been lovingly used in the furniture. The standard of medieval workmanship in this church is of a high order. Were craftsmen from Winchester Cathedral employed here? It was a living of the Bishops of Winchester. *Throope Manor* is Georgian; *Netton Farmhouse* and *Faulstone House* are flint and stone, 17th century with mullioned windows; the latter with a big circular medieval dovecote, built in bands of stone and flint. *Bishopstone House*, a big square building in greyish brick, dates from 1820. 17

Bishopstone (near Swindon). On the north slope of the downs, above the Vale of the White Horse. A place of gullies and sudden declivities, well-grown trees and well-tended gardens, with chalk streams and a pond. It takes a pride in its appearance: there is a constant trimming of hedges and re-thatching. There are attractive footpaths and tracks to back-lying cottages and farms about the village. In a fine churchyard, St Mary's, with its low west tower, is mainly Perpendicular, but there are Norman doorways and a tiny chancel arch, visually crushed by the huge organ case over it. In contrast, the 15th-century tower arch at the opposite end of the nave is lofty and graceful. The works of the old church clock, made by the local blacksmith in 1654, are kept in the tower. The interior is, in fact, much modernized, with green diamond-leaded glass in the windows: except for one which has some Perpendicular glass including St Peter holding his keys and St Anne with a book in yellow and silver. 6

Bishopstrow is where St Aldhelm's staff changed miraculously into an ash tree – "Bishop's Treow" or the Bishop's Tree. Both King Alfred and Oliver Cromwell are said to have camped here after fighting battles. A plain roadside hamlet on the western edge of Salisbury Plain, set below the twin Iron Age hill forts of Battlesbury and Scratchbury. Many overhead wires and TV aerials. The church is a simple nave-and-aisle building with a 14th-century tower and a well-kept interior, entered from the west under a strange arched arrangement. There were two restorations during the 19th century. The west door has enormous and elaborate Victorian hinges, a presage of what is to come inside, where there is much Victorian furnishing and stained glass (not very good: east window by H. Hughes, 1879) and two elaborate, Devon-style, Edwardian carved screens. There is a cosy-looking parsonage next door. Classical *Bishopstrow House*, in a park, was built in 1817. 10

Blackland is a hamlet outside Calne. The soil is indeed black. Beyond big trees is *Blackland Park*, an 18th-century mansion that once had a huge grotto in its grounds. St Peter's church is small and old with picturesque stone flagged roofs and bell turret. The interior is dark, much restored, partly scraped, and lacks interest. A late Georgian house next door has stables and barns of the previous century. 8

Blunsdon St Andrew, close to Swindon, has a greyhound stadium, and in and around the roofless walls of Victorian-Gothic *Blunsdon Abbey* is a well-laid-out caravan site. St Andrew's church is small and simple, at the end of a tree-lined drive. Norman doorway and an Early English arcade. Extensive restoration by Butterfield in 1868, when he built the west front, raised the walls and put on the elaborate new roof. Did the weight of all this cause the old walls and arches to lean over so frighteningly? Brass candle sconces and candles still in use, but there are modern spotlights. 2

Bodenham is to the south of Salisbury and one of the entrances to Longford Park is here. A hamlet with thatch and half-timber and one good Georgian house. The road through the village winds inside a cool green tunnel of trees out of which you suddenly burst upon a wide stretch of the Wiltshire Avon. 18

Boscombe. Here, by a mercy and a few yards, the Salisbury-Tidworth road by-passes the village. Richard Hooker, author of *Ecclesiastical Politie* was rector, 1591–1595. A later incumbent was Isaac Walton, son of the famous Izaak. The church gives a fair picture of what an English country church looked like in the 16th and 17th centuries: a simple nave and chancel with tiled roof and squat timber bell turret. The plain interior is full of Jacobean and Georgian box pews, three-decker pulpit (1633) and big squire's pew. The transept chapel, supposedly built by Hooker to accommodate the big congregations attracted by his sermons, is now disused. The old stone floor inside is attractive. The concrete-block churchyard path not so. 15

Bowden Hill stands beside Bewley Common, a National Trust open space from which there are views over the plain to Lacock and far beyond. Across the road from the church, the neat little conduit house was built by Sir William Sharington as part of the Abbey's water supply system. The church of St Anne, newly built in 1856, is in the Early English style with bits of pseudo-Norman and a Rhenish tower, like Sompting. Simple interior with ashlar walls and good timber roof. Memorials here to the Gladstones who still live in *Bowden Park*. This, designed by James Wyatt, was completed in 1796, and is a fine stone house on this dominating site. 16th-century gatehouse to the Victorian mansion of *Spye Park*, bearing the arms of Henry VIII, was re-erected here from Bromham House. Down in the valley, *Bewley Court* is a stone house flanked by trees; mostly medieval but "modernized" in the 17th century. 7

Bower Chalke. Among the Downs. A compact village with a flourishing watercress industry and big hedges everywhere, thick and lush in summer. Modern housing. The small church was built about 1300, but the tower and most of the other old work is Perpendicular. T. H. Wyatt re-built the chancel and added a south aisle in 1866. It is a dark pitch pine interior, not redeemed by the 1927 east window. Views of the downs from the churchyard. Old houses, including the 17th-century *Bingham's Farmhouse*, to the north. 17

Bowood is a 1000-acre estate and seat of the Marquis of Lansdowne. The first modest house was built here by Sir Orlando Bridgman in 1625. Taken over in 1754 by the first Earl of Shelburne, it was enlarged for him by Henry Keene and became "The Little House", which now contains the private quarters of the present Marquis around one courtyard and a series of flats for estate employees round the other. The second Earl employed Robert Adam to carry out further improvements. From 1760 to 1770, he added new porticos and built a new dining room, the library and an orangery, one wing nearly 100 yards long being known as the "Diocletian" range since its design is based on the palace of Diocletian at Split. Fifty years later a chapel was added by C. R. Cockerell behind the Adam block, and at the very beginning of the Victorian era Sir Charles Barry erected the tower. Much of the earlier work was pulled down in

1956, and "The Big House" of Bridgman, Keene and Adam is no more, although the Diocletian wing, the library, orangery and chapel remain. In the park, landscaped by Capability Brown and Repton, is Adam's *Mausoleum*, with cascades, temples, statues and other fine garden features. 8

Box, though hardly a town, is a scattered place whose many stone villas and large houses make it a proper neighbour for Bath. Extensive quarries produce Bath Stone. *Box Tunnel*, with its magnificent entrances, is one of Isambard Kingdom Brunel's great works on the old G.W.R. line. The church was enlarged at the cost and request of the railway company for the men working on the tunnel. Dedicated to St Thomas of Canterbury, it lies below the main road in a little precinct of old houses, including the tall and mullion-windowed *Old School*, built early in the 17th century. The church is mostly 14th century, with a central spired tower and later Perpendicular work. There are early Georgian windows and a classical porch. The south aisle, built for the navvies, was added in 1840, Box Tunnel being completed about a year later. Attractive Victorian chancel with elaborate reredos, and a window in mauves, reds, pinks and blues by Gibbs. There is a wonderful collection of tabletombs in the sloping churchyard. Along the main street is the village *Lockup* with domed roof; and here, too, the 19th-century *School* with startling Victorian clock tower. At *Chapel Plaster*, above the village, is a 15th-century hospice and church which was probably used as a stopping place for pilgrims making the journey to Glastonbury. *Hazlebury Manor* is a good restored Tudor house. *Rudloe Manor*, on the road to Chippenham is 17th century, with a medieval barn adjoining. 7

Boyton is quiet and well-wooded. The church, built of flint and stone in the chequer pattern typical of the area, is Early English and Decorated. Much restored by Wyatt in 1863. The sumptuous interior is newly furnished and very well done (1962). Here is the same use of subdued greens and golds that one sees at Compton Chamberlayne, where a similar modern scheme was recently completed, though it is doubtful if it was wise to paint all the stone-work white as well as the plaster. In the south chapel is a startling splash of medieval colour in the 14th-century tomb of Lady Margaret Giffard. Close by, the fine and well-preserved effigy of the Crusader knight, Sir Alexander Giffard (1265). His brothers Walter and Godfrey were respectively Archbishop of York and Bishop of Worcester at this time and each became Lord Chancellor of England. They were largely responsible for the splendour of the chapel. The north chapel now serves as a vestry and is comfortably furnished like a drawing-room. There is a large collection of bits of glass, English and foreign, of the 13th century onwards: some German, Flemish roundels, etc. A Gibbs window has been destroyed recently, and other Victorian glass cut about, and figures put on clear glass. All somewhat too drastic. The *Manor* overlooks the churchyard. The part one sees is early Georgian and newer than the rest, which dates from 1618. A handsome house, gaining from its situation. 14

Bradenstoke-cum-Clack. The best thing about Bradenstoke is the view from its single street across the Avon Valley towards the distant Cotswolds. There are one or two bits of half-timber here and there, but the whole village is rather depressed and shouldered aside by Lyneham R.A.F. Station. The church, by Hansom, in the Decorated style, has an elaborate interior and was built in 1866, the font coming from the Great Exhibition of 1851. *Providence Chapel* is a pretty brick building of 1777. Outside is the old village cross and over some fields the remains of the remains of *Bradenstoke Priory*, a foundation of the Augustinian Order which settled here in 1142. Until the 1930s there was a considerable range of half-ruined buildings, but Hearst, the American newspaper millionaire, took most of them away for the rebuilding of his dream castle in Glamorganshire, St Donats. 5

Bradford-on-Avon. A busy and fascinating town, much concerned with the present, rich with the past. The domestic architecture of all periods is carried out in the mellow-coloured Bath stone of the district. The streets are very steep, so that many buildings are seen from strange and surprising angles. The town is full of interest and unexpected visual pleasures. The church of *St Laurence* was built about 900 and its tall, mysterious interior is very moving. It was rescued in the 1860s from burial in a confusion of later buildings. Two sculptured angels, high up, are contemporary, and were part of a rood. Above the Old Town the *Hermitage* (or *Tory Chapel*) was a fifteenth century hospice, described by Aubrey as "the finest Hermitage I have seen in England". Later decayed, it was restored in the 19th century. The *parish church, Holy Trinity*, is by the Avon and contains features from every period from Norman onwards. It was much restored in the last century; the pillars on the north side of the nave have Victorian wreathed ribbons inscribed with pious texts. *Christ Church*, 1841, spired and added to later, is in the Perpendicular style. The *Town Bridge* has two of its medieval arches but was rebuilt in the 17th century. The little building in the middle was a chapel, but was used for generations as the town lockup. Among the more interesting of the older houses are *Old Church House* and *Old Priory*, both late 15th century, and there are Tudor houses in The Shambles. The 14th-century *Tithe Barn*, by the river at Barton Farm, is one of the finest and largest in the country and now cared for by the Ministry of Public Building and Works. *The Hall*, of about 1610, is an Elizabethan home, important in the history of English architec-

BOWOOD, *the Mausoleum*

ture. It was built for John Hall a clothier, and is related to Wollaton, Hardwick, Bolsover and Longleat in its relation of glass to wall and projection to related gable. The name of Robert Smythson has been mentioned in connection with The Hall. He was certainly connected with Longleat. "The great majority of Elizabethan houses," Sir John Summerson has said lately, "were probably copies, more or less, of other houses. Everybody copied everybody and everybody copied drawings or copies of drawings." The examples of fine building increase rapidly to almost overwhelming numbers. Of the 17th century are houses such as *Three Gables*; *The Chantry*, to which rooms were added by Inigo Jones; and the *Bell Inn* with adjoining cottages; but there are many others. Yet the architectural heyday of Bradford-on-Avon was undoubtedly the 18th century, when the growing prosperity of the cloth-men reached new heights of affluence. More and more cloth factories were built here: by the turn of the century, no less than thirty-two were recorded. This new richness of the town is clearly reflected in the excellence and amount of its Georgian architecture; fine classical houses are to be found in nearly every street. Of particular note are *New Church House*, the *Swan Hotel*, *Druce's Hill House*, *Abbey House* and *Little Chantry* in Church Street. In Woolley Street, *Old House*, *Moxham's* and *St Olave's*. Close to the Town Bridge is *Westbury House*, a big Bristol-fashion town mansion of the early Georgian period. It is possible to spend a good deal of time in Bradford without wasting any of it. 7

Bratton. The church of St James is isolated on the far side of a small and steep valley. It can be reached on foot by a long stepped causeway from the main village; the alternative approach is by a long climbing lane which stops at the churchyard gate. With the exception of the 19th-century Early English-style chancel, the church is Perpendicular, cruciform with embattled tower over the crossing, which has a tierceron stone vault. Good, symmetrical; somewhat over-restored. A late brass inscription but otherwise a curious lack of monuments. 18th-century houses: *Bratton House* (1715) and *Melbourne House* (1768). The *Baptist Chapel* (1734) is in the simple classical mode. *Court House*, on the way to Steeple Ashton, is partly half-timber and partly stone and dates from 1626. Leaving the village by the Westbury road, a finger post points the way to *Westbury White Horse*, on the downs. Close to this first and foremost of Wiltshire Horses is *Bratton Castle*, a hill fort of the Iron Age (see Westbury). 10

Bremhill is fringed with tidy Victorian houses and more recent estate-style developments. There are thatched cottages and a medieval village cross. Another cross in the churchyard. The church was originally Transitional Norman with an Early English chancel but all this early work was cut about by Butterfield in

BRADFORD-ON-AVON

1850 and again in 1864. Only the tower and the other Perpendicular work were left alone, and the church has an attractive texture outside. The interior looks Victorian, and has poor stained glass. There is a Norman font and an amusing and pleasing late-17th-century monument to George Hungerford, in which the arts of peace and war are depicted by violins, drawing instruments, cannons and pistols. Behind the church is *Bremhill Court*, the former vicarage. Basically a house of the 17th century, it was Gothicized by William Bowles, rector here from 1805 to 1844. Bowles was an *amateur* in the proper, old-fashioned sense of the word, poet, literary man, gardener. He was a friend of Tom Moore, wrote sonnets and epitaphs for many of the graves in the churchyard, entertained Wordsworth and Charles Lamb and had free access to Bowood House, where he met Madame de Staël in a famous encounter. 5

Brinkworth. The church, standing on a small hill on the fine ridge between Malmesbury and Swindon, is in a well-kept churchyard, with fine views. It is Perpendicular, with a Victorian chancel and tall slender pillars in the nave, on some of which are traces of painted figures and more than traces of other decoration. There is a Jacobean pulpit with tester and the gallery is Georgian. It is supported on thin, carved wooden animals. Are these modern Scandinavian, or what? The west end is dominated by a monster organ set up in 1905. One sensitive carved memorial tablet to John Weeks is mid-18th century and beautiful work. Two fine Royal Arms – one decayed but well designed, the other of George II (1728). 5

Britford. A hamlet in the Avon valley. *Bridge Farm* is a spreading 18th-century house close to the

BRADFORD-ON-AVON

river. There are a number of pretty estate cottages and *The Moat*, part Georgian and part 19th-century Gothick, with ogee headed windows has a moat in front and water, water everywhere. St Peter's church is at the end of the riverward lane. It stands beside a mullioned house of the 17th century which has a nice rhythm in its fenestration. The church is cruciform and very big for so tiny a place. Much remains here of an Anglo-Saxon building. The nave is tall and narrow with the small windows set high. At the east end of the nave are two arched openings like miniature transepts; one incorporates Roman tiles and one is carved with vine scrolls of the early 9th century. There is a good deal of Decorated work also, but the whole interior has been made brown and unappealing by Victorians. The monuments include one to G. P. Jervoise in the form of a huge open book in marble in which are listed members of the Jervys family from 1500 onwards (1820). 18

Brixton Deverill. Here was the "Ecgbryghts-stane" where Alfred the Great collected his militia together before the battle of Bratton Down. The church has a grey stone tower, square and short; a very tall and narrow chancel, framed by an Early English arch. The nave has a coved plaster ceiling of the Georgian period; and the atmosphere is attractively Victorian. There is respectable, if orthodox, stained glass. The Norman font was brought over from Imber church a few years ago. Among the thatched cottages nearby is *Manor Farmhouse*, 17th century, with mullioned windows. 13

Broad Blunsdon. A brash and bustling dormitory village with bright little developments all over the place but with roots deep in the past. *Castle Hill* is an Iron Age fort. Though over-restored in 1872 by Butterfield, St Leonard's church retains some 13th-century features. Jacobean screen and pulpit of the same period; wall monuments, including one by Peter Scheemakers (1733). A group of council houses has a view across the plain. 2

Broad Chalke. Full of thatch and well-kept houses. Modern farming development makes an eyesore on one side of the Ebble Valley. The church is big and strong in appearance; cruciform, with a tower over a vaulted crossing. The main building was begun in the 13th century and was completed by 1370. The windows in the nave and the battlements are Perpendicular.

There is good clear-coloured Victorian glass in at least two windows. Christopher Wood was buried in the churchyard in 1930. The farmers of Cranborne Chase regarded Broad Chalke as their "metropolis" to which they retired during the long winters, living in their "town houses" until the coming of spring. John Aubrey, the first Wiltshire archaeologist and antiquarian, lived in this village for a number of years, and served as a churchwarden. This fact is inscribed upon one of the bells. The *Old Rectory*, close to the church, was here before him: the entrance archway is 15th century and much of the house is Elizabethan. *Reddish House* is a diminutive grand manor house of the early 18th century, with a weathered pink brick and mossy stone north front, towards the road. It is a house of great character, noble yet rustic. 17

Broad Hinton is an unremarkable village on the way from Swindon to Devizes, relieved by one decent Georgian house and few thatched cottages. The church, among big yew trees, was heavily restored by the Victorians but retains a hammer beam roof of 1634, some 13th-century features and a number of excellent monuments. Of note is a fine six-poster standing memorial to Sir Thomas Wroughton and his wife (1597), the lady in widows' weeds; also the big monument to Colonel Glanville; his armoured figure stands like a giant beneath helmet and gauntlets. He was killed during the Civil War, fighting for the King at Bridgwater (1645). 5

Broad Town. Dropping down the very steep hill into the village there are tremendous views. In spite of a few old cottages, this is not really a pretty place; there are too many recent houses and bungalows, each trying to be different. Christ Church is the simplest of Victorian Gothic churches with plain lancet windows and remarkably unaffected. It was built in 1844 at the expense of the Marchioness of Ailesbury, who was also responsible for the churches at Savernake and Cadley. 5

Brokenborough is a hamlet on a hill with a tributary of the Avon winding through fields at the bottom. The pastoral, shallow valley eastwards from here is of great landscape beauty. The small church is long and low and stands in a neat churchyard overlooking it. The interior, mostly Perpendicular, is simple and attractive, but not exciting. A few hundred yards away is a big medieval tithe barn, stone, with two porches and massive buttresses. 1

Bromham is being gradually surrounded by mediocre housing. The church of St Nicholas is large and lofty with a tall Early English tower with a late 14th-century spire. The Beauchamp Chapel of 1492 is tierceron vaulted and ornate both inside and out. There are grand tombs in the chapel to Sir Roger Tocotes (1457) and Sir Edward Baynton (1578) and a number of other good brasses and memorials to members of the same families. The east window of the chancel is by Burne Jones. There are good churchyard table-tombs. Tom Moore, the poet, is buried in the churchyard, the spot being marked by a modern Celtic cross. He is also commemorated in the west window of the nave (not very good glass). Moore lived at *Sloperton Cottage*, a little way out of the village. An old lockup in the churchyard is built of timber. There are other half-timbered buildings, including the one now used as a workingmen's club. *Nonsuch*, on the Melksham road, is a classical house of the early 1700s. *Bromham House Farm* is all that remains of Bromham Old House, a huge Tudor mansion "nearly as large as Whitehall and fit to entertain a king". It was destroyed in 1645 during the Civil War; the gatehouse bearing the royal arms can be seen at Bowden Hill, where it was re-erected at the main entrance to Spye Park. 8

Broughton Gifford. A long, rambling village near Melksham with stone houses behind curving walls and much mixed development.

The church is simple and has a white-walled, red-and-black-tiled interior. Clean Early English arcades in the nave and a Perpendicular tower with a pyramid roof. Porch with a neat spiral stair leading nowhere and tiny slit windows that once gave a view of the south chapel. Two hefty Victorian boot scrapers in cast iron are boldly inscribed "Broughton Gifford Church". The big Rectory is Neo-Jacobean and dull; the Georgian house behind honest and pleasing. A little way out of the village, *Monkton House* is a stone gabled house of 1647. On the road to Broughton Common is the *Manor House*, another 17th-century building, L-shaped and gabled, behind its garden wall. The Common itself is a wide windy and reed-filled stretch of grassland, fringed with buildings. *Broughton House* and *Gifford Hall*, north and south respectively, are both 17th century. There is a round-headed Georgian box of a non-conformist chapel also. 7

Bulford consists of the old village and the huge mile-square military complex of Bulford Camp, a vast area of red brick buildings and huts. The garrison church, *St George's*, is big and brash (1927) but stands well enough above trees and downland. In the village the old church is far more impressive with a squat and enormously strong-looking Norman tower. Inside, much work of the 12th and 13th centuries. There is a sad contrast between this sturdy stuff and the terribly flat and weak-looking Gothick arch to the north transept, put there in 1855. The *Manor House*, along the road nearby, is a gabled 17th-century building with a not unhappy mixture of stone mullioned windows and later Georgian sashes. 12

Bulkington has simple Georgian houses. Later developments include a big Co-op Creamery and many modern farm buildings in

Reddish Manor, BROAD CHALKE

catalogue-style steel and asbestos. These make the small Victorian church look medieval by comparison. A depressing collection of ramshackle huts flanks the churchyard. 7

Burbage has a few old cottages and some dull modern housing. The church is pretty, flint and stone chequered, and it looks well against the equally pretty gabled, flint and brick, early 19th-century parsonage, although much rebuilt by T. H. Wyatt in 1854 and 1876. It has a low west tower and porch, both 14th century. There is charming patterned glass by Powell (of Whitefriars) with small figured panels in the east and some other windows. Outside the village, *Wolf Hall* has the remains of a house in which Jane Seymour, the third and short-lived wife of Henry VIII was born. The place has a curiously chopped-off appearance, emphasized by very tall Tudor chimneys which are all out of scale with the present building. 9

Burcombe. The village is off, but the church is on, the noisy main road. *St John's* stands well on a little hill and is small and inconspicuous, because of its truncated tower, now lower than the nave gable. The tiny chancel and narrow chancel arch suggest Saxon origins, and there is long-and-short work in the masonry outside. The tower dates from 1667 and T. H. Wyatt did restorations in 1859 and 1877. A multi-arched bridge over the slow-winding Nadder leads to the pretty village; grey and white houses with a background of low hills. 14

Burton, close to the Gloucestershire border, in the broken, Badminton hunting country of tall hedgerow trees and undulating fields, is a scattered village with a rambling Georgian rectory and a Decorated and Perpendicular church. The tower has a well-panelled upper stage, like West Kington. Norman font; 15th-century stone pulpit; wagon roofs, and some Georgian box pews. Others have been cut down, and the doors removed. Old stone floors. Early Georgian altar rails. No glass of merit. 4

Bushton is a straggling hamlet between Clyffe Pypard and Tockenham. There is one Georgian farmhouse, a few bits of thatch and some recent examples of Pop Art in the external decoration and general embellishment of certain houses along the main road. 5

Buttermere. A hamlet on top of the downs where there is a shallow valley full of fine trees. The church (*St James*) is remote and tiny; without tower or turret a like a cattle-shed in its simplicity. The oil-lit interior has pitch pine rafters and pews, and everything has been much renewed. Norman font with chevron ornament. 9

Cadley, on the edge of Savernake Forest, has a petrol station, a few cottages and a Victorian church by T. H. Wyatt; flint and stone among tall cypresses. It has a tower on the south side and low spire, and a wide interior from which most of the stained glass has been removed, though some bright patterned glass has been left in the west windows. The Victorian atmosphere is otherwise undisturbed. Robert Byron, editor of the first edition of this book, is commemorated by a tablet on the east wall, outside. He died in 1941, aged 35. 9

Calne. In the centre, Harris's Bacon Factory dominates the town like a north-country cotton mill. Its red bulk lords it over finer and more aristocratic architecture. For example, the *Lansdowne Arms*, 18th-century coaching inn with long and simple frontage. There are other Georgian houses. If the porker now holds the centre of the stage, it used to be occupied by the sheep: the parish church of *St Mary* was built by the prosperous clothiers and wool men of the district in the Perpendicular period. Approached by a vaulted porch at the end of a yew walk, the interior is impressive in scale. The grand arcades of the nave date from 1160. The clothiers built their 15th-century church around this nucleus. In 1638, the big crossing tower collapsed and was replaced by the present one; Gothic Survival, rather than Gothic Revival. Ornate organ, all silver and gold and Arts and Crafts movement, made by C. R. Ashbee's Campden Guild in 1904. Two vivid windows of the early 1850s – otherwise the stained glass is brownish and unattractive. No notable monuments, but some decent tablets. Churchyard stones well carved. Dr Townson's Almshouses, 1682, are near the church. Here also are the 17th-century *Church House* and the *Youth Hostel* is in a house of the same period. Some of Calne's best Georgian buildings are to be found around The Green; *Adam House* is notable. Across the way, the very pleasing Gothick of the *Boys School* and the *Girls School* (1829). The Girls, building is smaller than the Boys, and the two are separated by a row of cottages. A good town for architectural perambulation.

Calstone Wellington near Calne, is a scattering of thatched cottages in a romantic setting on the lower slopes of downland, with big hedgerow trees and steep declivities. The small 14th-century church almost completely Victorianized, is at the top of a grassy lane, its simple square tower framed in trees. Some fragments of glass in the chancel. The "Norman" font is Georgian. The 19th-century gabled and pantiled rectory neighbours it in green, well-planted, surroundings. 8

Castle Combe. This village, once a centre for cloth weaving, lies in a wooded hollow through which a river twists and turns. High above, the few remaining fragments of the old *Castle* moulder among "green battlements". Houses and cottages cluster about the focal point of the Market Cross, and all is warm mellow stone of a golden hue. The *Manor House* – now a hotel – stands in wooded grounds and is dated 1664. Its gabled *Dower House*, built thirty

Graffiti in BROMHAM church

BROUGHTON GIFFORD

years later, has a shell porch and stands among charming little cottages. The church has some 13th-century work, but is mainly Perpendicular, the fine chancel arch with its canopied saints looking remarkably like French Gothic. The great tower was erected in 1434 "at the expense of the clothiers of the district". Carvings of shuttles and other weaving implements were added to one face in 1576. There was extensive restoration in 1851 but St Andrew's is still a splendid building. Monuments of various periods. 13th-century font. Fan-vaulting. *Weavers House* stands at the bottom end of the village by the river, with the early-Victorian vicarage beyond. Here also is a recent block of conveniences. In 1966, there was a great to-do in Castle Combe when a film company took the place. Temporarily, the village was transformed into a little seaport, with new harbour walls and jetties and boats all over the place. It is now back to its more normal tourist existence. 4

Castle Eaton. Stone houses. The *Red Lion* is an attractive Georgian building in brick, with stone tiled roof, dormers and big brick chimneys. The church is beside the river Thames, down a long path. Norman doorways, Early English chancel, large and remarkable 14th-century bell turret as well as western tower. Butterfield restoration, 1862. Timber columns to the arcade. Jacobean pulpit. There is some pretty glass by Gibbs of the early 1860s. The blues, pinks and ruby of the east window are an addition to this agreeable interior. 3

Chapel Plaster. See Box.

Chapmanslade is a long village strung along the road between Westbury and Frome, with some 18th-century houses. See also *The Wheelwright's Arms* and the *Dead Maids* at the Warminster cross roads. The church was designed by G. E. Street. An excellent essay in Early English. Nave and chancel under arc-gable-western turret. Very spare in details. 10

Charlton (near Upavon) lies just below the Downs and has thatched cottages and a church. The original Perpendicular tower and a chapel remain. J. L. Pearson rebuilt the body of nave and chancel in flint and stone and brick in 1858. In a side chapel, small brasses to William Chancey (died 1524) and his wife, and tablets. Stephen Duck, the "thresher poet" who received a pension from Queen Caroline was born here. She made him a Yeoman of the Guard and he later became vicar of Byfleet. He drowned himself in 1750. An annual dinner in his memory "for threshers and labourers" is still held at *The Charlton Cat*. 11

Charlton (near Salisbury) has an unremarkable brick Early English style church, by T. H. Wyatt, 1851. There is a charming schoolhouse of 1622, and the *Manor*, seen among trees from the Salisbury road, is a mid-Georgian house. 18

Charlton (near Shaftesbury). The church was designed by William Walker and completed in 1839. Outside, Norman Revival with twin castellated towers, as straightforward as an engine shed. The interior is plain, honest and impressive, with king-post roof trusses, a simple west gallery on engineers' cast-iron columns and some recent and unpretentious ritual furnishings, Worth seeing. Nearby, the smaller church hall is an echo of the main building. Much recent and undistinguished housing. 16

Charlton (near Malmesbury). The cream-washed inn, *The Horse and Groom*, is a charming building with a deep bay window. The church, near the park-gates, is much restored but has a tall round-arched, early 13th-century arcade. There is a big, rather forbidding monument of 1598 to Sir Henry Knyvett. His daughter married the first Earl of Suffolk, and there are other Suffolk memorials, including 20th-century ones.

Charlton Park is a big square house, facing south-west down a well-grown avenue and built round a central court, the entrance side of which originally had an open loggia. It was built in 1607, and altered perhaps later in the same century, certainly in the next. It has corner turrets with pointed caps like the Tower of London, or Blickling Hall, Norfolk, and flame-like stone shapes lick the parapets, and run up and down the gables. Suffolk's son-in-law, the poet Dryden, having, like Boccaccio before him, fled to the country to escape the plague, sat and talked with his friends: they were Sir Charles Sedley, Lord Buckhurst and Robert Howard, and Dryden then and there wrote down their discussions in his *Essay of Dramatic Poetry*. It is a big, gay, palatal design, originally built for the first Countess of Suffolk, and altered for the twelfth Earl in the 1770s by Matthew Brettingham, whose name appears in the house. He closed the open loggia, and did a great deal inside. The original Jacobean long gallery remains. It was last occupied (as a girls' school) in 1931. 2

Cherhill lies below the Downs near Calne; a big village with much recent messy development and an older part near the church. *St James* and the *Manor House* stand together, the public footpath to the church leading across the front of the manor garden. A simple church with a tapering Perpendicular tower. The interior is mostly Victorian, including the gallery and the brownish stained glass. Nice brass chandeliers, 1702. The beautiful tithe barn mentioned in the last edition of this Guide was demolished in 1956. From the church porch is a view of the Cherhill *White Horse* cut in 1780, and of a Lansdowne memorial column, this one commemorating an ancestor-economist of the 17th century, Sir William Petty. 8

Chicklade. All Saints was re-built in 1832 and has a Georgian-style bell turret; well-meaning renewals and "improvements" since have removed interest and beauty. The old rectory next door is much bigger than the church itself. Nearby is an unexpected and prim block of 19th century villas in warm stone, and a manor house, all on the main road. 13

Chilmark. The home of Chilmark stone, the fine creamy freestone used in the building of Salisbury Cathedral and many of the churches of Wiltshire. It has been quarried since Roman times, and the old quarries are the size of a cathedral. Now used by the R.A.F. as an ammunition dump. There is messy fringe development but the main village has many 17th-century houses and cottages built in this local stone. A clear stream is crossed by miniature bridges. The *Manor House* has mullioned windows looking on to a tiny courtyard with a scrolled wall. *Chilmark House* is late Georgian and set within a walled garden. The Elizabethan *rectory* had a large wing added in the Trollopian days and is in parklike grounds. The church, dedicated to *St Margaret of Antioch*, is a cruciform building, large and well-kept. Beautifully arched Early English crossing, simple and sturdy, with a rib vault under the tower. Stone spire. All in Chilmark stone, of course. The interior is very Victorian. The churchyard tombs are handsome, good table-tombs among them. People from this parish emigrated to America in the 1600s. When Mayflower II, the replica of the Pilgrim Fathers' ship made the commemorative voyage to

CASTLE COMBE

New England in 1957, a scroll was sent from here to the people of Chilmark, Massachusetts "which was undoubtedly founded and named by emigrants from this village". 14

Chilton Foliat. An attractive village in the Kennet water-meadows, well timbered; somewhat marred by through traffic. A few Georgian brick houses and some variously-styled cottages in thatch and tile. The flint and stone church is basically Early English and was much rebuilt by Benjamin Ferrey in 1845. Painted Jacobean roof, and a screen of the same period. There is an effigy of an armed knight, and a Popham baby of 1861, sculptured by another Popham. The Victorian stained glass is bright and pleasing. Next door is the big 18th-century *Rectory* and at a little distance, *Chilton House*, also Georgian, with an octagonal entrance hall and a small domed lantern over the main staircase. The River Kennet is dammed here to form a wide pool. *Bridge House*, close by, is a 17th-century house with Georgian additions – tall round-headed windows in the front facing the river. Eastward, *Chilton Lodge* dominates the valley from its Berkshire knoll. Pedimented, in stone. Pretty row of thatched estate cottages. 9

Chippenham was a market town in Saxon times, was frequented by Alfred the Great, received mention in Domesday Book as a place of importance and sent representatives to the Parliament of Edward I. It is now a busy, noisy, modern town, full of motorcars and heavy transport and traffic jams, with too little architectural evidence of this historical past. The big Perpendicular church was almost entirely rebuilt in the 1870s and even the impressive tower and spire, which look old, are of 1633. The Hungerford Chapel is, however, genuine 15th-century work. The monuments in this, from the 13th to the 19th centuries, include one of the early 17th century with kneeling figures. The older parts of the town centre are round Market Place, a big irregular square. Two hotels, *The Angel* and *The Bear* present bold fronts, the one Georgian and the other "thoroughly Tudor Gothic". There is no great architecture, but a pleasing profusion of buildings that at least are easy on the eye. The *Old Yelde Hall*, standing in the central island of buildings once known as The Shambles, dated originally from the 16th century. Across the way, the new *Post Office* completed in 1959 rounds off the corner. There are Georgian houses here and there, and at *The Grove*, in St Mary's Street, is a garden pavilion and the last remains of a medicinal *Spa* which was started here in 1694. *Ivy House*, along the Bath road, is an 18th-century house, perhaps the best in Chippenham. A great deal of industry has grown up around the town in recent years, the factories and buildings of the Westinghouse Brake Company having really industrialized it. 4

Chirton in the Vale of Pewsey is a thatched village with a few country-Georgian houses among the smaller cottages. Grey-stone church, with a big golden weathercock on a low square tower. An impressive Norman entrance, the mouldings of the arch delightfully punctuated with carved heads, hands, beasts and little men. The nave has a fine late-Norman arcade, re-worked by Butterfield at his restoration of 1850, and much of the pleasure of the interior is spoiled by later over-conscientious plastering. A Norman font is carved with figures of the twelve apostles. The ancient timber roof of the nave is believed to be the original one, dating from 1200. Some tolerable Victorian glass with clear colours, and hatchments under the tower. At *Conock* are two manor houses. *Conock Manor* is an early and mid-18th-century house of brick and stone, with handsome stables behind with a cupola. A good composition in flat meadows. There is a pair of Gothick lodges, 1820, with big quadruple chimneys and attractive estate houses. *Conock Old Manor* is of brick, of about 1710. 11.

Chiseldon is within commuting distance of Swindon. But the old village nucleus around the church has some character and some thatched cottages. A wooded gully west of the church, in which ran the railway, opens out as it descends northwards into a beautiful open valley. South of the village is the big army establishment of Chiseldon Camp and at the hamlet of *Hodson* can be found a pretty collection of old cottages. Holy Cross church has a Perpendicular tower unusually placed half-way along one side of the nave, with an entrance porch beneath. Transitional-Norman arcades in the nave. The Early English chancel is darkened by bad late Victorian glass, and dark woodwork. Traces of Anglo-Saxon work. A light and lofty nave with a profusion of wall monuments in delicate coloured marbles. Some poor modern glass, and very new pews in light oak. *Burderop Park*, a big early-Georgian house, stands in wooded grounds nearby. 6

Chitterne. New housing on the outskirts is almost hidden by a screen of big trees lining the main road. A stream runs alongside and through the village. In the centre, a triangular green with smaller houses. The flint- and stone-chequered church was built by T. H. Wyatt in 1863. Big, apsidal, Perpendicular, but not impressive. Dull inside, with dull stained glass. Some good decorative wall monuments are collected together on the walls under the tower, the best of them skied. A few hundred yards away is St Mary's, the 15th-century chancel of the old parish church. The rest was pulled down in the 19th century. Windows with very slight fragments of old glass. The L-shaped *Manor House* next door is a much-altered Jacobean building. It is of beautifully textured brick with some stone mullioned windows. *Chitterne House*, against the road, has a stone gateway into a courtyard flanked by 17th-century buildings in flint, stone and half-timber,

Charlton Park, CHARLTON: the south-west front

with mullioned windows. The gateway is wide and handsome, like the entrance to many a manorial and farm courtyard in western France. 11

Chittoe. A few thatched cottages in a valley. Church by T. H. Wyatt, simple Decorated. On the hillside beyond is a 17th-century farm, with a smaller half-timbered house below. *Spye Park*, a rambling Victorian mansion, is hidden in woods. 7

Cholderton. Neat houses. The Bourne gives character to the village street. *The Crown* is an agreeable 18th-century inn, all whitewash and thatch. *Cholderton House* is of flint and brick, Georgian. T. Mozley, Newman's brother-in-law, became incumbent in 1836. In 1839 he heard of a church roof lying on the quay at Ipswich, going cheap. He had it brought by sea, canal and turnpike road, and with it came a little colony of Ipswich woodcarvers and carpenters. T. H. Wyatt designed the church to accommodate it. Mozley searched for suitable designs for windows and found them at Old Basing, where he spent two days drawing and measuring. After three years he ran out of money. Church was completed in 1850, after he had left the living. It cost over £6000, of which he paid £5000. The seats are by the Suffolk carvers. All stonework came ready cut from Tisbury, except bosses and corbels, which were done by the stone carvers at Wilton church. The Rev. James Fraser succeeded in 1847. He planned the glass and wrote (1849) "The east and west windows are being executed by O'Connor, and promise to be as handsome glass as I ever saw. The two side windows I have entrusted to Clutterbuck. If life is spared I hope to fill every window by 1851". All is still there. (T. Mozley. *Reminiscences, chiefly of Oriel College and the Oxford Movement.* Vol. II.) 15

Christian Malford. A lane peters out at the church on the banks of the Avon. There is a little brood of recent council houses. Churchyard has daffodils and primroses in spring. A wartime pill-box still stands near the river. All Saints has Early English work and a 14th-century screen. Old stone floors. It was much tidied up by Victorians. Fine medieval consecration crosses, one carved on south buttresses. 5

Chute. In *Lower Chute* the cottages are in good trim. *Standen House* is a late 18th-century mansion of greyish brick and stone with a wide pedimented front. Thatched boundary walls have straw birds perched along the top. In *Upper Chute*, the brick and flint church serves both places and was built by J. L. Pearson in 1872. It has a rich and rather beautiful east window by Clayton and Bell: Entombment, Resurrection and Mary at the sepulchre, with Instruments of the Passion above and below, in three lancets. Heavy timber roof trusses and much pitch pine inside. The Norman font looks out of place. Halfway between the two villages is a Victorian school. 12

Chute Forest is a large parish scattered with many cottages and farms. The forest is no longer recognizable. It was once a royal hunting ground of which Savernake formed a part. St Mary's church, by J. L. Pearson, 1875, and is a much finer building than St Nicholas at Chute. Flint and brick with a tall pyramid spire. The nave arched across inside, making a curious roof structure. Another good Clayton and Bell east window, contemporary with the church – Crucifixion, Agony in the Garden, Ascension, etc. Not so rich in colour as at Chute, but well drawn and full of character. Near the road is *Chute Lodge*, a handsome big brick mansion of the 1770s, designed by Sir Robert Taylor. It has endured many changes of fortune and fashion. It had an elaborate double staircase, but this was mutilated, and the Victorians did some re-roofing and left the place with unpleasantly wide eaves. It was used for some years as a Borstal institution. There are prefab classrooms and rugby goal-posts in the grounds. 12

Clatford. *Clatford House* is multi-dated from the early 17th century onwards and a good many smashed-up sarsen stones went into its construction. There are Georgian sash windows and porch. A pretty house, said to be on the site of one of King John's hunting lodges. 9

Clarendon. There was a royal household here soon after the Norman Conquest and at the beginning of the 12th century Henry II and later Henry III built and enlarged the great house which became Clarendon Palace. It remained and was used as a royal palace until the end of the 15th century and played a considerable part in the political history of England: the Constitutions of Clarendon, an attempt to limit the secular power of the Pope, were framed here by Henry II and Thomas à Becket. By the time of Henry VIII, however, the huge complex of buildings was beginning to fall into disuse. In the 17th century it was already a complete ruin and served as a quarry for building materials during the next two centuries. The site became overgrown. In the 1930s, excavations were begun by Professor Borenius, but the outbreak of war and the Professor's death brought the work to a standstill. It has not been resumed and Clarendon Palace is once again "a wilderness, hidden in woods and difficult even to find". *Clarenden House* by Thomas Archer (*see* Verey). 15

CHOLDERTON church: A Tractarian interior of 1850, by Newman's brother-in-law, T. Mozley, and T. H. Wyatt architect

17th-century gateway at CHITTERNE House that resembles the yard entrances in the Charente area of Western France

COLERNE from BOX

Clyffe Pypard. Well set below Clyffe Hanging, the steep hill ridge that rises 400 feet. Sloping streets are lined with cottages. The church was restored by Butterfield, who re-built the chancel in 1860 and came back to do more work in 1874. His lavish painted decoration is fading and looking shabby. The font, of 1840, was carved by a vicar. Jacobean pulpit. The great set-piece of the church is the monument to the carpenter and builder Thomas Spackman, who died in 1786. Eighteen feet high, in marble, by John Devall, Jnr. Spackman left this, his native village, to make a fortune in London. At his feet lies an open carpenter's bass displaying the tools of his trade and he is flanked by a little boy and a little girl, pupils of the Chantry School which he endowed with "£1000 in Bank three per cent annuities". 5

Coate. Richard Jefferies was born at *Coate Farmhouse* in 1848, a 17th-century building. The house has been much changed since his death. *Coate Water* is now owned by Swindon Corporation and is used for pleasure boating. 6

Codford St Mary. The changing levels of the plain flow above and behind. The church has been twice restored, first by T. H. Wyatt in 1843 (one of his earliest restorations). A few old features survive: Early English chancel arch, 14th-century tower, Norman font and Jacobean pulpit. The elaborate tomb of John Mompesson, rector from 1612 to 1645, has fluted columns. The much fragmented effigy inside it is not the parson, but a much earlier gentleman (14th century). 14

Codford St Peter is linked to its twin village by a street of small houses and cottages. *Woolstore,* is mid-Georgian, with round arched windows. T. H. Wyatt re-used bits of the old Norman work in the church in 1864 and was content to leave some of the Early English chancel in position, together with the Perpendicular south aisle and the tower, but the structure has a Victorian atmosphere. Preserved in the church is one of Wiltshire's art treasures: part of a 9th-century carved stone cross. It is interesting as a link in the story of early carving; but – more important – it is beautiful and moving as a work of art. The subject is easy to recognize though hard to interpret: a man, his head thrown backwards, holds a tree in one hand and a hammer in the other (*see* p. 16). 14

Colerne stands high and bleak across the valley from Box. It is a big village with an R.A.F. airfield which, unlike Lyneham, does not dominate the scene. In the centre is an open space with two memorial columns and good houses. Nearby, the *Manor House* is of 1689. Everything is stone here: flat-topped garden walls with curved steps cast sharp shadows, balls on gate-posts, carved details, gables and roofs are all of a piece in form and colour. The church is light and lofty and its slender Perpendicular tower is a landmark. During the Victorian restoration, the Early English capitals and arches of the nave were heavily re-cut and now have an unpleasantly fresh look. The walls were scraped of their plaster, too. Entry is by way of the tower under a tierceron vault and there is a splendid and immediate view of the interior framed by the lovely tower arch. Old grisaille glass, and a window of 1850. Museum of memorials and wall tablets in the north aisle. Pieces of a 9th-century cross shaft with interlace carving are presented here. 7

Collingbourne Ducis. A village of straggling cottages at the junction of two main roads with a thatched barn in the middle. There is a neat new Rectory and a Victorian-Gothic house nearby. The flint and stone church is 13th-century with a later Perpendicular tower, the upper stages of which are formed as a dovecote. 12

Collingbourne Kingston. Big thatched farm buildings here; a pleasure to behold after so much concrete and corrugated asbestos. A good church with big round pillars and pointed arches in the nave dating from the beginning of the 13th century. An extensive restoration in 1862; this is the date of the chancel arch, and the naughty little hexagons and pentagons of the clerestory windows. The big monument to members of the Pile family (1626) is impressive. *Brunton House*, down a lane in the hamlet of Brunton, is a brick house of the early 18th century. 12

Compton Bassett. A sign announcing R.A.F. COMPTON BASSETT leads one past a huge broken area of demolished and derelict buildings. On a slope looking north is *St Swithin's*, an

CORSHAM Court: the centre of the south front, 1582

The Hungerford almshouses, CORSHAM

exquisite church which was enhanced by the Victorians. In the nave are late-Norman pillars and arches which stand below the curving wagon roof. The east end, and the whole atmosphere of the church, are due to Henry Woodyer who rebuilt the chancel and chapels and restored the rest in 1866. The east window is by Hardman. The painting of features in the figures has mostly disappeared, rendering them no less acceptable to the taste of our time. There is a gallery against the lofty Early English tower arch. The rood screen is carved in Caen stone with figures of the Apostles on the pilasters. The

"*The Flemish Cottages,*"
CORSHAM

pulpit has a big 18th-century hour-glass. The big stables of *Compton House* were built about 1670. The mansion was demolished after the First World War and the present house dates from the early 1930s. The village has many thatched cottages and rows of Victorian estate houses. The schoolhouse is charming. 8

Compton Chamberlayne. The long street has a half-timbered post office and thatched cottages. A lodge like a miniature castle marks the entrance to *Compton Park*, for 400 years the home of the fighting Penruddockes. The house itself is of stone, and the long façade looks towards the lake. It is of the 16th to the 18th centuries – the parts visible outside are mostly of the latest date. There is Grinling Gibbons carving inside. Sir Edward came to these parts from Cumberland in the early 16th century and one of his descendants, the romantic Royalist Sir John, was executed for treason against the Commonwealth at Exeter in 1655. The family gave up the house in 1930. The well-kept church stands within the park and is approached down a curving yew walk. Tower and north transept are late 13th century; nave and chancel Perpendicular. The floor level between nave and altar pace here was lifted to accommodate the Penruddocke family vault. A recent re-furbishing and re-decoration has left the interior spruce, if a little dull. No stained glass. White walls. Excellent lighting fittings. 14

Coombe Bissett. The river is spanned by an 18th-century bridge and downstream is a late-medieval packhorse bridge, (rather spoiled by heavy modern railings). The church is big with Norman south door and fat pillars carrying Norman arches along the south side of the nave. The opposite arcade is Perpendicular, like the tower. It has old stone floors. There was Victorianization in the 1840s, but it is a pleasing building, with good texture and colour outside: an addition to the landscape on the main road from Salisbury to Dorchester. It is without exciting monuments, stained glass or furniture. 17

Corsham. The outskirts are rather dull, with much nondescript Victorian and later development. The population has enormously increased since the last war. Admiralty establishments and other causes of accretion, have swelled the population to over 14,000. In the older centre are many good 17th- and 18th-century buildings, including weavers' houses. It has been said that "Corsham has no match in Wiltshire for its wealth of good houses". Most are built of warm honey-coloured stone. *Hungerford Almshouses* and *School*, form a gabled block of 1668. The

CORSHAM Court: The Folly

school retains its original seating and master's "pulpit". *Porch House, Alexander House* and *The Grove* in High Street, are all Georgian. There is another beautiful 18th-century house in *Church Street* with humble, but charming cottages alongside. In its garden, the "ancient ruin" with its "Norman" broken arch, oval chimneys and church-like windows is sham, a folly put there by the Methuen family at the end of the 18th century. *St Bartholomew's* is a fine big church, originally Norman but drastically dealt with by G. E. Street in 1876. He pulled down the central tower and erected the present one with its spire on the south side, removed the galleries, destroyed windows and arches and added the present Methuen Chapel. To the left of the church gates is the monumental entrance to *Corsham Court*, for more than two hundred years the seat of the Methuens, who are still in possession. (House and gardens are open to visitors throughout the year.) The earliest parts of the present building date from 1582, when the first house was built by "Customer Smythe", a wealthy London haberdasher. After passing to the Hungerford family and then to the Thynnes, it was purchased by Paul Methuen, of Bradford-on-Avon, in 1745. Within five years, he had remodelled the frontage and called in Capability Brown in the somewhat unusual role of architect to develop the south wings. In 1800, John Nash carried out further alterations and, at the same time, Humphry Repton was working on the layout of the grounds, following on from earlier schemes by Brown. The building history did not stop until the 1840s, when the architect Bellamy re-built a good deal of Nash's work which was found to be unstable. Apart from its architectural interest, Corsham Court houses a fine collection of 18th-century furniture and pictures by Italian and Flemish masters. Much of it now houses the Bath Academy of Art. At *Pickwick* to the west of the town, is a manor house of the late 1600s with traces of a medieval dwelling. Here are other cottages of the period. *Hartham Park*, to the north is a big mansion built by James Wyatt (1790–1795) but added to in the 19th century. *Neston*, south-west, has a Victorian–Gothic church and *Neston Park*, a big late-Georgian house. At *Moor Green* not far away is *Jaggards*, of 1657, with twin porches and well designed façade.   7

Corsley. Has a tall church on a hill, with a Perpendicular tower. St Margaret's is in fact more like a Nonconformist chapel or an assembly hall than a parish church; it was rebuilt in 1833 to accommodate a sudden influx of cloth workers to the district. The ornate reredos and surrounding decoration are of 1891, and the glazing scheme in side windows very recent. There are twin entrances – chapel style again – on each side of the tower. *Manor Farmhouse*, adjoining, is a late Elizabethan house, brick and stone. Opposite is the Victorian *school* and teacher's house. The church of St Mary Temple, at *Corsley Heath*, belongs to the Arts and Crafts school, and is by W. H. Stanley, 1903. *Corsley House*, in the same district, is Greek Revival.   10

Corston is a rather messy main road village just outside Malmesbury. A few older houses stand uncomfortably among the more recent developments. There is a simple church, mostly of 1881, its chief feature a big 15th-century bell turret. The porch is old also. 18th century tablets.   1

Corton, a Wylye valley village, is pretty, if unassuming, with many pleasant 17th-century cottages and a few larger houses in stone, brick and colourwash. Thatched garden walls everywhere. A lane takes a circular route round the best parts and the circumambulation is worth while: gardens and unexpected vistas at every turn. At the western end is a recent, good modern house.   14

Cricklade. An attractive main street of stone and plaster, with mainly stone tiled roofs. The church visible for miles across the flat landscape. A place large enough to have minor suburbs and continuing post-war estate development. People may one day admire the 19th-century cast-iron memorial clock, at present painted very dark green. The old town is within a square enclosure, the boundaries of which follow the lines of ancient fortifications. Alfred the Great is held responsible for these, although Roman and Saxon sherds have been found among the footings. There

CRICKLADE tower

is a mixture of 17th-century and Georgian buildings. Of earlier date are *Robert Jenner's School*, a mullion-windowed building of 1651 and *The Priory*, a block of small houses concealing the medieval remains of the Hospital of St John, a hospice for destitute travellers. *Lloyds Bank*, in the High Street, is an excellent mid-18th-century building and there are other Georgian houses nearby. But the big building of Cricklade is the parish church, unusually dedicated to *St Sampson of Dol*. The fat-turreted tower built by the Duke of Northumberland in 1553 dominates the town. There is work of many periods, from Norman times onwards. The interior is lofty and stony, somewhat cold and arid, and wanting in colour. There is a good deal of redecoration work and re-furnishing by Martin Travers, 1930, including two windows with glass by him. A second church, *St Mary's*, near the town bridge, is small and basically Norman with Perpendicular additions.   2

Crockerton. About Crockerton is a modern outburst of bungalows and detached residences, like a built-up part of the New Forest, or parts of Southern Germany. The church stands apart and looks out at them across a small valley. It is in the Norman style, by T. H. Wyatt (1843); but he did a much better job in the same manner at Dilton Marsh. Here the exterior has the right massiveness, but the inside is a disappointment, with the apse too tiny and the flimsy roof trusses too weak. Nor is the curious chancel "screen" a success. In the vestibule, modern lighting slits have an abstract medley of coloured glass.   13

Crofton is of note because it stands at the highest point of the Kennet and Avon Canal, about 400 feet above the source of the Kennet. A pumping station was established here in 1812. The engine house is in simple Industrial Revolution style, with the remains of a big chimney. Within are a beautiful pair of beam engines by Boulton and Watt operating an enormous cast iron beam. This machinery used to pump 11 tons of water per minute but now has ceased to function and the future of the installation seems to be in doubt. Efforts are being made by the Kennet and Avon Canal Trust to preserve the Crofton pump house.   9

Crudwell. Between Minety and Crudwell is a beautiful stretch of woodland road. In the village itself are green lawns guarded by spiked chains and, round the church, stone buildings. Medieval barn. *School House* of 1670, very much better than the Victorian school to which it is necessarily, if tenuously, attached; the *Old Rectory*, 17th- and 18th-century with a circular dovecote, and the Georgian *Crudwell Court*. The church incorporates some work of the Early English period, but the tower is Perpendicular. Aubrey much admired the "substantial" box pews here and they are still to be seen (Jacobean). Unfortunately, all the inside walls are scraped. There is a window with splendid 15th-century glass – the Seven Sacraments. The Victorian glass (east and west windows) is dull, though the west has some colour.   2

Dauntsey. The Avon flows beside the church and manor house. St James has a Gothic Survival tower well built in the medieval tradition, but as late as 1630. A misguided heating engineer has clamped a huge flue pipe to the outside. The interior is delightful, with much to see. In the north aisle, painted wooden panels of a 16th-century Doom: a monstrous dragon-fish clearly enjoys his meal of lost souls. Jacobean box pews and screen (with earlier parts). Pulpit with carved panels. 15th-century stained glass. Big Royal Arms. In the 17th-century Danby Chapel a very large tomb to the first Earl. Many others, with and without brasses, against the wall and in the floor. Epitaph by George Herbert, who courted Ann Danvers in the village. From the chapel, views of the gardens of

Part of the flight of 29 locks on the Kennet and Avon at DEVIZES

Dauntsey House, which is plain stone Georgian. 5

Dauntsey Green is a busier little place than Dauntsey itself. Here is a Victorian school with elegant flèche and *Good Mondays Farm*, a Georgian house on the road to Brinkworth. 5

Derry Hill. The church of 1840 has a plain interior with a short chancel that it was intended to lengthen, but the extension never took place. The naive but attractively colourful east window is half obscured by the reredos. The small *Zoar Chapel* down the road is simple and pleasing. There are a few Victorian estate houses and the main entrance to Bowood House – Barry's splendiferous "Golden Gates" with their inscribed blessing of PAX INTRANTIBUS ET HABITANTUS. Across the road is the 19th-century Tudoresque *Lansdowne Arms*. 8

The Deverills form a string of delightful villages along the river Wylye, the five being linked together by the road from Mere to Warminster. They are described under their respective names: *Brixton Deverill; Hill Deverill; Kingston Deverill; Longbridge Deverill* and *Monkton Deverill*. 13

Devizes. A medley of streets and architectural styles and a place in which it is a pleasure to walk. Some new shopping developments by men from London, but the old country-town bustle does not seem to be greatly altered. Even the street names are charming: *Wine Street, Little Brittox* and *Snuff Street* are typical. The list of good buildings is a long one. There are a few 16th- and early 17th-century cottages, some half-timbered, tucked away down little alleys, but the best architecture of Devizes is undoubtedly Georgian. In the Market Place the *Black Swan Hotel*, the *Bear Hotel* and a number of houses are all 18th-century work, and the *Post Office* is accommodated in a splendid brick house of the same period. The classical *Town Hall* in St John Street is an elegant

Long Street and Brownston House, DEVIZES

The Market Place, DEVIZES

building; *New Hall*, on the corner of Wine Street, is no less delightful although long used as a laundry. New Park Street has the imposing *Castle Hotel* and a few yards away, one of the finest houses in Devizes: *Brownston House*, of 1720. There is decent early 19th-century building to be noted: Benjamin Wyatt's pinnacled *Market Cross* is well done; so, too the *Market House* of 1835 and the stately *National Provincial Bank*. The Victorians are well represented with *The Corn Exchange*, the Gothic *Masonic Hall*, once a girls' school; *St James's Hospital* and quite a few pleasant villas. And, of course, the *Castle*, which originated in early Norman times as a simple motte-and-bailey affair and was massively developed by Bishop Roger of Sarum. After playing an important part in political manoeuvrings for most of the medieval period, it fell into disuse. Re-fortified during the Civil War, it was "slighted" – i.e. blown up – by Oliver Cromwell. Any ancient remains are now hidden within the romantic castellated structure built by the architect H. E. Goodridge, of Bath, in 1842 and greatly enlarged in the 1870s. The town possesses four Anglican churches, one Roman Catholic church and a number of Nonconformist chapels. *St John*'s is a big Norman building with a crossing tower and 12th-century arches. Looking towards the altar from the west end, there is a vista of groined vaulting. In the Beauchamp Chapel a sumptuous Tudor roof and many monuments. *St Mary's* has Norman vaulting in its chancel, and is a big, light and simple church. *St James* was re-built in 1832, but retains its original Perpendicular tower and some interesting memorials. The last of the four, *St Peter's*, in the Bath Road, is entirely Victorian, by Slater and Carpenter, 1884. 8

Dilton (or *Old Dilton*). A pretty wooded lane climbs out of Dilton Marsh and drops more gently down into this hamlet with its background of downland. Suddenly framed within a railway arch, the surprising little white church of *St Mary* is basically 14th century, with a stone spirelet, and since Georgian times little has been done to it inside. The building shows how a simple country church looked two hundred years ago. 18th-century furnishings, plain, bleached box pews, three-decker pulpit, big family pews and two small galleries, one looking directly into the chancel. Very pleasing; usually locked up, but the key is next door. Back on the main road, *Chalcot House*, early Georgian, is seen across its parkland. 10

OLD DILTON church interior

Dilton Marsh is rather dull, but in the long village street the one-time *Apple Tree Inn* is a late 18th-century house in the Adam manner. *Holy Trinity* church is one of T. H. Wyatt's exercises in Norman, and very well done. Nothing timid here; a big building full of strength with its massive short tower. By contrast, the small Victorian Gothic *school* next door seems shy and retiring, as if over-awed by its big neighbour. 10

Dinton is an open, south-sloping village, beautifully disposed in and off the Salisbury to Warminster road. *St Mary's* church is a handsome building, Decorated but with some earlier work and was finished in the 15th century with the top stage of the tower. The square Norman font on its stumpy legs is of Purbeck marble. There have been recent renovations; the wavy lines where the new plasterwork has been "cut in" against the window openings give a somewhat flippant effect, and the clear glass throughout and the whitening of everything a somewhat glaring one. *Hyde House*, birthplace of the first Earl of Clarendon, can be seen over the churchyard wall and has a pleasing 18th-century front, formal and pedimented. 16th-century work behind; the big dovecote is medieval. *Little Clarendon* is a 17th-century house in lichened stone. Close by is *Lawes Cottage*, once the home of William Lawes, composer friend of John Milton. Both are National Trust properties, as also are *Hyde's House*, near the church and the big late-Georgian *Philipps House*. This with its huge Ionic portico stands in Dinton Park, and was designed in 1816 by Sir Jeffrey Wyatville. The entrance drive is up the hill just to the north of the village. On the same road over the brow is *Marshwood House*, a stone and stucco late Georgian building of character in a sweeping landscape of open fields and small copses. 14

Ditteridge, over the valley from Box, is a pretty hamlet of thatched cottages and farms. *Cheyney Court* is a gabled Jacobean house. *St Christopher's* church all in stone, stone-tiled, is small and simple, with a Norman doorway and window and an Early English chancel. Over-restored in 1860. Lower down into the valley is *Spa House*, Middlehill; all that remains from the late-18th century of a medicinal establishment that failed. There used to be a little pump room and a boarding house here, but these have disappeared. 7

Donhead St Andrew. In a hollow among winding lanes this stone village with some thatch has a church among chestnuts, yews and manor-house *Macrocarpas*. It is a Perpendicular building, with aisles and tower, and a chancel of 1837, and a delightful atmosphere of that date. It is

Marshwood House, DINTON

dominated by a well-coloured east window with figures under delicate canopies of 1847 – early enough to retain the influence of Gothick, and genuinely pre-Victorian in feeling. In the churchyard is a well-carved, elaborate Cotswold-style table tomb of 1921. *Donhead House*, opposite, behind a high stone wall has old parts, but is mostly of 1892. 16

Donhead St Mary. Above the Nadder, with a splendid pastoral view, towards Wardour, of the clumped and copsed landscape of the Dorset–Wiltshire border. Road up to the church goes between deep grass banks and overhanging yews. *St Mary's* has not suffered too much from Victorian improvements, and is well cared for. Trans-Norman arcades in the nave, ribbed stone porch, and Norman font. Under the Perpendicular west tower a modern spiral stair leads to the ringing loft. A recent and very simple curtain setting for the altar is effective. Undistinguished stained glass, but a pleasing interior. The big rambling house nearby is the *Old Rectory*, looking 18th-century but much older in parts. It was once an overnight halt for pilgrims journeying to Shaftesbury Abbey. *Donhead Hall*, to the south, is early Georgian with a bowed central feature, facing eastwards down its sloping park, and there is a handsome stone non-Conformist chapel. In *Chilver Combe Bottom* is a Quaker burial ground, dating from 1678. 16

Downton. Turn off the main Salisbury – Fordingbridge road and you are in *The Borough*, a long and very wide street with a great swathe of grass down the middle, now unfortunately marred by lines of black electricity poles, which could easily have been hidden behind the parallel rows of cottages on each side. There is a neo-classical *Memorial Hall*, and, at the far end, three bridges across the Avon take the road into Downton. *The Tannery*, which has a river frontage, has flower beds and virginia creeper to soften the brickwork. There are some 18th-century houses and at the top of the hill *The Moot*, a house of about 1700, brick, with formal gardens with clipped and unclipped yews, and well-grown beeches across the road on the site of an old earthwork. There is a classical summer house here, and stepped seating cut into the turf, supposedly in the manner of the Saxon meeting place which was once here. Beyond, in *Moot Lane*, a new bungalow estate has been laid out in an open lawn treatment. The church of *St Lawrence* is big and of scintillating flint and stone, though in the 18th century the height of the nave was increased by building up part of the walls in red and purple brick; unfortunate, from the outside. The interior is spacious and impressive. Transitional columns and later medieval features give it character, which is enhanced by old stone floors, (with patterned slate in the chancel), five great 18th-century wall tombs, with pyramid slate-coloured marble backing (form symmetrically placed in the chancel), and decent glass in the east window of 1867. The monuments are by Peter and Thomas Scheemaker and others. 18

Draycot Cerne. A group of stone houses on the fringe of Draycot Park. At *Upper Draycott* is a brick cottage designed by a Mr Brick which was awarded a prize and gold medal by the Society of Arts in 1864. *Draycot Park* is overgrown, the mansion having been demolished since the war. Great Edwardian house parties were held here, with skating on the lake by the light of Chinese lanterns and orchestras playing until dawn. The church of *St James*, in the park above the river, has an Early English chancel, lower than the floor level of the nave. There are a stone effigy of a knight, and a fine double brass with three-foot figures (15th century), Gothick box pews, Jacobean stalls, squire's pew with fireplace and other monuments, including a good composition of 1710, (John Young) and a bust of a sleeping child, Adelaide Cowley, 1843. 4

Durnford (or *Great Durnford*) is the place "sweetly watered and abounding in troutes", which John Evelyn speared on his way to Stonehenge. The road curves between flint-and-thatch cottages of the 17th century, and there are later houses and a Georgian farmhouse. The 18th-century manor in the wooded cleft to the north of the village has big additions of 1913. The church (*St Andrew*) has beautifully textured walls without and within. It is of nave and chancel, of Norman proportions, and foundation. Outside of stone, flint and plaster, with flat Norman buttresses at intervals, and there are two Norman doors (north and south) with 17th-century porches to protect them. The north doorway has a charming decoration: round the dark green and white stone chequered tympanum is a semicircular sequence of large seedpods, of budding whitebeam or chestnut. Not much building after Norman times, but alteration and enlargement of openings and other details. Old wooden doors. Inside, remains of good 13th-century painting – patterns and remains of a Doom – Perpendicular bench ends, Jacobean pulpit and Communion rails and big painted Royal Arms. There are also medieval tomb recesses, old stone floors and stained glass fragments, including a well-drawn late 14th-century crucifixion. 7

Durrington, north of Amesbury and with army camps all around, is now nearly all suburb. The old village street survives and preserves its character and older buildings. There is some thatch and Georgian work, although a few recent bungalows popped up overnight opposite the church. *All Saints* was extensively restored in 1851, but (like the church at Allington) is reputed to be a faithful copy of what was here before and not some restorer's dream of the ideal medieval church. Norman doorway and pillars and re-set Early English windows in the chancel. It is quite easy to distinguish Victorian from original work. At the end of the street, the medieval village cross base is a huge affair. There is some bright glass. The interior is very dark. Below, the Avon runs through meadows. The prehistoric temple of Woodhenge lies to the south, by the side of the main road. 12

East Chisenbury. Thatched cottages with gardens along the river and, on the outskirts, *Chisenbury Priory*, a Jacobean house with a most elegant 18th-century front. 12

East Coulston. The church is now almost hidden from the lane by a "contemporary" house built in front of the churchyard; a most unfortunate planning decision. The church (St Thomas à Becket) has old stone floors, wall tablets, a decent Victorian east window, and a pleasing atmosphere. The dark stain removed from the pews has improved the appearance. Norman and 14th-century bits. Next to the church, *Baynton House* is late 18th century, with yellow plastered exterior. *Coulston House*, nearby, is also Georgian, of stone.

Eastcourt. *Eastcourt House*, half-a-mile to the south, is a mid-17th-century manor, added to later. 2

Easterton. A long narrow village below the Downs with all but two of its better buildings hidden from the main road. The exceptions are *Eastcott Manor House*, 16th-century black-and-white half timber reminiscent of Cheshire "magpie" work, and the *Manor*, also half-timbered. The two stand at opposite ends of the village. Up little side lanes are old stone and timber houses; the *Royal Oak Inn* and early Georgian *Kestrels*. The nave and chancel church is Victorian, 1875, brick, dull. 11

East Grafton. Fine trees, and a big village green with thatched

EAST GRAFTON|

cottages in brick and half timber widely spaced around it. Some simple Georgian houses also. Newly built in 1844 and designed by Benjamin Ferrey, the church is Norman Revival with a Romanesque campanile; Norman arches even in the lychgate. A pleasing interior. On the horizon, a sail-less windmill. See also *West Grafton.* 9

East Grimstead. Victorian villas; a Gothick cottage and some stolid modern housing. The flint and stone church stands by a small bridge and dates from 1857. It has a bellcote and is conventional, but attractive and appropriate to the site. Patterned glass of 1857 in east window. 18

East Harnham. Over the river from the centre of Salisbury. Anthony Trollope conceived the plot of *The Warden* on the bridge.

All Saints is Victorian, by T. H. Wyatt. A row of cottages near the church has rustic thatched porches supported on tree-trunk pillars. The *Three Crowns* is a restored half-timbered pub of early origins. See *West Harnham.* 15

East Kennett has a stone and flint Victorian church of 1864 with chequered walls. Small and simple, with spired tower and the interior finished with fine ashlar. Many monuments and tablets to the Tooker family retained from an earlier church. Charles Tooker (died 1716) wears a turban. In the village, the *Manor House* is good late Georgian; *Manor Farmhouse,* mullion-windowed, is a century or so earlier. Beyond the church, on open downland, *East Kennett Long Barrow* is a fine example of a large prehistoric chamber tomb.

Unexcavated, and sarsen stones stick out from one end. See also *West Kennett.* 8

East Knoyle. There is a fine approach from West Knoyle, the road plunging through leafy cuttings and thick woodlands. Above the village is the marvellously-sited *Clouds,* the house designed for the Wyndhams by Philip Webb. Completed at a cost of £80,000 in 1886, it was burned down three years later and quickly re-built for a further £35,000. Now used as a Church of England Babies Home and somewhat spoiled by utilitarian alterations (many of them done in 1938) and additions. Sir Christopher Wren was born in the village, his father, Dr Wren, being appointed rector here in 1623. The church is notable apart from this. Bits of Norman, and more Early English work, with many 19th-century alterations. The plaster "inventions" in the chancel use 17th-century representations of Biblical scenes devised by Dr Wren, which were quoted against him at his trial by the Commonwealth authorities. They were carried out "by one Brockway of Quinton in Dorset". (*Vide* Byron or Olivier in the first edition of this Guide.) At the time of his father's trial in 1647 Christopher was fifteen. The church has been recently re-decorated and is as white as a wedding cake; the organ is a pretty piece of painted nonsense. The original rectory was pulled down in 1888. On the main road, the village store calls itself "Wren's Shop" and there is a plain memorial stone to the architect on a bit of grass across the way. See also *West Knoyle.* 13

Easton Grey. Stone houses and cottages near a bridge over the Avon. *Bridge House,* restored 17th-century, has gardens along the river. The Georgian *Manor House* has three elegant façades, and has lately been well-restored and newly furnished. From it are picturesque views of the Avon which winds through meadows below, among well-grown trees planted romantically in relation to it. Church re-built in 1836

EAST KNOYLE: Plaster decoration devised by Sir Christopher Wren's father when he was incumbent here

except for the Perpendicular tower, pleasantly irregular. Tiny chancel with decorative wall monument, box pews in pitchpine. Unfortunate electric fittings much in evidence. There is a Jacobean pulpit and an 18th-century organ. In the vestry, a drawing of the old church. The outer door of the porch is in white-painted decorative palings, 1836, and a simple version of the one at Sherston. 1

Easton Royal. A few low mounds outside the village hide the foundations of a Friary, founded in 1245 as a hospice for travellers. Except for a great deal of overhead wiring this is a neat and pretty village, sloping its way down a long street to the church. There are many thatched cottages and Georgian houses with the Downs a sweeping background. The very late Perpendicular church was built by the Earl of Hertford in 1591. It has been sadly, and badly, Victorianized. 9

East Tytherton. Here is a Georgian church, built in 1792 by the Moravian brethren who settled here fifty years earlier. It is flanked on one side by the "sisters' house" and on the other by the minister's, all equally charming. A delightful composition in mellow brick and stone. The church retains original organ and gallery inside. The corrugated iron village hall next door is ugly. 5

Ebbesbourne Wake. On a north-facing slope in the downy Ebble valley, among lanes. Thatch. The flint and stone church has a Perpendicular west tower and nave and chancel all in one. The interior has yellow walls and green glass, and pitchpine. An ugly chancel screen belonging to some Victorian improvement and is not attractive – all mid-19th-century. Norman font. 17

Edington. A magnificent church stands below the Downs looking like a cathedral – or as Dr Pevsner says "like a fortified mansion", on account of its many battlements. It has a multiple dedication to *St Mary, St Katherine and All Saints*. It was attached to a college, later Priory, founded in 1351 by the Bishop of Winchester. It shows the transition from Decorated to Perpendicular, and was built in a continuous operation between 1352 and 1361. Later work does not detract from its nobility, nor from the unusually sensitive and convinced-looking medieval craftsmanship. The ceilings of nave, tower crossing and chancel are a great enhancement of the interior: the white one in the chancel is 18th century, the other two 17th, and coloured brown and white, and pink and cream respectively. Pulpit 17th century. The floors are patterned in dark and light marbles, black and white and grey and white, and the altar rails are splendidly – even aggressively – Jacobean. The screens are very much renewed, and lack texture. There is old glass: five or six figures, and bits. One Victorian window has figures like Reynold's at New College, Oxford; but most of the glass is clear, and the church light. Big painted Royal Arms (also from Imber). Furniture mostly modern; but a few old stalls. The monuments include two 14th-century knights (from Imber church), and large later monuments including one of the 17th century with a white angel fluttering over two alabaster effigies under a canopy, and other angels flanking them. The big house below the church to the north is *The Priory*, on the site of the original foundation; and in its garden the fishponds remain. There is very little of Edington village: the houses are scattered about the lower downs' slopes, approached by undulating lanes. 10

Enford. The peaceful village described in a previous edition of this Guide is being spoiled. Harsh terraces of houses now stick above the skyline; bad planning and bad placing indeed. A fine church; the exterior of flint and stone in bands, is clean and sharp and looks as fresh as many a Victorian re-building; but it is of the 12th century and later. South side of chancel, attractive brick and flint, 18th century. A splendid interior, white and plain, where everything can be seen clearly. Plain dark benches. Wide Norman chancel arch and arcades with square piers in the nave. The blank arcading in the chancel is 13th century, and remarkable. So is the hexagonal building joined to it on the north. The church looks monastic. Was it connected with Chisenbury Priory? *Longstreet House* and *The Grange*, are Georgian houses near the river. 12

Erlestoke. H.M. Detention Centre, *Erlestoke Park* is surrounded by high fences. The remains of the Georgian Mansion can be seen on the wooded hill above the main road. Its main entrance gateway, with urns, is close to St Saviour's church, designed by G. E. Street in the Perpendicular style – very unusual for him – and completed in 1880. The new church has a clean and satisfying interior, ashlar walled and parquet floored, with a Kempe east window. Across the road is a group of thatched Gothick cottages, and further on in the village street are many architectural bits and pieces of sculptural ornament built into the walls of houses and cottages. They were supplied by Joshua Smith, builder of Erlestoke Park. 11

Etchilhampton, pronounced "Ashelton", is a truly-rural hamlet near Devizes. The church, simple nave-and-chancel, basically Decorated; restored, and chancel of 1866. 14th-century effigies of a knight and his lady, box pews, Norman tub font and good nave roof. Archangel Gabriel figure in stone, 14th century. The figure of a lion on a pedestal is at the crossroads,

EASTON GREY: Table tomb, one of many of this kind in north-west Wiltshire churchyards

EDINGTON

west, where the road to Devizes branches. 8

Everleigh was "once a market town and is now a hamlet" being entirely re-built on a new site in 1810–1811. The old church, a simple squat-towered building was replaced about the same time by the present St Peter's, a pretty little Gothick design of 1813. The apparent loftiness is emphasized by the very short chancel and narrow nave. An elegant west gallery and neo-medieval hammerbeam roof. Unfortunately much evidence of damp. Wet rot and woodworm are both causing much concern (1966). On the outskirts of the village, the early-18th-century *Crown Inn* used to be the Dower House of the manor. Originally simple white-wash but now duo-tone, in contrasting colours, and a bit forced. The *Manor* itself is now occupied by the R.A.M.C. as laboratories; a plain Georgian mansion, much re-windowed. 12

Farley is distinguished by a classical church (All Saints) in the design of which Sir Christopher Wren may have had a hand. The founder was Sir Stephen Fox, one of the Commissioners for the building of Chelsea Hospital and the builder was Alexander Fort, master joiner of the Office of Works. Both men worked closely with Wren. It is satisfying both inside and out. Splendid proportion of solid and void on the exterior, and perfect symmetry of plan. The fine arches are still marred by painted Biblical texts in red and black Victorian Trajan lettering. Most of the furnishing is original, though the pews have been cut down. Many memorials to members of the Fox family, that to Sir Stephen himself being inscribed in medieval French. The famous Charles James Fox, buried in Westminster Abbey, is here remembered by a tablet set up by his widow to "the best of husbands and most excellent of men". Across the road, the big block of *Fox Almshouses* dates from 1681 – ten years before the completion of the church. 15

Fifield Bavant has a row of cottages, a farm or two and one of the smallest churches in Wiltshire, (St Martin). It is on a knoll, the only approach to it through a farmyard. The walls are chequered in flint and stone, 13th-century, with one or two windows of later periods. Recent electric lighting has caused an unpleasant outbreak of meters and switches at the back of the nave, and four white lampshades are nearly as big as the church itself. The altar table is 17th-century. The font is perhaps 13th-century. It is generations since there was a burial in the graveyard. 17

Figheldean. An old mill and many thatched cottages, the newly renovated group at *Ablington* being most picturesque. Recent extensive tree-felling along the river has somewhat spoiled the approach to a village in which almost every house has a roof of straw. The church has traces of Norman work. J. W. Hugall restored it in Norman–Revival style in 1851. The tower arch and balcony and the top stage of the tower are his work. The chancel is raised high above the nave: there are five steps up to the choir and another two up to the altar pace. Powell glass in the chancel. *Syrencot House*, secluded at the end of a tree-lined avenue, is an early Georgian manor, no longer occupied as a dwelling. The setting has been ruined by Nissen huts and piles of junk. 12

Fisherton Delamere. Stone and thatch cottages, with the river below. A flight of narrow steps climbs to the church between two old houses. Battlemented 14th-century tower and traces of original work of all periods, but two Victorian restorations (or re-building) removed much of the medieval structure. Among other monuments a sad little memorial to the Crockford children who died in the 1620s; one baby in bed, the other wrapped in a shroud. 14

Fittleton. Winding lanes among flint and brick cottages with the thatched cob walls of the district. The flint church has a big west tower of the 14th century. It was built clear of the earlier nave arches to avoid interfering with the original structure. 14th-century arcades. A simple, whitewashed interior. Most of the stained glass has been removed. Wall tablets. Church and churchyard well maintained. Early Georgian rectory in brick and stone with the date 1743 on a key stone. *Fittleton Manor* is of the same period. 12

Fonthill Gifford. The rise and fall of Beckford's Gothick dream palace was short and dramatic. Construction beginning in 1796, the huge building grew apace, with 500 workmen working round the clock in the later stages. Even so, the enormous tower was still not completed when Nelson and Lady Hamilton visited the site in 1800. Beckford took up residence in 1807, but the builders were in occupation for another five years. In 1823, he sold it for £330,000 to John Farquhar, after warning him that the stability of the Abbey was not all that it ought to be. In less than two years, the huge tower, 276 feet high "quietly subsided" one night and the whole place soon became a ruin. Beckford, meanwhile, had retired to Bath, where he lived until 1844, building another tower. In 1859, on a different site, a second "abbey" (the fifth house in the series) was built nearby in the Scottish Baronial style, this time for the Marquis of Westminster.

Detail of the monument to Sir Edward Lewys and his wife, 1630, EDINGTON

The final house, still existing, is a Jacobean-style building by Detmar Blow completed in 1904. The centre section incorporates part of a 17th-century manor, brought here in pieces from Berwick St Leonard and re-erected.

In the village, the famous author of *Vathek* is commemorated by the *Beckford Arms*. Here also are thatched cottages and *Holy Trinity* church, a lavish Victorian structure by T. H. Wyatt. With all its pinnacles and spiky spire among the cypresses it looks like a cemetery chapel. The previous church was a classical building founded by William Beckford's father before he built the big Palladian mansion that preceded Fonthill Abbey. The splendid *Gateway* at the Bishop's Fonthill entrance to the Park, with flanking walls capped with giant urns, may be by Inigo Jones. 13

Ford (near Salisbury) is a watery place on the River Bourne, which often spreads itself in flood over the low-lying fields. The bridge is on the site of the ancient crossing. There is a concrete block manufactory, R.A.F. housing and a group of old cottages with the river gushing beneath them. 15

Ford (near Chippenham) has some 17th-century houses and a Perpendicular-style church by Ponting of 1897, one of his last before he adopted the Arts-and-Crafts manner. The sharp little spire and red tile-hung gables give it a domestic-cum-village-hall air. 4

Fosbury. A few brick and flint houses with odds and ends of building up the hill behind. Out of the village along the road to Oxenwood an avenue of trees focusses on the porch and spiked tower of the church: a big gaunt structure in the Decorated style, by S. S. Teulon, 1856. The neighbouring vicarage is by him also. *Fosbury Manor*, close by, is a classical stone house in parkland. In springtime, fields of daffodils. The interior is under a wide and tall single gable, with a hammer-beam roof. Greenish amber impressed glass, by Powell. Not unattractive. 9

Fovant was an army training area during World War I and huge regimental badges are cut into the chalk of the Downs. A long village with much recent speculative housing and more in progress (1966). The *Cross Keys* has mullioned windows (17th-century). The church, much restored by T. H. Wyatt, has an impressive tower of 1492. The side chapel was once used as the school. The interior is completely Victorian and dominated by a rich-coloured but over-theatrical east window. Nearby are the Georgian *Rectory* and a small *Manor House*. 14

Foxham, on the line of the old canal near Chippenham, has a scattering of houses and a tight little church of 1880 by Butterfield. His characteristic forcefulness can be noticed in the hefty chancel screen. *Cadenham Manor House*, nearby, was built towards the end of the 17th century. 5

Foxley is a hamlet of stone cottages on the edge of Malmesbury Common. The church is mainly Early English but the unusual T-shaped interior is fitted out with Jacobean and Georgian furnishings. Knobbed 17th-century pews, and a panelled reredos of a century later. The wall monument to George Ayliffe (1722) is impressive; grey and white marble with garlanded twisted columns. There is a dashing, arty window, perhaps influenced by G. F. Watts, of 1901. *Foxley Manor* is 18th-century, with an earlier dovecote. At *Cowage Farm*, near the river, is a medieval mortuary chapel, recognizable by the little bellcote on its roof. This was once the nave of Bremilham church. 4

Froxfield. Bath Road village. The *Somerset Hospital* is a group of buildings dating from 1694; "Almshouses for 30 Poor Widows, founded and enlarged by the right noble Sarah, Duchess of Somerset, deceased." A fine composition in warm red brick, enlarged in 1775 and completed by the addition of a Gothick gateway and chapel in 1813. Flint church (All Saints). Plain nave-and-chancel, mostly Early English, restored. Victorian bell turret. The chancel is planned at a pronounced angle with the nave. Greenish glass gives a gloomy effect. 9

Fugglestone, on the outskirts of Wilton has St Peter's church, an early medieval building which has not been much changed since the 18th century. Late-Georgian box pews and gallery and a font of the same period, which looks like a classical bird-bath. Lighting by gas. 14

Fyfield (near Marlborough). In a fold of the Downs and watered by the Kennet valley with pastoral views, though within sound of roaring traffic of the Bath road. There is a simple late-Trans-Norman church. Plain whitewashed interior (too much so – the stonework has been whitewashed as well as the plaster) with a good roof to the nave and a very tall tower arch; the tower itself 15th-century in dressed stone. Restored, but not greatly harmed, in 1849. Fyfield Down is a nature reserve full of "grey-wethers" (sarsen stones) and old thorn trees. 9

Fyfield (near Pewsey). *Fyfield Manor*, is a big rambling house, much older than it first appears, when one might assume it to be Georgian. The brickwork is 16th-century and there are many gables and in-and-out bays overlooking a charming courtyard. The sober sash windows replaced mullions in the 18th century. In the grounds a flint dovecote. Across the lane a range of barns and stables. 9

Garsdon has a Tudor manor house modernized in the 17th century and once occupied by the Washingtons, kinsmen of George Washington. Their arms incorporate stars and stripes and are found in the 17th-century wall monument, with twisted columns, to Sir Laurence Washington (died 1643) in the church. The building is Victorian, with an old tower with big gargoyles. Fine

FARLEY

view from churchyard. In the pastoral village is a quaint little *Hall* with a picturesque Swiss–Victorian verandah. 2

Grafton *see East Grafton and West Grafton.* 9

Great Bedwyn. A big village in a hollow. An ancient settlement: the Romans were here; the Saxons called the place a "city" and fought a fierce battle in the district; it was later a borough which became "rotten", sending two members to Parliament from the time of Edward I until the passing of the Reform Bill. Along the main road, the establishment of *Lloyd – Stonemason and Stone Museum* has monuments, gravestones, portrait busts and sculpture in profusion, some dating from the 18th century. There is a fine tradition here which has been carried on into the present day.

The church is an excellent landscape feature by the canal, with flint and stone walls and pierced stone parapet to the tower. It is large and cruciform, largely Early English but with some remaining Norman work. The solid tower is over the crossing. Fine big pillars in the nave. But a disappointing church, spacious but terribly over-restored, and with gloomy Victorian and Edwardian glass. The window in the south transept, designed by G. E. Street

FONTHILL: *The Bishop's Fonthill entrance gateway (a detail of the keystone is on the title page)*

the architect, is better. There is a cross-legged knight and a tomb in the chancel to Sir John Seymour, moved here from Easton Royal in 1590. He was the father of Jane Seymour who married Henry VIII in 1536, a few days after the execution of Ann Boleyn. She was born at Wolf Hall, *Burbage*. There is also an early 18th-century tomb with a bust and big cherubs. 9

Great Chalfield. The early Tudor Manor house with arched gateway to courtyard and church, all moated and among otherwise uneventful fields, form a memorable medieval group. The house was built by Thomas Tropenell about 1480. It has a picturesque asymmetrical front facing northwards, with oriel windows against its grey-yellow stone walls. The hall is in the middle and the porch has a groined roof. During the 19th century the house fell into disrepair, and was much pulled about structurally. It was restored in the present century, and has belonged to the National Trust since 1943. (Open to visitors between April and October on certain days.) The church has Early English features. The south chapel and stone screen were built by Tropenell, and are contemporary with the house. The Neale chapel eastwards is 18th century. There is an attractively worn old stone floor, wagon roofs, 17th-century pulpit, communion rails and chandelier, and Perpendicular and later stained glass, all re-leaded in window heads as picturesque jumbles. The organ, a pretty piece of faking, was built by a vicar in the 1880s, the gay "Italian primitive" panels of the case being painted by a Miss Maurice. 7

Great Cheverell. *Glebe Farmhouse* with pleasing oval windows, was built about 1700. The early-Georgian *Manor* is of a few years later. The flint-and-rubble and stone church with its short 15th-century tower was originally Early English, but is very much restored. In a side chapel, an elaborate wall-tablet to James Townsend, 1730. Old roofs. Part of the nave ceiling is charmingly

Cottage by the railway and canal, GREAT BEDWYN

painted with clouds. Well carved headstones have been removed to form the inappropriate flanks of the churchyard path. Great Cheverell was once noted for the manufacture of sheep bells. 11

Great Durnford *see* DURNFORD.

Great Somerford. An ancient ford across the Bristol Avon here linked this village with Little Somerford. It was guarded by a motte-and-bailey castle on the site of which now stands the *Mount* farmhouse which originated in the 16th century. The elegant Georgian gate piers deserve a better gate. There is a 17th-century *Rectory* and *Bevis* is a half-timbered house opposite. The church is by the river, Perpendicular, in warm stone with external staircases (tower and rood loft) giving a boldly sculptural effect along the south wall. The chancel has a pretty painted ceiling, designed by F. C. Eden. Stained glass fragments, and a rather dominating but colourful east window by Lavers and Barraud (1865). A number of wall monuments in black and white marble. 5

Great Wishford. The things to see are all near the church. The *Grobham Almshouses*, a row of cottages with steep roofs and mullioned windows, were built in 1628 for "Four poor people and One Housekeeper". Adjoining them, the *Howe School*, founded by Sir Richard Howe in 1722 for the instruction of 20 poor boys and 20 poor girls in reading, writing and the casting of accounts. Also there is a severe and handsome brick and stone parsonage in South Street, early 18th century and attractive small houses opposite. The river is wide and swirling here; near the bridge, the *Swan Inn* is big, pleasing and late Georgian. The church was thoroughly restored by Wyatt in 1863–64. The interior is prim Victorian. Norman font and two man-and-wife monuments to Sir Thomas Bonham (died 1473) very handsome, with attendant allegorical figures and Sir Richard Grobham, who built the almshouses. The face of Sir Thomas is that of a modern-looking man. His wife was delivered of seven children at one birth after the knight had gone on a seven-year pilgrimage to the Holy Land. Fine Jacobean chest. Pretty Victorian brass chandeliers, with real candles. The people of Great Wishford have immemorial rights in the matter of collecting free firewood from Grovely Woods; this privilege, together with the right of shouting before the High Altar, in Salisbury Cathedral, is preserved and guarded. Every Oak Apple Day (May 29) there are great goings-on in the village. The poster announcing the 1966 festival stated:

GROVELY, GROVELY, GROVELY
AND ALL GROVELY!

A Procession of Oak Boughs will leave the Townend Tree at 5.30 p.m. Headed by the Shaftesbury Town Silver Band ...

Following the "Annual Re-Affirmation of Rights at the High Altar" there was a long list of attractions, including Dancing Round the Maypole and "Chick – The Comic Cyclist!" 14

Grittleton. Has a monster of a house by two quarrelling architects who in turn both quarrelled with the owner. Now a school, it was begun in 1848 for a millionaire Member of Parliament, Joseph Neeld. It is part pseudo-Jacobean, part Italianate, part Venetian and part-Byzantine; was still unfinished when he died in 1856. The main front, seen at the end of an avenue of tall trees, seems to have acquired a sort of monstrous charm. The church was over-restored by Blomfield in the 1860s. The elaborate carved panelling of the Neeld family pew was brought by Joseph from Italy. The gold and bright colours of the reredos are supposedly in "ancient" mosaics. The interior is heavily furnished and there is a lot of indifferent stained glass. Much Tudor-style Neeld estate housing in the neighbourhood. *West Foscote Farm*, half way between Grittleton and Castle Combe, is a towered folly, with barge boarded gables, characteristic of the estate building. 4

Ham. Thatch, brick cottages, a whitened Georgian house and an old church. There were restorations and rebuildings here in the 18th century that changed the medieval character of the structure. The little brick porch and dormer window gives the place a domestic air. Mid-19th-century alterations, too. Simple interior; except for the deep blue of the reredos wall in the chancel, all is dark wood and white paint. Georgian furnishings; gallery, pews with doors (mostly altered), and a cut-down three-decker pulpit and communion rails. Wall monuments, including one with brasses. In the churchyard a vast yew tree, a group of table tombs and a quaint tomb beside them with a truncated obelisk. 3a

Hankerton. Some fine farm buildings with round stone pillars and sagging flagged roofs, some much the worse for wear and being replaced by corrugated iron. A few old cottages, and a church attractively sited among flat meadows with tall hedgerow trees. It has 13th-century features with a 15th-century tower, and a small early 20th-century chancel. Plaster on the walls, but no furnishings or glass of interest. There is a memorial by Nollekens to Miles Earle, set up in 1775, and good churchyard tabletombs. In the lanes hereabouts some houses of the 1930s in the Cotswold style. "Superior Detached Residences" in course of erection are not quite so good. 2

Hannington is a countrified place. The village centre has pea-green council houses; and *The Jolly Tar* (far from the sea) is in pale pink. *Hannington Hall* dates from 1653, with various additions of the 18th and 19th centuries, and is of stone. It has a fine elm avenue, pointing towards developing Highworth. The church is a mid-Victorian rebuilding by Slater and Carpenter who re-used Norman and Early English features. Wall monuments. The short drive north to *Hannington Wick* gives a sight of the Manor there; a 17th-century house, gabled and of mellow stone. 3

Hardenhuish (pronounced Harnish) is now a suburb of Chippenham. The classical church by the younger John Wood of Bath, 1779, stands on a steep knoll and is saved from semi-detached engulfment only by the wide expanse of Hardenhuish Park in which a number of modern schools have been built. The big late-Georgian mansion of *Hardenhuish House* is a part of this educational complex. Two Venetian windows give the church a domestic air; so do the elegant candle glasses on their brass wall brackets, now electrified. The pews have been painted blue-grey, and there are wall monuments in elegant coloured marbles and Royal Arms. An attractive interior. In the churchyard is a Greek Revival monument to David Ricardo, the economist. In the *Rectory* across the main road, Francis Kilvert, the diarist, was born in 1840. 4

Harnham see *East Harnham* and *West Harnham*. 15

Hartham Park. A mile north of Corsham is a big late-Georgian mansion, designed by James Wyatt. Easily seen from the road to Biddestone it is now occupied by a company concerned with scientific agriculture. Close to one of the entrance lodges is the Victorian "chapel" of the old estate, with a big neo-Perpendicular tower. Quite as large as many a rural parish church. By P. C. Hardwick, 1862. 7

Monument to Ricardo the Economist, and the church, HARDENHUISH

Hazlebury, *see* Box.

Heddington. Under bold hummocks of the Marlborough Downs, where there are many cultivation terraces. Half-timbered cottages and a thatched pub, *The Ivy Inn.* The church has 13th-century arcades and Norman fragments in the chancel arch, but is essentially a Perpendicular church, and a simple village model of its kind. Charming little 18th-century organ carved with trumpets, horns and sackbuts. A pleasant, light church, over cream-washed (stonework and all) but with clear glass and old stone floors. 8

Heytesbury. Splendid downland country all around. Much traffic, but still pleasing and full of interest. The charming *Hospital of St John and St Katherine* is a block of almshouses, built in the 17th century and rebuilt after a fire in 1770 in their earlier manner. Nearby, octagonal lockup. There are late-Georgian *malthouses* along the street. Behind the church, the Jacobean *Parsonage Farmhouse.* The church is big. Restored by Butterfield in 1865–7. There is much interlocking of ancient and modern in both exterior and interior. The chancel is Early English, with detached Purbeck shafts to the windows – immensely tall and impressive inside; in its present form the creation of Butterfield, whose red and black tile decorations are an addition. Seven windows have Victorian glass by Gibbs, for Butterfield – very attractive. There is less good later glass also, and 17th-century kneeling figures. *Heytesbury House,* away from the village, and seen from its entrance gateway, has a long plain front of 1782 concealing parts of a 17th-century house behind. But one of the earlier Lords Hungerford "was building a mansion here when he was arrested and beheaded by Henry VIII". And the Empress Maud, mother of Henry II, is said to have had a palace on this site. In 1083, certainly, she had a hand in the foundation of the little church at Tytherington a mile away. Until the passing of the Reform Bill in 1832, Heytesbury was one of England's "rotten boroughs", returning a member to Parliament. 13

Heywood. The gloomy Victorian church has a plain east window of 1876 with a plethora of angels (15) in the tracery lights. Not good, nor very bad. Opposite the church is *Heywood House,* built in the Jacobean style in 1869. 10

Highway. Butterfield did a cheap re-build of the church here in 1867, retaining a Norman doorway and a few medieval bits and pieces, and making much use of his favourite geometrical tiling as decoration. Long disused. 5

Highworth. An old hill-top town. A cross-roads place with inter-war developments on all its four approaches, and much new house-building. But, for all this, a charming town and "mostly a Cotswold-coloured place with a few Georgian red brick houses looking as ripe as autumn apples among all the silver stone of the streets . . .". There are excellent stone houses of the 17th century and *Highworth House* and the *Jesmond House Hotel* are part of an elegant 18th-century group. St Michael's is a fine big church, with lofty nave and aisles. There is some 13th-century work in the arcades, but most of it is Perpendicular; anyway, most of what escaped Victorian restoration. Huge parish chest, and huge splendid Royal Arms (north aisle). A Cromwellian cannon ball, which hit the church when it was held as a strong-point by a Royalist garrison in June, 1645, is preserved. Among a number of monuments are those to members of the Warneford family in the chapel of that name. These include one to Sub-Lieut. Warneford, V.C. who shot down a Zeppelin in 1915. The church is over-furnished, and the stained glass poor. Among the newer buildings of Highworth are a Methodist church and a carpet factory; both incorporate a number of the fashionable design clichés of the 1950s but are not unreasonable. 3

Hill Deverill. The church of the Assumption is a charming bell-coted building 1843, opposite some council houses. Furniture, including gallery, largely of that date. There was a restoration in the '90s. There are three pretty 17th-century tablets. A big table tomb in the chancel is that of John Ludlow (died 1520). His ancestor William was butler to the three Henrys – IV, V and VI. Edmund Ludlow, on the other hand, became a regicide. *The Manor*, across watercress beds, where the family lived, is a big farmhouse, late 17th-century square and of stone with mullioned windows. It has a long and splendid barn of timber on a stone base, tiled, attached to it. There are other old barns here, too. 13

Hilmarton. Here are neat cottages built by the Poynder Estate, school with tall bell tower, and inn, *The Duke*. Standing as part of this group of Victorian buildings is the church, altered and given a new tower in 1840, and heavily restored by G. E. Street in 1879. The Transitional–Norman nave arcade survives. An alabaster and black marble memorial has skulls and bones carved at its base. Above the nave arches are a good series of hatchments. Outside the village, *Hilmarton Manor* is a pleasing 19th-century house in Elizabethan style. 5

Hilperton. A big village. In spite of recent housing developments it has considerable character. In the main street are houses of the 17th and 18th centuries and about the little square a group containing the Georgian *Hilperton House*, stone-tiled, the Victorian *school*, the domed *lock-up*, and the *church*. *St Michael's* retains its medieval tower and small broach spire, but the rest of the structure was drastically dealt with by T. H. Wyatt in 1852. There is nothing of interest inside. Some fine trees in the churchyard. Those in the square have been brutally chopped about. 7

Hindon has a wide and pleasant street climbing uphill to the church, with regular houses of the 18th century on each side. All are handsomely built in stone from the quarries at Tisbury and none are earlier than 1754, the date of the Great Fire of Hindon which destroyed most of the village. St John's church, by T. H. Wyatt, has been compared with the church he designed for the Marquess of Westminster at Fonthill Gifford, but Hindon church – though quite attractive as a village feature – is clearly the cheaper utility model with none of the lavishness of its counterpart. Simple Early English style with lancets and a rose window. The trees planted to commemorate the marriage of the Prince of Wales (later Edward VII) and Princess Alexandra have been terribly lopped. On the edge of the village is *The Lamb*, an 18th-century inn. Hindon was once a town, sending two members to Parliament, but drifted into the corruption of a "pocket borough" with the electors doing as they were told. 13

Hinton see GREAT HINTON (7) *and* LITTLE HINTON. 6

Hodson, *see* CHISELDON. 6

Holt. The extensive green in the centre is encompassed by pleasing 17th-century and Georgian houses and several Victorian ones. All live happily together, but two garages are somewhat vociferous with advertisements. Holt was once far enough from, yet near enough to Bath to have its own Spa. The lodging house for those taking the waters has now been pulled down, but the well building is still in existence, tucked away inside a local bedding factory. It is possible that the *White Hart Hotel* with its early Georgian assembly room was catering for those who, with the Lady Lisle, "patronized this spring and rendered it famous in the year 1720". *Holt Court*, of about the same period, is a big house in beautiful gardens to the north of the village. Now belonging to the National Trust, this exuberant – some purists say vulgar – example of early 18th century architecture is open to visitors. (Wednesdays for the house; Tuesdays, Wednesdays and Thursdays for the gardens, April to October.) A neighbouring nonconformist chapel has slim white glazing bars in Gothick windows. There is another chapel, spired and ugly, next door. The church has a Perpendicular tower, and other medieval fragments, but is otherwise by C. E. Ponting, 1891, and quite good. There is a lot of undistinguished stained glass, the best being a dashing design of the '90s in the east window, all regal robes and crowns and heavenly angels. 7

Homington. A farming hamlet on the slopes of the Downs south of Salisbury. The simple church, with an Early English chancel and tower of the 17th century, is largely of 1860. New-plastered inside. No stained glass. 17

Horningsham is a diffused and spread-out village with its buildings widely spaced along a beautiful valley on the edge of Longleat Park. Distant glimpses of the house. *The Bath Arms* is a big country inn with twelve pleached lime trees in front. Across the road are thatched cottages and the old post office. The long church is below the road. It has a 15th-century tower, all battlements and pinnacles, but the rest dating from the re-building of 1844. It is not interesting inside, and rather arid. In the lane called Chapel Street, well sign-posted, is the *Meeting House*, possibly the oldest Dissenting chapel in the country. There is confusion as to its exact date; tradition holds that it was provided by Sir John Thynne, builder of Longleat, for the use of his

Tips from ancient chalk quarries on the edge of the Marlborough Downs above HEDDINGTON

Scottish Presbyterian workmen (1566). Some authorities, however, place this small thatched building firmly in the 17th century. The interior has a gallery round three sides and a Georgian pulpit, but otherwise it is Victorianized. Hat pegs along the ceiling on one side. Fine countryside all about here and splendid woodlands on the surrounding hillsides. 13

Horton, a little roadside village on the Kennet and Avon Canal near Devizes, has pretty half-timbered cottages, some thatched and "modernized" many years ago by the insertion of tiny bay windows and oriels. Surprisingly, the experiment has come off and the work is now nicely matured. 8

Huish, on the Marlborough Downs, has a scattering of simple cottages and a few farms and the small church of St Nicholas, 1879, with a bellcote. The interior is plain and unattractive, owing to the tiles and green-edged glazing in the windows. The late Georgian rectory, with mansard roof and bow windows, is pleasing. 9

Hullavington. Many new bungalows and a medley of overhead wiring, but also pretty stone cottages and some modest houses of the 18th century. The church is not over-restored, although Sir Arthur Blomfield put in new windows and built the neo-Perpendicular tower in 1880. The nave arcades are early 13th-century and the fine north chapel with its lancets not much later with forward-standing shafts to window openings is also Early English. A rood screen with part of the loft still remains. The north wall leans outwards, the most upright thing here being an iron stovepipe. There is a big carved panel of Abraham and Isaac, and another framed panel of medieval needlework. Like many in Wiltshire, the nearby R.A.F. airfield is now disused. *Bradfield Farm*, to the north, is a Jacobean house with a medieval great hall. 4

Idmiston. Plenty of new building, but the village is well placed above the Bourne, and off the main Salisbury–Tidworth road. The church is a mixture: Norman, Early English, Perpendicular. The top of the tower and spire modern. The Perpendicular roof is the best feature. Purbeck marble font and 17th century kneeling figured monument. The old parsonage is 17th-century with later alterations. 15

Iford. A romantic hamlet with a stone manor house in a lush wooded valley near Bradford-on-Avon and Freshford. The house is of the first half of the 18th century, and is at the bottom of the carefully landscaped and terraced garden which has balustrades, loggias cloisters and sculptures disposed here by Harold Peto at the beginning of the 20th century. He and his fellow-architect partner, Sir Ernest George, had a strong influence on English country house and garden design. A figure of Britannia crowns the parapet of the medieval bridge over the river opposite the front of the house. The whole complex demonstrates the unremitting love and conviction of the connoisseur–artist–architect of sixty years ago. It is still beautifully cared for. 7

Imber. Only the most intrepid travellers, careless of life and limb, now make their way to Imber. It is an Army battle-training area and on the most desolate part of Salisbury Plain. General access is prohibited. The village is abandoned and half destroyed, and the little medieval church of St Giles has been stripped of its valuables, which have been moved to safety in other churches. 11

Inglesham. A short narrow lane passes a rather plain grey 18th-century house and ends among farm buildings and the ancient church, St John Baptist, "repaired in 1888–9 through the energy and with the help of William Morris who loved it", is now again in poor state (1966) owing to damp and dilapidation. Late Norman and Early English work and the interior looks much as it must have done two hundred years ago. Perpendicular screens, Jacobean box pews, Elizabethan pulpit, wall paintings, early stained glass fragments and an 11th-century (or earlier) sculpture of the Virgin and Child, with the hand of God above. Much weathered, but now re-built inside. Like the fragment behind the altar at Toller Fratrum, Dorset, it is a small but precious example of early sculptural invention. 3

Keevil. A charming village with interesting buildings. *Talboys*, on the roadside, is a half-timbered house of the late 15th century, modernized in Victorian times. *Keevil Manor* is a triple-gabled stone house built in 1580. Here Ann Beach scratched her name in the window of the room in which her father imprisoned her for two years for daring to fall in love with the curate. She later married him, but died three months afterwards. There are timber-framed cottages, some thatched. The church is a big, light one, Perpendicular, with a painted roof. A large and unusual signboard records a number of Benefactions. Among others, the clergyman is enjoined to preach on Easter Wednesday each year "a sermon suited to the capacity of children and young persons". After the preaching of this sermon, the vicar and his wardens are instructed "to provide a four-penny cake for each teacher and a twopenny cake for each scholar". It resembles Steeple Ashton, and is, in its setting and exterior texture, a model of a late medieval village church. The interior has been hopelessly vulgarized by a restoration in the 80s or 90s.

KINGSTON DEVERILL

Inappropriate reredos, poorish glass. There are wall monuments, and a fine Royal Arms under the tower. Churchyard table-tombs. 7

Kennett, *see* EAST KENNETT and WEST KENNETT. 8

Kellaways. *Maud Heath's Causeway*, a raised stone path 4½ miles long, runs from Wick Hill almost to Chippenham and is raised over the flood-prone fields near the Avon on 64 medieval arches. Maud was a pedlar woman born at Langley Burrell. On her death in 1474 she left enough property to pay for this still useable work of civil engineering. There is a little pillar to her memory at the end of the causeway and on Wick Hill a more pretentious monument erected in 1838 by the Marquess of Lansdowne. Kellaways church is a tiny late 18th-century building with a delicate bell turret, and old pulpit and remains of benches. Much alteration and redecoration. Across the road, a stone-roofed farm. 5

Kilmington is a very strung-out village with a big timber yard, much modern housing and far too much wiring overhead. The approach to the church is by way of farm buildings. The Perpendicular tower was restored in 1906 following an earlier Victorian re-building. A plain well-kept interior, and not a bad setting for the furniture: an ornate Jacobean pulpit in black oak with golden cherubs and coats of arms, and the reader's desk, assembled from old bits and pieces, are quite good. Entrance is under the tower and here a dreadful electrical mess greets you. The *Manor House* adjoining is much altered, but an attractive stone house. 13

Kingston Deverill. The Downs flow beautifully about the village, which has cottages and *Pope's Farmhouse* at the northern end. This is a long house with an early-Georgian front and 16th-century fragments. The church has a Perpendicular central tower, but the rest was rebuilt in 1846. It is, in effect, a fine Victorian church, with elaborate and successful timber roofs inside, and an impressive vista from the west end. There is a Pugin-like east window. The architects were Manners and Gill. In the nave is the effigy of a long-haired bearded man, with his feet on a smiling animal. There is a fine wooden carving of the Virgin and Child on the tower arch, medieval and foreign. There is a big stone house behind the church which has mullioned windows – some old – and a spire. Perhaps also restored by Manners and Gill. 13

Kington, *see* WEST KINGTON. 4

Kington Langley, separated from its neighbour Kington St Michael by the main Chippenham–Malmesbury road, has a poor and insignificant Victorian church looking timidly over a vast triangular green. But widely spaced among big trees are some good houses, including the Georgian *Greathouse*, now one of the homes of the Cheshire Foundation. An unusually pleasing Victorian school and schoolhouse, and a nonconformist chapel of 1855. The original church here was converted into a private house in 1670. 4

Kington St Michael. The outskirts have drab undesigned bungalows, but there are old parts. In the main street, the *Lyte Almshouses*, a gabled and mullioned block of 1670, stand near to other houses of the same period. The church is much restored, though the south doorway and strangely flat chancel arch are Norman. The freshness of some of the "13th-century work" in the nave arcades makes one suspicious as to its real date. A memorial window here commemorates those two famous Wiltshire antiquaries, John Aubrey and John Britton. Aubrey was born in this parish, at Easton Piercy, in 1626. Britton, who edited the *Beauties of England and Wales* was born in the village in 1771. At *Priory Farm*, north, are the remains of a Benedictine Nunnery, founded in 1155. Parts of the medieval buildings are incorporated in the present 17th-century farmhouse. 4

Knook. Name is the Celtic "Cnwc" – a hillock – describing the situation by the Wylye. A Norman church, with early carved tympanum with interlace work (p. 19). The church was restored by Butterfield in 1876. The two surviving 12th-century chancel arch capitals carry an incongruous Victorian roof truss. The double-storey porch forms the massive base of a Norman tower that was never built. There is glass by Gibbs in the small chancel windows, of Christ in Glory and the Evangelists, of the date of Butterfield restoration – 1876. From the churchyard is a view of *Knook Manor*, by the river; an L-shaped building in silvery stone. It is mostly of the mid-17th century, but there are both medieval and later works. A recent modern timber house lives agreeably with its older neighbours. 11

Lacock. Acclaimed as one of the most beautiful villages in England. The whole now belongs to the National Trust. In its little twisting streets are examples of houses and other buildings of every period from the 15th century, medieval half-timber and Tudor mullions mixing most happily with Georgian and later work. The following might be picked out: the 14th-century *barn*, once part of the abbey estate; the half-timbered *Porch House* in the High Street; and in West Street, the *Angel Hotel*, late 16th-century, and the Georgian *Cantax House*. Also of the 18th century is the *Red Lion Hotel*, with a frontage of mellow brick. The two big buildings of Lacock are St Cyriac's church and the Abbey. The *church* is magnificent. Cruciform, it has nave with clerestoried aisles and stone spire and pinnacles in the battlements of nave and aisles. Perpendicular, light and airy. Entering under the tower, there is a vista of the lofty nave with a traceried window high above the slender chancel arch, and beyond, the fine altar and sumptuous east window. The

Maud Heath's causeway and monument, KELLAWAYS

LACOCK Abbey

fan-vaulted side chapel of about 1430 with Jacobean monument of Sir William Sharington is splendid and faded colours here have so far mercifully escaped re-painting or touching up. There are remains of original glass in the north-east chapel, and remains also of colourful glass of the early 19th century in other window heads, which add necessary bright colour along with the 1855 window with characteristic bright glass and flowing figure drawing in the south transept. There are good brasses. The churchyard has excellent table-tombs. *Lacock Abbey*, just outside the village, is an ancient foundation with a long architectural history. (Also a National Trust property, it is open to visitors through the year.) The Abbey began as an

Church Street, LACOCK

Augustinian Nunnery in 1229 and was occupied as such until the Dissolution of the Monasteries, when the property was bought by Sir William Sharington (1540). It later came to the Talbot family by marriage, and stayed with them until 1958. W. H. Fox Talbot, the father of photography, carried out his experiments here in 1839. The present building has a great deal of medieval and Tudor work. Sharington improved and added to the nunnery buildings and, in the 1750s, Sanderson Miller carried out further extensions in the Gothick manner for the Talbots. It is his work, the hall, with the double staircase and ogee-headed windows, that meets the eye on approaching the house. It is full of crests, a chimney piece, niches, vaulting and doorways all in the 18th-century Gothick pattern-book

taste. There are some strange and exciting terra-cotta niches by a German artist called Sederbach. It was Miss Matilda Talbot who presented both Abbey and village to the National Trust in 1944. 7

Lake. *Lake House* is of 16th-century origin, but has been much altered. At the end of the Victorian era it was beautifully restored by Detmar Blow. Gutted by fire in 1912 and again rebuilt, it is gabled and impressive and is in the local style of square chequering in flint and stone. It has topiary in its forecourt. River valley views. 15

Landford has a brick and stone-banded church by Butterfield with much stained glass by Clayton and Bell, with lively pinks and blues. Re-set Norman doorway and Norman sculpture. A gallery of Georgian wall-tablets to members of the Eyre family is collected

LANDFORD Church, by Butterfield, 1858

in the south transept. The church shares a hill with the manor house and both overlook a pleasant countryside. *Landford Manor* is an impressive house with back quarters of 1599 and an early-Georgian front. *Landford Lodge*, down a lane to the west of the village, is of 1767 and has elegant brick pedimented facade of brick and stone. 18

Langley Burrell. A roadside village outside Chippenham, known to readers of Parson Kilvert's *Diary*, in which it is well described. Kilvert, born at Hardenhuish in 1840, helped his father here as curate. The church is among park trees – and has Norman arcade and Early English work. The medieval architecture is attractive and rewarding, but the interior has been scraped of its plaster and is not improved by the brownish, dull stained glass in some windows. There are pretty 18th-century wall monuments. The oil lamps mentioned in the last edition of this Guide have given way to naked electric bulbs. Good churchyard headstones and table-tombs. From the churchyard is a view of *Langley House*, a four-square Georgian house of warm creamy stone. Across the traffic-laden road, the pretty school is Gothick. It was built for a "Squarson" – Kilvert's great-great-grandfather. 4

Larkhill. Big Army complex on Salisbury Plain, started after the First World War and much developed during and since the Second. An array of low buildings huddle the skylines, following the slow risings of the Plain. Neatness and order in all this, with tree-planting and neo-Georgian permanent buildings standing among acres of hutments. New buildings of the '50s and '60s are emerging; more rational and functional than the earlier War Office designs, and more pleasing. The garrison church of St Alban is brick, pre-war and very large. The congregation comes not singly but in battalions. A jarring note is the messy group of shops along the road into Amesbury. 11

Latton. A main-road village with old stone houses and some new development. Spoiled by an excess of poles and wires. The church has some Norman remains – the big tower has the proportions – but after a Butterfield restoration it looks mostly Victorian. He built the chancel (1861). There is glass by Gibbs, Kempe and others, and the interior is darkened by it and by the smooth, cemented walls. There are a few Cotswold-style table-tombs in the churchyard. There is a cross and a Victorian school and a little green shed housing the local Women's Institute; and down the road a large Co-op Creamery. The small Thames and the weedy bed of the Thames and Severn Canal are close at hand. On the canal is one of the stone round houses that grace it hereabouts. 2

Laverstock, on the outskirts of Salisbury, has pleasing old houses as well as mixed modern development. The little *Manor* is late-Georgian. T. H. Wyatt's multi-gabled church of 1858 incorporates a Norman doorway from the original St Andrew's. It is in an attractively-planted churchyard, with old yews and new trees and shrubs. Several windows are filled with well rearranged fragments of glass, 13th–18th – and 19th-century, some from the town ditch in Salisbury, and therefore from the Cathedral. Schools and new blocks of flats have been built here recently. 15

Lavington, see MARKET LAVINGTON and WEST LAVINGTON. 11

Lea. Scattered about a junction of minor roads. The unremarkable church stands on one corner; tower and east window Perpendicular, the rest of 1880. Several good farmhouses to be seen along the lanes. 5

Leigh. Spread-eagled across a flat and watery landscape. Two churches. *All Saints* incorporates the re-erected nave of the original church, carted here from half-a-mile away. The architect, C. E. Ponting, protested vigorously at

LITTLECOTE

this violation, but still did the job (1896). The Early English chancel of the *old church* is still standing. 2

Leigh Delamere. Neeld estate village near Grittleton. Charming mid-19th-century almshouses by James Thompson, who designed *Grittleton House* for Joseph Neeld M.P. The big parsonage next door is more stolid and less pretty. The old church here was pulled down in 1846 and its re-usable parts taken to Sevington, where they form features in the strange village school. Thompson also designed the present St Margaret's, whose Gothic bell turret is a fair copy of the one that Neeld had previously pulled down!
The interior is very much as it was left in 1846 – and very impressive in a theatrical way. There are big figures in niches in the gloom behind the altar, and a small, skied, circular window away above them. Tremendous colours of the west window – magenta clouds are looped above the three crosses in the Crucifixion against a brilliant blue, very much in the manner of some abstract expressionism of today. The painting and carving of the organ, the round-arched arcades that are neither Norman nor Classical, but all of a piece with everything else – these provide a splendid example of the drama that early High Church Victorianism was after. 4

Liddington. Old thatched cottages and a simple 17th-century manor house; the outskirts now rather "garden suburb", with undistinguished, if well-kept modern houses. The church stands on a high knoll and has an attractive stone-tiled exterior. It is basically Early English, but much restored, scraped and dark inside, with green and pink cathedral glass and indifferent Victorian glass. Tub font. Above the village is the towering Iron Age earthwork of *Liddington Castle*: strategic siting, with views over three counties. 6

Limpley Stoke. Built on the slopes of the steep Avon valley, the wooded hillsides are peppered with the residential developments of earlier generations. Bath stone everywhere, and the general atmosphere is not unlike that of parts of Bath itself. The little church of St Mary has escaped the attentions of Victorian restorers. A tall, narrow arched opening in the south arcade of the nave may be pre-Norman, and not much later in date than the Saxon church at Bradford-on-Avon. The rest of the building is mainly 13th-century. Gallery has Jacobean panelling. There is an old stone pulpit, and thirteen medieval coffin lids. *Limpley Manor* is 17th-century, with a Georgian front. John Rennie's fine *Dundas Aqueduct* carries the Kennet and Avon Canal across the river (p. 36). 7

Little Bedwyn is a picturesque village with some Victorian estate housing along the lane to the church (St Michael), of flint and stone with a stone spire looking attractive among dark yews. There are big Norman arcades, Early English tower and chancel arch and Perpendicular chancel. The very tall nave under a steep gable gives the interior strong personality. The east window, signed "Barnett, Newcastle", of about 1880, is strange and mannered but not at all uninteresting. It must be by a Belgian, or Netherlandish, designer. Across the railway and canal, which run parallel here, the *Manor House* is a pedimented Georgian building of chequered brick.
On the hill westwards *Chisbury* has a small, brick Georgian manor within the ramparts of a camp, and a ruined, thatched chapel of St Martin among neighbouring farm buildings, visible on the approach from Little Bedwyn. 9

Little Cheverell. The church, except for the 14th-century tower and porch, is Victorian. There is a gloomy Edwardian east window. Good painted Royal Arms. *Hawkeswell* is a neo-Georgian house nearby, designed by A. C.

Martin, one of the early 20th-century architects engaged on Dauntsey's School. 11

Littlecote. If not quite so romantic-looking as Compton Wynyates, this Elizabethan mansion is comparable. Seen from the axial main entrance drive from the south its front of mellow brick and stone mullions is impressive. The scene of a baby-murder in the 16th century, the haunted room where the child was flung into the fire is still shown. "Wild" William Darell, the alleged murderer, later broke his neck while hunting in the park; his spectre, accompanied by a pack of hounds, returns. The house, with paintings and collections of Cromwellian armour and weapons, is open to visitors. The Great Hall, the whole height of the house, has screen and plaster ceiling with pendents, and there is a lot of (foreign) stained glass of the 16th and 17th centuries. The Dutch Parlour has 17th-century paintings. The chapel is a rare and rather beautiful example – there are a few parallels in the north – of a Cromwellian place of worship, with galleries and a pulpit in the altar's place, and original seats. The early 19th-century conservatory has been converted into a swimming pool. 9

Little Hinton (or *Hinton Parva*). Cottages of whitewash and thatch. The church of St Swithin is simple and old. The interior has big cylindrical pillars and Norman capitals and arches in stone against the white plaster of the walls. With the exception of the porch and clerestory, which are 15th century, nothing is much later than about 1300. The Norman font is carved with birds, beasts and knotwork. Jacobean pulpit and reading desk. Kempe glass in east window. Old roofs of lead and stone. 6

Little Langford. Beautiful open site. It was rebuilt in 1864 by T. H. Wyatt, in flint and stone chequerwork. The south door has a tympanum and lintel of the 12th century, rather worn, with a lively carving on the lintel – four collared dogs are biting a boar. Above, in the tympanum, are a bishop and three birds in a tree. Victorian atmosphere remains inside. Tomb of an Elizabethan rector. South of the church, among well-disposed trees, is a Tudor-revival house of stone with a turret and bay windows, like a lithograph in a mid-19th-century pattern book by P. F. Robinson, or another architect of the period. 14

Little Somerford. Nave and chancel run through in the church, separated only by a Perpendicular screen. West tower. Jacobean woodwork, including choir stalls and a pulpit of 1625 with reading desk attached. Royal Arms of Elizabeth I on the tympanum above the screen. Victorian east window adds colour. 5

Littleton Drew. A farming hamlet with some good stone buildings. The church is small, with a slender central tower, 15th-century; most of the rest dates from a rebuilding by T. H. Wyatt in 1856. There are two large sections of carved stone in the porch: parts of a 9th-century Saxon cross, possibly one of the crosses set up every seven miles on the route of St Aldhelm's funeral procession from Doulting in Somerset to Malmesbury Abbey. Inside, a 13th-century effigy of a lady, wearing a wimple, surprisingly modern. 4

Littleton Pannell. Two big houses; one Georgian and one neo-Georgian. The *Manor House* is late 18th-century and now used in connection with nearby Dauntsey's School. The other, *A' Becketts*, is a classical composition of 1904. 11

Lockeridge, near Marlborough, is a village of mainly Victorian cottages and one elegant Gothick residence of the early 19th century. There is a maze of overhead lines on poles all over the place here. *Lockeridge House* is early-Georgian. 9

Longbridge Deverill. The most beautiful of the five Deverills, standing about a crossing of main roads by a calm stretch of the River Wylye. Here are the *Thynne Almshouses*, founded in 1655 by Sir James Thynne of Longleat, and the interesting church above the winding river. The impressive interior is much older than the apparently Victorian exterior implies. North arcade early Norman; south 14th-century, and a lot of Perpendicular work. There is an assortment of furnishings and fittings: painted Jacobean screens and panelling, genuine and "reproduction"; a green and gilt triumphal arch framing an Art Nouveau memorial font by Gilbert under the tower; an ornate chancel and north chapel, both in the High Victorian manner; a richly handsome west gallery of the 18th century, and a collection of ancient and modern helmets and weapons. Monuments include the simple slab that marks the resting place of Sir John Thynne, who died in 1580 and was the builder of Longleat House, and a monument by Chantrey. The general effect is richly Edwardian. Stained glass in keeping, i.e., baroque 19th–20th century. 13

Longford Castle is a strange and exciting triangular house in the water-meadows of the Avon, south of Salisbury. It was built between about 1575 and 1590 by Sir Thomas Gorges, who was fascinated by astronomy and the occult, and whose tomb in the Cathedral has astrological signs. The ashlar walls of the house have a big masonry pattern in stone and flint. There are squat round towers at each corner of the triangle; a double-storeyed open loggia on the entrance side (restored by Salvin in the 19th century) and an array of chimneys and little domes on the roof, like an apprentice Chambord. "It is", as Mark Girouard says, "a kind of pocket encyclopaedia of Elizabethan ideas. It became a 'castle' only in comparatively recent years, but the change of name reflects something in its nature...." Longford and Wollaton are like architecture described in *The Faerie Queene*. Longford was actually built by patrons of Spen-

LITTLE LANGFORD: *Romanesque tympanum; a boar-hunt below*

ser, and it is even possible that he had it in mind when he described The Castle of Temperance:

> The frame there of was partly circular
> And part triangular – O work divine . . ."

(Sir Thomas Tresham built the Triangular Lodge at Rushton, Northants, in honour of the Trinity.) The first building was completed in 1591 with the help of treasure salvaged from a Spanish galleon wrecked off Hurst Castle. Extensive alterations were carried out in the 18th century and still more was done in the early 1800s, by David Alexander. Anthony Salvin was brought in by the fourth Earl of Radnor in 1870, and during the next ten years did much to restore the house to something like its original form. Longford has splendid furniture and paintings. One original circular room has a Gothic rib-vault on Corinthian columns, showing a characteristic Renaissance combination of Gothic and Classic motives. Many of the great decorators and cabinet-makers of the Georgian period worked here, including Rysbrack, Cheere and Cartwright, designing and building pieces specially to fit the circular rooms in the three round towers. The park and gardens, originally laid out by Capability Brown, are outstanding, though simplified in recent years (pp. 30, 116–17). 15

Longleat. Completed about 1580, the house stands on the site of an Augustinian priory acquired by the original builder, Sir John Thynne, whose tomb is in the church at Longbridge Deverill. He spent many years converting the priory buildings into a comfortable dwelling, but much of the work was destroyed by fire in 1567. He then brought in Robert Smythson as master mason, who was also employed at Wardour Castle and Hardwick Hall. Outwardly much of the building seen today is Smythson's work. If you look at the south facade the building appears an impressive, symmetrical, smallish palace; but take a few steps to west or east, so that part of another wall of the quadrangular design is visible in perspective, and you see that it is vast, and a more formidable, interesting and revolutionary building than it seemed. It is not to be properly comprehended as a facade at all, or even as a regular arrangement of four facades, but as a complex sculptural whole, an ordered progression of projections and depressions, of mouldings, niches, doorways and window openings, the whole crowned by a balustrade with figures that bounds a great parade of chimneys and small domes. It justifies Englishmen in feeling a little European, this

pp. 118/119:
LONGLEAT HOUSE
p. 120: *Figures on the parapet, of later date than the house*
p. 121: *"Banqueting Houses" on the roof*

great Naples-yellow monument in an undulating Wiltshire park. "It is perhaps the first Elizabethan home to have more than the charm of naivity or freshness. It is a work of art, noble, delicate and intelligent" (*Girouard*). At the very beginning of the 19th century, Wyatville re-built the north front, added the fine stables and the Orangery, and did an extensive re-modelling of the interior. During the Victorian period nearly all the state rooms were decorated with Italian marble doorcases and fireplaces, marquetry doors and painted and gilded ceilings, all done by Italian workmen for little money, with a profusion of ornament. The result is gorgeous, if not specially original. There are fine pictures and furniture, while some of the walls are hung with Genoese velvet and old Spanish leather, and there are some splendid 16th-century tapestries. Crace and Wyatville were the chief restorers and decorators. Owned by the Marquess of Bath, who has done much to develop it as a show-place, Longleat has been open to the public for a number of years. Bishop Ken's Library, at the top of the house, dates from the 1690s and is little altered – one of the few interiors here left as it originally was. The park and gardens were worked upon by Capability Brown and Repton. There is a two-mile-long approach drive from the main entrance on the Warminster road, with a dramatic downhill descent to the house. Another, through woodland, from the south. The Longleat lions are now in residence. 10

Lower Woodford. Chequerwork houses and cottages. The *Wheatsheaf* is a small and pretty inn;

LONGFORD CASTLE

LONGLEAT STABLES: Victorian, by Wyatville

the *Manor House* Georgian. Valley scenery with woodland and, across the river, *Little Durnford Manor*. 15

Lower Wraxall is an extension of South Wraxall now undergoing invasion by bungalow. *South Wraxall House*, is a late 18th-century house. *Mison's Farmhouse*, Tudor, has mullioned windows. Over a doorway: *God Save Our Queen Elizabeth* 1575 – *And John Mison & Elizabeth his wife*. 7

Luckington is a pretty place in the Beaufort country. Georgian houses and a tiny lockup. Parts of the nave and tower of the church are 13th century. Sir Arthur Blomfield restored it in 1872. 18th-century north entrance. *Luckington Court* is a Queen Anne house with a long garden and two magnificent trees that overhang the church walk. Referred to in Domesday Book as the Peach House, a hunting box of King Harold. Peach coloured stone and Queen Anne sash windows with thick glazing bars. 4

Ludgershall. The modern village is a ribbon development. New speculative houses and bungalows. The older village is a relief. In Castle Street is a badly eroded cross protected by elaborate railings. Nearby, a row of dilapidated 17th-century almshouses and the crumbling flint ruins of the once royal castle. The big church rambles externally, but the interior is simpler. Some Norman work, but the chancel Early English; the rest Perpendicular with a 17th-century tower. The large ornate late-Renaissance (1558) tomb of Sir Richard Brydges is one of the most beautiful and least-known in Wiltshire. It has reclining figures side by side, in a table-tomb under an arch, below which flutters an angel. There is delicate 16th-century carving, and painting. The kneeling children on the base facing into the south chapel are surprisingly "pictorial" in their attitudes. 12

Lydiard Millicent. The approach to this quiet village is along a processional way of red council houses and bungalows and it now lies within the expanding shadow of Swindon. There is a new Village Hall, stone-front and brick back; and much recent building, some good. Before the next edition of this Guide is published there may well be a large satellite town here, anyway. Unpretentious church, mainly Decorated but much restored. Attractively cleared and refurbished recently. Norman font with band of arches. The Victorian pulpit was carved by the curate and choirboys in 1862. Kempe east window. 5

Lydiard Tregoze church takes one's breath away. Standing in a beautiful park, it looks outwardly like a typical 14th-century village church, but inside one quickly realizes why Aubrey said "here is little that savours of venerable antiquity but for modern ornaments and monuments it excels all the churches in this countie". Sir John St John (died 1648) was the chief adorner. First, he commemorated his parents by an elaborately-painted folding triptych, with genealogical tables painted on the outside, and splendid portraits of the family inside. He then put up the gorgeous and fanciful monument for himself and two wives in the newly-decorated south aisle. The painted screen, the pulpit, the elaborate gilded wrought-iron altar rails, the reredos and the extraordinary glass in the east window (perhaps Flemish – St John the Baptist and St John the Evangelist flanking an olive tree, the whole a rebus on the name "Oliver St John") are other features of his embellishment, and his last grand addition was the strange and beautiful gilded figure of his son under a canopy on the north wall – Edward St John, who was killed fighting for the King at the second battle of Newbury (1645). There are earlier monuments to the family, and one later one of distinction: by Rysbrack to John, Viscount St John (1748), who remodelled the house. There are good fragments of 15th-century glass and wall paintings. The Gibbs glass in the west window is colourful and not at all bad. The old house of the St Johns and Bolingbrokes borders the churchyard. It is a rebuilding of 1745 of an earlier house. It has Georgian ceilings, furniture and pictures, which are in excellent order under the present owners, the Swindon Corporation. They have adapted parts of the house, and repaired it carefully, as a conference centre. 5

Lyneham is dominated by the R.A.F. Station. Barbed wire and high fencing, and planes constantly overhead. The church was practically rebuilt by Butterfield in 1860; clean, neat and tidy inside. Ugly roofing in the nave. A lot of colour. Glass in east window by Gibbs. The Perpendicular chancel screen is well painted; but a similar treatment on the font is garish. There is a fine, plain 18th-century marble tomb with columns and broken pediment. Near the porch a churchyard yew supported on crutches. One very well-carved table-tomb. New brick Church Hall. 5

Maddington adjoins Shrewton. *Maddington Farm* has late-medi-

p. 124: *LYDIARD TREGOZE: Edward St John monument, 1645*

p. 125: *St John family triptych, 1615*

eval buildings and a barn that may have been part of the nunnery that once stood here. Next to the church, a vicarage in flint and stone chequerwork is dated 1704. St Mary's is inside a walled enclosure and approached by a narrow walk from the main road. Restored in 1852, it has Decorated work remaining. The curious trussed roof of the nave is of 1623: the date appears in plaster wall in the west gable. The interior is mostly Victorian, and is darkish and dullish. 11

Maiden Bradley is tidy and well-kept, with many trees, The post office is of the 17th century; it was first a private house and later an

LYDIARD TREGOZE Park

MALMESBURY from the water-meadows

inn, and has a late-Elizabethan fireplace. The church is of many periods. The basic plainness of the interior is relieved by the dark richness of Jacobean box pews, and some of the monuments. A large and elaborate memorial to Sir Edward Seymour (died 1707) is by Rysbrack. Over the churchyard wall are the remains of *Bradley House*, the mansion of the Seymours built about 1700 and, except for the present occupied wing, largely demolished in the early 19th century. At *Priory Farm* are fragments of a 12th-century leper hospital, later taken over by the Augustines as a priory. *New Mead*, another farm, was the birthplace of Edmund Ludlow, one of the judges who condemned Charles I to death. 13

Malmesbury. A small town clinging to the rock which rises impressively out of the plain, crowned by the Abbey. In the centre, the space about the Perpendicular market cross is quite theatrical, although rarely free of traffic. Leland said that the purpose of the cross was *for poore folkes to stande dry when rayne cummeth*. The Abbey, though but a fragment, is magnificent. Originally a vast cruciform building, what now remains is little more than the nave and porch. The fine space of the nave, of about 1160, is enough to indicate the scale of the original. What Leland called *a mightie piramis* of a spire, taller than Salisbury Cathedral, stood above the crossing until 1500, when it collapsed. A few years later, about the time of the Dissolution, a massive western tower also fell. Of recent years, there has been some criticism of the very plain and simple treatment of the blank wall which was built to close off the ruined east end. In fact, the finish of this reredos wall is honest and effective. The south porch with its carvings is the glory of Malmesbury. The sculptures form one of the best displays of Romanesque art in the British Isles, though the medallions on the outer porch are badly weathered. Some of the figures are much elongated, and their poses and implied actions are clearly the work of an internationally-minded and experienced sculptor. The Six Apostles on each side, inside the porch, have influenced 20th-century English sculpture and painting very clearly, being easily accessible examples – and very fine ones – of the 12th-century European style. There are many good buildings; the narrow streets are full of pleasant surprises. *Abbey House*, *Old Brewery House* and the *St John's Almshouses*, are all of the 17th century. The Georgian period is well represented: there are many small houses of the 18th century, as well as *Athelstan's House*, *The Bell Hotel* and *The Priory*. From the time of King Athelstan, whose empty tomb is in the Abbey, until 1832, Malmesbury returned two members to Parliament. Until the decline of the wool trade in the 18th century it prospered as a weaving centre. 4

Manningford Abbots. Thatched cottages along a twisting lane. On a sharp bend and lying across lawns is the *Old Rectory* of 1812, a bow-fronted brick box with big ranges of stables. A sweep of trees takes the eye to the simple Victorian church, less imposing and hidden in a coppice. It has nave and chancel with bellcote, 1864. No stained glass. One good early 19th-century table-tomb in churchyard. 8

Manningford Bohun is on the main road to Pewsey, but its church (All Saints) is some distance away, across Bohune Common towards Woodborough. A bellcoted, slated building of 1859, down a "No Through Road" beside a firwood, it is by J. B. Clacy. The exterior stonework is set in irregular chunks, like crazy paving. 8

Manningford Bruce. St Peter's is a remarkable early Norman church of nave and semi-circular apse. J. L. Pearson did a sympathetic restoration here in 1882, building a wagon roof over the nave and an ingenious herring-bone half-dome of timber over the apse; an echo, perhaps, of the flint herring-bone work of the outside walls. Pearson designed the reredos;

pp. 128/129: *The twelve apostles, six each side, in the abbey porch, MALMESBURY. The larger photographs are details*

Clayton and Bell made it, and at least one window. There is a modest wall memorial to Mary Nicholas, who helped Charles II to escape after the Battle of Worcester, thereby gaining the privilege of incorporating part of the Royal Arms of England in the Nicholas family arms. Daffodils are cultivated in the fields here. 8

Manton. Overspill for Marlborough. The old nucleus of the place is pretty with whitewash and thatch cottages and a charming old post office. 9

Marden. Thatched cottages. The much restored church retains its richly decorated Norman doorway and beautiful and big chancel arch, with Royal Arms over. There is a Jacobean pulpit with tester, many wall tablets to the Hayward family, and an old

MALMESBURY Abbey, from the south

MARLBOROUGH

door. Though much restored, the interior has an agreeable, old-fashioned atmosphere. The Peter and Paul window by J. and M. Kettlewell, 1958, is a lively piece of modern stained glass. The *Manor House*, standing in parkland at the south end of the village, is late Georgian. *Marden Circle* is a big oval earthwork of the New Stone Age. 8

Market Lavington. Once considered a market town. The big church stands on a steep knoll, a clean and well-kept building with 13th-century chancel with some Decorated work, and also much Victorian work in wood, tile and stone. There are many wall monuments, including one to Thomas Saintsbury (died 1797) by Flaxman. There is a Georgian vicarage. The Tudor Revival *Manor House* of 1865 was designed by Ewan Christian, who restored the church three years earlier. Westward, some unpleasant pre-War housing, and *Clyffe Hall*, an early 18th-century house, with much creeper. 11

Marlborough. The English country town at its best. A grand, wide sloping street with a fine church at each end. This High Street has a great variety of buildings; hotels, guest houses, shops, eating places aimed at the visitor and tourist; but visually speaking, they go about the business quietly and do not shout. Along the north side, the shops are colonnaded; the predominant style Georgian, with many tile-hung fronts; little passages and alleys to explore everywhere and most are worth plunging into, those on the south side of High Street running down to gardens along the river. Marlborough had a Great Fire in 1653, when much of the old town was destroyed. The few surviving medieval structures can be seen in the twisted half-timber cottages in some of the minor streets. Among the more notable buildings in the centre are *The Castle and Ball Hotel*, *Ivy House Hotel* and the *Georgian Restaurant*, all 18th-century buildings. The *Town Hall* at one end, built in 1901 in late-17th-century style, fits in remarkably well with its neighbours. So does the new Woolworths, a decent modern design with no attempt at "reproduction". The latest Motel Units at the *Ailesbury Arms* across the way are also well done. In *Kingsbury Street* are still more Georgian houses with a further collection disposed about the wide stretch of grass known as *The Green*. Without doubt the best house of the period is *Poulton House*, just outside the town. Both of Marlborough's two old churches suffered in the fire, *St Mary's*, at the eastern end of the High Street, being gutted. There is some surviving Norman work here, but the general style is rebuilt Perpendicular with some strangely classical columns of the late 17th century and a chancel of 1874 by G. E. Street. *St Peter and St Paul*, at the opposite end, is Perpendicular also, with a stone-vaulted chancel and porch; restoration by T. H. Wyatt in 1863. An impressive tower and a number of interesting monuments. *Marlborough College*, beyond St Peter's, seems to stand quite separate from the rest of the town and in ways other than architectural is its own world. Founded in 1843, near the site of the old Norman castle, its building history is older. One of its "houses" is the mansion built by the sixth Duke of Somerset in 1700. Fifty years later it became the Castle Inn, which received and despatched forty coaches a day. This fine building remained a coaching house until 1843, when the formation of the College was in progress and plans were made for receiving the first 200 boys. In the ensuing hundred years, many architects were engaged in works of extension and alteration. Blore, Blomfield, Bodley & Garner, Sir Aston Webb and W. G. Newton all were employed in their turn. Cardinal Wolsey was ordained priest at St Peter's. During the Civil War, the Royalists stormed and captured Marlborough, and both Charles I and Cromwell passed through. After the Restoration, Charles II was entertained at the original Seymour mansion and to the later building came many 18th-century wits and men of letters. 9

Marston. There is a scattering of new and old cottages and farms, some half-timbered. Comfortable scenery. 11

Marston Meysey. An attractive village, in flat country but of a Cotswold type. Meanly designed council houses. Spoiled also by a profusion of television aerials mingled with the general mess of overhead wirescape. But there are many happy vistas of gardens and old stone gables, and three excellent 17th-century farmhouses with good barns. The church is Victorian (1876) by James Brooks. Stone, with simple nave and chancel under one gable, without tower or spire. Vaulted chancel, careful mouldings, elaborate tiles and door furniture. Low stone screen. High chancel. Glass by Kempe and Clayton and Bell. Close to the now derelict Thames-Severn Canal is a *Roundhouse*, one of several in this district, dating from 1789 when the canal was opened. 2

Melksham. Not a large town, but with the exception of Swindon the most industrialized in the county. The big rubber factory has been long established and several new works have appeared in recent years. In the centre are new shopping developments. Good buildings are few. In *Cannon Square*, a precinct near the church, is a pleasing jumble of 17th- and early 18th-century stone houses and also the curious *Round House*, once used as an ammunition store by the Volunteers. *Melksham House* is a much altered 17th-century town house. Nearby, a big buttressed tithe barn has been turned into a school. In 1815 the discovery of a chalybeate spring led to serious attempts at turning Melksham into a spa; a half-crescent of villas and a bungalow made out of the original Pump Room along the Devizes road show where the enterprise failed. The big Perpendicular *church* of St Michael has traces of Norman and 13th-century work and a scraped interior much restored by T. H. Wyatt in the 1840s. All is brownish and in need of colour – and plaster. In the churchyard a vast and ancient yew tree has its limbs supported on a pergola of stout poles, shading a fine collection of table-tombs. 7

Mere is a charming little town. On the outskirts is *Castle Hill*, the site of a medieval fortress, and on the slopes of the downland to the east a series of strip lynchets, or terraces, may have been vineyards planted by the Romans. In the town, the *Ship Inn*, with a fine wrought iron sign, was once the mansion of Sir John Coventry. To the now-modernized *George Hotel* across the way came the fugitive Charles II diguised as a servant after the Battle of Worcester in 1651. Both were famous coaching inns. In the centre of the town a rather grim Jubilee Clock stands in front of the Queen Victoria Memorial Hall, now converted into motorcar showrooms. Not far away is one of the buildings of which the great Sir Gilbert Scott was so ashamed in his later years: one of his utilitarian workhouses. The best bit of mid-19th-century work in Mere is undoubtedly Walton's shop in the High Street. The pinnacled tower of the parish church stands proudly over the town; as at Westbury, the small Georgian cottages grouped around the churchyard give St Michael's the feeling of a cathedral precinct. A vaulted porch leads to a light and lofty interior; here are rood screen and rood loft, the screen Perpendicular work, the other parts more recent, but well done. The fine Jacobean pews were made and carved by "Walter the Joiner" of Maiden Bradley in 1638, the total cost being £86. 11s. Among the monuments is a brass of 1398 to Sir John Berreshorne in the south chapel. Noteworthy stained glass, 15th century and pre-Raphaelite. The game of fives was once played regularly in the churchyard. It was also used for archery practice. Against the wall can be seen the chantry house used as a school by William Barnes, the Dorset poet; nearby is the 15th-century charnel house. 13

Middle Woodford. Some prim but not unpleasant council housing; better than nearby speculative-builder housing. The church, near to a big bend of the Avon, was rebuilt by T. H. Wyatt in 1845, although he left the Perpendicular tower alone. Surprisingly, he also left untouched the small and elegant Jacobean gallery; perhaps because it is built into the tower. Otherwise the church is decent but fairly dull. Stained glass of the 20th century with saints on clear backgrounds. 14

Mildenhall – known as "Minal" – is a village of brick and thatch, tile and slate. Here is a most unusual Gothic school, designed by Robert Abraham and built for the Rev. Charles Francis in 1823. A notable exercise in early educational planning: octagonal central hall with radiating wings and the whole building crowned by a lantern. At the opposite end of the village is the church. Not only was it untouched by the Victorians, so that the work of all medieval periods is left, but it retains all the late-Georgian Gothic furnishings introduced in 1815: gallery, two three-decker pulpits symmetrically arranged on each side of the chancel arch, font, reredos; one walks between the high box pews as down a narrow street. Fragments of 15th-century glass in east window. Moulded plaster ceiling, Jacobean. Among other monuments, a memorial to the Rev. Harris, who built the school and was the "Squarson" of Mildenhall. Two wall monuments with palms in white marble, in the chancel, are by Harris of Bath, and admirable. Nearby is the site of the Roman town of Cunetio. There is also a Belgic war cemetery here from which a number of skeletons were removed in 1952. 9

Milford, on the outskirts of Salisbury, has a medieval double bridge over the Bourne with a kind of causeway between. Here is an 18th-century mill house with weeping willows in a garden, the river running underneath. *Milford Manor* is a rambling Victorian house. 15

Milston is by the Avon above Salisbury and between the military areas of Larkhill and Bulford. A recent invasion by modern housing has so far been halted on the outskirts. The charming little flint and stone church was restored in 1860, but retains many of its medieval features. There is an unusual tubby font and 16th-century woodwork in the porch. Good Royal Arms. Joseph Addison was born here in 1672, when his father was rector. The mullioned house beyond the churchyard dates from 1613. 12

Milton Lilbourne. A tidy village with Victorian, Georgian and earlier thatched buildings blending well together. In the main street is *Manor House*, built in two stages during the 18th century. *King Hall*, further down, has Georgian entrance gates but is Victorian and crude by comparison. The church is on a green knoll above the street, with an early 19th-century vicarage next door. Flint and stone chequerwork with an Early English nave, Decorated chancel and Perpendicular tower, restored in 1875 by J. L. Pearson. Jacobean pews, reader's desk and pulpit. Bits of Perpendicular glass. 9

Minety. From Silver Street and the pretty Victorian railway station at one end to the church at the other is 1½ miles. There are many undistinguished bungalows among a few good houses and cottages, and the public buildings are remarkably divergent. The church, St Leonard, is Perpendicular with battlements and lead spouts. It has a carved pulpit of 1627 and much woodwork of the same period in pews and reader's desk. The screens are earlier (Perpendicular). There is a fine brass chandelier. The only unfortunate thing is the brownish stained glass in several windows – as dull as can be. The best window (? O'Connor) is behind the organ. The churchyard is rich in stones, table-tombs and an urn on a pedestal. *Mansells*, on the roadside north of the village, is a mid-17th-century house with later additions. 2

Monkton Deverill. The compound Old English – Old Welsh origin of "Deverill" is "Dubro-ial", meaning cultivated water field; the name is therefore most appropriate for the five Deverill villages in the Wylye valley where watercress cultivation is a local industry. *Monkton* has a church with nave, chancel and 13th-century tower, the remainder being simply rebuilt by T. H. Wyatt in 1845. All is now lichenous, and old-looking. Thin rafters to the roof inside, pitchpine and (later) Victorian glass. The original dedication being lost, the church was rededicated in 1950 to "Alfred, King of the West Saxons", who "camped for the night in the Deverill valley before giving the Danes a sound beating at the great Battle of Ethandune". 13

Monkton Farleigh climbs up a steep little street of stone (partly estate) houses, passing a big Gothic rectory, bigger than the church next door. *St Peter's* is plain and simple with a 13th-century tower and Norman north door, but was largely rebuilt in 1844, by T. H. Wyatt. There is a Jacobean pulpit and linenfold

MILDENHALL Church, interior, 1816

NETHERHAMPTON

panelling at the back of the nave. Lighting, by electrified oil lamps, is quite well done. *The Manor*, originally a Cluniac priory, is a big golden stone house looking down a tree-lined ride across the countryside. Medieval fragments remain, including effigies of knights and ladies, but the main facade is early 19th-century Georgian. *Monks Conduit*, to the north, is a pretty little stone structure housing the spring that formed the priory water supply. 7

Neston see CORSHAM. 7

Netheravon. There is military housing all round this Avon valley village, which possesses one big house and a good ch rch. *All Saints* is remarkable for its appearance, antiquity, and development. The original Saxon building was very much larger, cruciform in plan, with the tower over the crossing. The nave we see was the big chancel of the old church, whose crossing tower with its majestic Norman arch, with carved cushion capitals, now terminates the west end. The nave, which has completely disappeared, stood in the present churchyard. The base of the tower, with its signs of two *porticus* – rudimentary transepts – in the walls is Saxon, the main part Norman and the easily distinguished upper stage Early English. There are two bright Victorian windows, but most of the stained glass has been removed. The 19th-century wit, Sidney Smith, was curate here in 1794. Close by can be seen *Netheravon House*, an 18th-century mansion now under Army occupation. In the grounds are many huts and a large dovecote. The big stables have charming lunettes and one quite enormous oval window. 12

Netherhampton, on the edge of Wilton Park, has gabled estate cottages and across the road from the church an elaborate group of stables and barns (see also *Quidhampton*). The church (St Catherine) has an 18th-century brick tower but all the rest was newly built by Butterfield in 1876 in Decorated style. Interior rather attractive, in a simple severe style, and little disturbed since he left it. Stained glass by Gibbs. The church is dangerously close to the busy main road. *Netherhampton House* has an early-Georgian facade stuck on to a much humbler cottage block of the 17th century and is very charming in a swagger sort of way. Nice wrought iron gates. 14

Nettleton is a scattered place with no real focal point, houses and farms being dotted about a network of lanes. The Fosse Way runs close by and here was discovered the site of a Roman temple to the goddess Diana, recessed into a small cliff. At *Lugbury*, the burial chambers of a long barrow yielded up 28 skeletons in the 19th century. The church of the parish is at Burton, under which name it is described. 4

Newton Toney. Toney is the modern version of Tosny; a family of that name and town in France were lords of the manor here in the 13th century. A pretty village with cottages of thatch and colourwash along both sides of the Bourne. The flint and stone church is by Wyatt and Brandon, and a good village feature, with a short spire and bright and attractive figures on rich grounds under Gothic canopies in the 1845 glass of the east window. There are some wall tablets. Norman tub font. New bungalow estate on the hillside behind the main street; at one end a good gabled and mullioned farmhouse, 17th-century. Here too, the entrance gates to *Wilbury House*, a Georgian mansion which can just be glimpsed among the trees. 15

Newtown is a plain village with some splendid views over the countryside of southern Wiltshire. *Hatch House* is partly 17th century and well restored by Detmar Blow in 1908. *Pyt House* is a late-Georgian house in the Palladian manner, open to visitors. The church is Gothic, and simple, of 1911. The chancel arch came from a ruined chapel at Pyt House. 13

DINTON: Philipps House, 1816

North Bradley is on the Westbury road just south of Trowbridge. Outside the village a signpost points the way to Scotland and Ireland: twin farming hamlets nearby. In spite of the dereliction of *Vicars Poorhouse*, the neat row of almshouses built by the incumbent Charles Daubeny in 1810, North Bradley is a quiet and well-kept place. The big church has a Perpendicular tower and was restored by T. H. Wyatt in 1862. Monuments of the 18th century to members of the Trenchard and Long families. The elaborate north chapel contains the tomb chest of Emma Stafford, who died in 1446 and was the mother of John Stafford, an Archbishop of Canterbury. A simple Baptist church of 1775 is now joined by a second, modern one. Good views of Westbury White Horse.   10

North Newnton. The church is near the Avon and a millstream, backed by willows. Nice cottages here, one with its drooping thatch pulled down over one end like a thick shawl. A mill race slides over a weir into the foaming river. But the picture has been spoiled by the new concrete roof tiles, the tarmac car-park and the ranking together of a group of well carved tomb-stones at one side of the churchyard, like giant's teeth. St James is simple and has a 13th-century chancel, recently well refurbished in white and gold. The nave was a Victorian restoration and one of the arches leans outwards. On the Perpendicular tower, the strange little projections with their lean-to roofs are the projecting ends of the old bell cradle beams. There are a couple of delicate wall-tablets inside and two or three good stone table-tombs in the churchyard. On the road to Woodborough, *Hillcot Manor Farmhouse* is half 17th century, half Georgian, with straw birds perched along its thatched ridge.   12

North Tidworth. Writing in the last edition of this Guide, David Verey commented: "This place has become entirely military and is surprisingly ugly despite its fine situation between tree covered hills. The late Victorian and Edwardian barrack buildings have a fine suburban flavour with tennis courts and privet hedges. The enormous extensions of hutted camps cover the surrounding horizon and a scattering of bun shacks and garages make a living for the hangers-on near the church...." The description is still very accurate, although some of the buildings erected in the last five years or so are far more pleasant, particularly the newer housing. The church, overlooking a sea of this eastwards, is Perpendicular and Victorian and

NEWTOWN: Pyt House, begun 1805

has an unusual Norman font in the form of a column capital. *South Tidworth*, which is part of the single Tidworth Barracks area, is across the county border in Hampshire. 12

North Wraxall is on a hillside and just clear of the main Chippenham–Bristol road. A pleasing place with a pretty Gothic school and schoolhouse below a steep rock face with a miniature playground. The church is unrestored. It has a Norman doorway, but is mostly of the 13th century. White plastered ceilings throughout, that in the Georgian Methuen Chapel is elaborated with painted heraldic devices. Old stone floors. Jacobean pulpit. A noble white marble sarcophagus, designed by Westmacott, commemorates Paul Methuen (1837). Attractive and colourful glazing scheme of the 1840s. Patterns, with small scenes inset. Churchyard table-tombs. Near the church is a small medieval *Chantry House*. 4

Norton. A small farming village at a crossing of lanes near Malmesbury. The little 13th-century church is much rebuilt, with an over-sized bell turret that was a throwout from Grittleton House in 1858. On a shelf over the west door is a tiny Bates Mechanical Organ that plays a handful of set hymns. Norman font, Jacobean pulpit and a bit of 17th-century panelling have survived the restoration. Cheap modern panelling round the chancel. The *Manor House* is a modernized house of 1623 with formal gardens split into two by the roadway. 4

Norton Bavant. Described by William Cobbett in 1830 as "one of the prettiest spots that my eyes ever beheld". Much of its charm remains. Rebuilt ten years after Cobbett came here – 1839–1841 – the Church, except for the Perpendicular tower, is among yews and huge fir trees along the chestnut drive leading to Norton Bavant House, a handsome building with a Queen Anne front and shell porch. There is colourful glass (not very competent), of about 1845 in two windows. The Bennet family vault is on the south side, and has wall tablets, brass and indented floor slabs. 10

Nunton. South of Salisbury, has a lot of overhead wiring and a thatched Gothick cottage. A newly erected block of council houses is called "Ebbleside Villas". *Nunton House* is a pedimented mansion of the early 18th century near the church. St Andrew's was restored by T. H. Wyatt. It is in flint and stone, tiled. There is a Christopher Webb east window (1937) and a monument by Westmacott with standing figures – full of early 19th-century sentiment. 18

Oaksey. There is a drab estate on the edge of the village and there are also rather ugly Victorian villas, but the rest is pleasing, with a number of 17th-century stone cottages and farmhouses. At *Dean Farm*, to the north, are the remains of *Norwood Castle*, a Norman motte-and-bailey fortification. The church has 13th-century fragments and a Decorated porch, and tower and clerestory, but the total effect is Perpendicular. The cream interior is relieved by some colourful 15th-century wall paintings, among them St Christopher and a Christ of the Trades. There is good 15th-century glass in one window. The east window of 1862 in bright and welcome colours, is by William Warrington. A good rustic church. Over the entrance doorway, an admonition to "Remember the Poor" is painted in the style one expects to see in Bavarian country churches. There is a Sheila-na-gig carving, and another of the Virgin, both medieval. 2

Oare has a church by S. S. Teulon, 1857. Both academic and eccentric; but it is easy to exaggerate its ugliness. Romanesque, red and blue brick. *Oare House*, nearby, is a small mansion of 1740 built by a London wine merchant; elegant and with wings added in the twenties by Clough Williams-Ellis, the architect and creator of the "Italian" village of Portmeirion in North Wales. He also designed the thatched *Cold Blow* and a row of white cottages in the village. Near to the Marlborough road and superbly sited below Oare Hill is *Rainscombe House*, late-Georgian. 9

Odstock in the Ebble Valley. At one end of the village, *The Parsonage* is an unusual and pleasing tile-hung house, once an inn at which Oliver Cromwell stayed. Further along the same road is the *Manor House*, early 17th-century, of brick stone-dressed, seen from its entrance gates between big trees. The church has some attractive flint and chequerwork; it is of 13th-century origin, over-zealously restored in 1875. The base of the Jacobean pulpit bears the date 1850 and the carved inscription:

God Bless and Save our Royal Queen,
The lyke on earth was never seen.

a couplet which is usually considered Elizabethan double-talk.

*St Mary, ORCHESTON.
Re-styled in early 19th-century Gothic*

There is also an Elizabethan stone-arched monument against the tower arch. On the downs above the village is the plantation known as *Great Yews*, one of its boundaries being the ancient Grims Ditch and the border between Wiltshire and Hampshire. This wood is of prehistoric origin and seven dark yew tunnels meet at its centre. It can be approached from a downland track from Hornington. The yews are now overgrown and intermingled with thorns and brambles. The site is more primeval than one has a right to expect in our urbanized civilization. 10

The Ogbournes, Maizey, St George and St Andrew, are three villages below the Downs north of Marlborough, linked by the road to Swindon which follows the valley of the Og. 6 & 9

Ogbourne Maizey, smallest and southernmost of the three, has no church, but there are pretty cottages and by the river bridge a small *Manor House*. The broad flint and stone-banded front is Jacobean, with mullioned windows and later Georgian sashes. 9

Thatched wall, NUNTON. These capped boundary walls round gardens and farm-houses are less common than they used to be

136

Ogbourne St Andrew is a well-looked-after village, off the main road from Swindon to Marlborough, with a rural atmosphere. There are many old thatched cottages with walls of sarsen, and a good deal of later make-do-and-mending in brick. Two late-Georgian houses with open lawn layout in front look towards the church. The church has the tierceron-vaulted base of the Perpendicular tower open-arched, the big pillars supporting it exposed to view in the nave: a splendid arrangement. Restored in 1873, but much of the Norman nave survives. There is a pretty 17th-century monument with chubby busts of husband and wife holding a skull between them.   9

Ogbourne St George. Along the main road, the newer parts are a dull straggle, but, leading to the church, the High Street has some thatched cottages in stone and brick. Some of the houses spoiled by the use of cheap off-the-peg windows. The church is Perpendicular, behind a high wall. The interior has recently been re-plastered. There are Victorian pitch pine pews and poor decoration and glass in the chancel. Decorative text (Victorian) over chancel arch. Fine late Royal Arms and Commandment boards. Excellent carved table-tombs in the churchyard. Over the wall can be seen the *Manor House*; Georgian at the front and Jacobean at the back, in mellow brickwork. On the downs above, an old-established Army camp.   6

Orcheston St George is green and pleasant enough, though "development" threatens. The flint and stone church has a Norman doorway and 15th-century tower with deep mouldings and tall panelled arch framing the view of the Early English chancel as you enter under it. Branching brass candlesticks attached to the pews are effective. The general atmosphere, however, is rather dark and dull.   11

Orcheston St Mary enjoys the blessing of no through traffic. A few old houses and the Victorian village school, now converted into a cottage. A small inn and a water meadow setting; all very pleasant. John Aubrey reckoned that the famous "Orcheston Grass" used to grow to a height of twelve feet and more. It is still said to be record-breaking. *St Mary's* church has one or two late 13th-century features (doorway, arcade) but is in total effect a church of about 1840, and looks like a model picturesque church of the period. Spiky pinnacles, saddleback tower, all in pale stone and lively flint. The interior is less good since everything has been painted, stonework included, but it is a good period piece, all the same and has contemporary pews, dark roof structures and bright glass of about 1850.   11

Overton, *see* WEST OVERTON.   8

Patney stands in the flat Vale country between Pewsey and Devizes. An unremarkable village and church. *St Swithin's* is almost entirely Victorian (1877), the oldest things within being the base of the font and the Jacobean pulpit. There is a pretty, mostly blue east window of 1862, and some small wall tablets. The magnificent cedar tree in the churchyard must come near to outdating everything else.   8

Pertwood. A wonderful site, high on rolling downland. A little road from the general direction of Mere winds over a shoulder of the downs and drops into Pertwood. Here, the potholed lane comes to an end at a modest group of cottages and the forecourt and facade of the *Manor House*. The church is behind the back gardens of cottages; the approach is along the side of the Manor Farmhouse, an unassuming 18th-century building. St Peter's is a very simple and pretty nave and chancel of flint and stone, of 1872; now dilapidated. There are medieval fragments: Norman font, 14th-century piscina, Perpendicular pulpit. The oldest church bell in Wiltshire (c. 1290) hangs in the bellcote.   13

Pewsey. A small country town. At the cross-roads in the centre a statue of Alfred the Great. The local cinema has been turned into a factory. Buildings of note: the early-Georgian *Old Rectory*, now the offices of the R.D.C.; *Court House*, half-timber with a thatched roof; the old house known as *Ball*, also timber-framed; and – a little way out of the town – *Pewsey Hospital* which used to be the workhouse and still looks like one: grey, grim and classical, built in 1836. The church (St John) stands high above the main road with a new and complicated system of approach steps, and a recent red brick retaining wall. There are Norman arcades founded on great sarsen stones, but with the exception of these and the Perpendicular tower, most of its structure is 13th century. A tactful restoration was carried out by G. E. Street in 1861, when he rebuilt the chancel and designed the pulpit and choir stalls. The interior is remarkable for the competent workmanship of the reredos and font cover and the "lady angels" painted in sickly pinks in the spandrels of the nave arches. The same hands were responsible for both, Canon Pleydell Bouverie (rector, 1880–1910) being an amateur carver and painter. There is some rather poor stained glass.   9

Pickwick is made up of *Upper Pickwick* and *Lower Pickwick*, twin hamlets outside Corsham and mentioned in the description of that town. It is possible that there is some connection here with Dickens. The firm of Moses Pickwick & Co. ran coaches from London to Bath through Lower Pickwick.   7

Pitton. East of Salisbury. Cottages thatched, slated and tiled. The flint church has Norman doorways and a 13th-century porch under the tower. The simple interior is the result of Victorian restoration. There is an attractive milky-white and greenish east window by Kempe: Crucifixion with the Virgin and St John. Electric radiant heaters and electronic organ.   15

Porton. Standing high above the

Wilton Estate Model Farm, QUIDHAMPTON. A picturesque group of Italianate buildings of the mid-19th century

river, the village has a miscellaneous collection of houses and cottages, in the rural suburban styles of the past seventy years. They are served electrically by the inevitable webs of overhead wiring. The church, by J. L. Pearson, dates from 1876. Nave, chancel, western turret, south porch. Flint with stone dressings. Interior dark, with careful but dull glass. 15

Potterne has a church which stands high and majestic over the little town, dominating everything. Built at the same time as Salisbury Cathedral and in the same single outburst, St Mary's is pure Early English. It is cruciform, with tower over the crossing. The stone roofs, and the exterior of the imposing tower are attractive. (This tower was altered in later medieval times.) But the church has been ruined inside by the introduction of dark pitch-pine woodwork, tiles, and stained glass that is mostly brownish. Colour is sorely needed. The fine proportions remain. Moses and Aaron paintings, and tablets. The churchyard is excellent, on different levels, with stone flags, limes, well-carved tombs (especially table-tombs) and a fine wall on one side of black clinker and brick. A number of good buildings cluster about the church. In the High Street the half-timbered *Porch House* is a 15th-century building, well-preserved. George Richmond, R.A., father-in-law of Samuel Palmer, came here to live in 1875 and restored the house. A row of old half-timbered cottages adjoins it. Nearer to the church gates, *Church House*, with its pretty garden, is a mullion-windowed building of 1614. 8

Poulshot. A quiet village near Devizes. On the outskirts is a pleasing black and white half-timbered inn, and then the road cuts across the middle of a huge green, surrounded with attractive little cottages set among trees. There are new houses and bungalows on the outer fringes, and the church is nearly a mile away. The tower with its pyramid roof is Victorian, but the rest is old. Wide nave and very narrow aisles, separated by uncommonly big span 14th-century arches. Bits of Norman capitals are built into the walls here and there and one of the big arches is stiffened by a sort of flying buttress. The interior has been scraped, but the temptation to finish off the stonework with the usual prim pointing has been resisted. 8

Preshute is by Marlborough. The tower of the church is original and 15th-century, but the exterior is otherwise all the work of T. H. Wyatt; inside, however, he did preserve the Early English arcade of the nave. The "enormous sinister font" was carved out of a huge block of black Tournai marble and is reputed to have come from Marlborough Castle; tradition holds that King John was baptised in it.   9

Purton is a straggling place with conglomerations of buildings, mostly Victorian. The original village is a good half-mile away from the High Street and here are cottages, church and manor house of c. 1600, of stone with brick chimneys, and tithe barn making a delightful group. St Mary's is a beautiful building with a central tower and spire; there is a second pinnacled tower at the west end. The interior is of the 13th and 14th centuries, tall and with slender pillars, the soffits of the arches being enriched with colour making altogether a light and happy effect, in spite of restoration. There is a good deal of medieval stained glass, a medieval wall painting of the death of the Blessed Virgin Mary and several good wall monuments. Fine collection of churchyard table-tombs, including a severe oval one, which occurs elsewhere locally.   2

Purton Stoke. A cross-roads hamlet about a mile-and-a-half north of Purton itself. Here is the Bell Inn, with one or two nice Georgian houses nearby, some fairly recent speculative houses and among them one or two bits of decent Regency architecture; bright red brick council houses and a corrugated iron youth club complete the scene. In the middle of the 17th century, someone tried to start a Spa here and the funny little Pump Room still exists.   2

Quemerford. A suburbanized extension of Calne, along the main Marlborough road. There is a riverside mill building, erected at the beginning of the 19th century and then used for spinning flax. The church is Victorian (1853).   8

Quidhampton. On the River Nadder outside Salisbury and a patchy, nondescript village much uglified by overhead wiring. *Wilton Estate Model Farm* is a pretentious curiosity in an Italianate style, built in careful random stonework. It has many arches and gables in the barns and a picturesque dovecote, in all this resembling another Wilton Estate farm at Netherhampton. *The Grange*, not far away, is a house of 1675, with mullioned windows; picturesque in a rambling sort of way.   14

Ramsbury. Thatched cottages and brick houses. The approach is delightful, particularly from Froxfield; here the Kennet runs wide and clear beneath a long low millhouse. There are Jacobean and Georgian buildings; *Parliament Piece* is a square late-17th-century house with elegant cross windows, standing on the road above the church. The flint and stone church with massively-buttressed tower is impressive. Partly built on Saxon foundations, it is mainly Early English and Decorated; the chapels and some of the arcading Perpendicular. After recent decoration, the nave is light and airy and makes a splendid impression; the choir stalls, screens and other woodwork have been "limed". Among the furnishings and fittings are the remains of one, or maybe two, crosses of the 9th century, and other Saxon stones. The pieces of cross are beautifully carved with interlace and other designs. They relate to other Wiltshire carvings at Colerne and Knook. Brass chandeliers of the mid-18th century and Gothick organ. Many monuments. Sir William Jones of Ramsbury Manor, who died in 1682 and was Attorney-General to Charles II, has his well-composed and swanky tomb next to the altar, with reclining effigy. There are also two monuments by van Gelder (1786 and 1801). Another grand coloured marble composition signed by J. F. Moore with bust and cherubs (1775). The east window in the south aisle (made by Powell) is of bright saints under stylized foliage – very pretty. The *Manor* is easily seen from the road to Marlborough. Jones employed John Webb, son-in-law of Inigo Jones, to design it, and it was completed in 1680. It is in parkland flanking the river, which is dammed here to form an ornamental water, with a handsome five-arched bridge.   9

Redlynch, in the far south, in the coppice country, has a lot of suburban-style development near the main road. The old village is much pleasanter. Redlynch has two churches, both Victorian; *St Mary's*, yellow-brick Perpendicular, dates from 1837. Fifty years later, C. E. Ponting did the strange Arts-and-Crafts Movement church of St Birinus, all tiles and half timber with a shingled bell tower. At one end of the village is the 19th-century Gothic lodge to *Redlynch House*, a Victorian mansion. The lodge has been recently colourwashed bright pink.   18

Rockley is a very pretty hamlet below the Marlborough Downs. There is a small Victorian church chequered in flint and stone and *Rockley Manor*, a stuccoed late-Georgian house in a small park with fine trees.   9

Rodbourne, near Malmesbury, is a scattered hamlet with a huge water tower dominating everything, the church not excluded. There is a rusticated Victorian school, its roof hidden under a thick layer of mosses and lichens, and *Rodbourne House*, where Thackeray stayed. The church of *Holy Rood* has a 19th-century saddleback tower with a distinctly Continental appearance, but the rest of the building is much older, and has atmosphere, though the walls are partly scraped. Old wooden roof. The tympanum of the Norman south doorway is carved with a Tree of Life. East window: stained glass by William Morris (early).   1

Rodbourne Cheney is a growing suburb of Swindon. Its growth

RODBOURNE: Stained glass by William Morris (1870s), Adam and Eve and the Serpent, and the Annunciation

is reflected by recent developments at St Mary's church which has two priests and a deaconess and many extra and intra-mural activities. There are interesting alterations and extensions to the building itself. Among these are a new reinforced-concrete west gallery, sloped and stepped like a cinema balcony; new vestries and an extension of the north aisle. Not badly done. Of the old structure, traces of 13th-century and Perpendicular work remain, but much was altered in a rebuilding of 1848. *Manor House* and *Manor Farm* are two 17th-century stone buildings nearby. 5

Rood Ashton, *see* WEST ASHTON. 10

Rollestone, in a wooded fold of Salisbury Plain, is in the hands of the speculative builders. Until recently it was no more than a Georgian farmhouse and a fistful of cottages. The church, a small flint building, has an Early English chancel and Perpendicular windows with Jacobean heraldic glass. 11

Rowde. Much modern main-road development. The church stands high with a tall thin tower of the 15th century; the rest, rebuilt in the 1830s, lacks interest. The font was designed in 1850 by Sir Matthew Digby Wyatt. He lived

for a time at *Rowdeford House*, a big square classical mansion of 1812, now a school. At *St Edith's Marsh*, the *Bell Inn* is a simple hostelry dated 1698. Opposite is a monster of a Victorian country house. 8

Rushall is mostly a main road village in the Vale of Pewsey, but at the end of a no-through-lane are pretty cottages and the church. St Matthew's has a Perpendicular tower and 14th-century chancel arch, but the rest was rebuilt in brick in 1812. The Norman font sits on a piece of an old pillar. Old benches. Small panels of foreign glass: 16th-century. 12

Salisbury. "New Sarum" came into being with the laying of the foundation stone of the new cathedral on April 28, 1220. The old town – "Old Sarum" – had previously been growing for centuries around the castle and ancient church of St Osmund on their hill-top site to the north. This fortified hill was always a bleak and exposed site afflicted by "too much wind and too little water." The growing population was already moving down to the gentler meads about the Avon when, following a final dispute with the civil authorities holding the castle, Bishop Poore decided to pack up and follow them. A papal bull of 1219 authorizing the move speaks of those *plains where the valley abounds in corn, where the fields are beautiful and where there is freedom from oppression.* In less than a year, the cathedral was under construction and Salisbury had come into being. By 1227, the city had received its first charter from Henry III, making the Bishop absolute overlord. *Harnham Bridge* was built over the Avon, the secular town to the north of the cathedral was laid out in a regular grid of spacious streets and, largely supported by the prosperous wool trade, the place grew rapidly. Kings and princes came and went; the noble and ignoble were executed here; Nell Gwynn came to buy scissors and

SALISBURY: Mompesson House in The Close

Samuel Pepys stayed for a while. These years of history are reflected in Salisbury's hundreds of old buildings. From medieval times onwards there are buildings great and small, of every style and period: delightful half-timbered houses of the 14th and 15th centuries with quaint overhanging gables are hidden away down little alleys, or stand between elegant Georgian facades. Ancient city churches, the halls of the old craft guilds, the fine houses of the wool merchants, almshouses, coaching inns and the original public buildings of the town can all be seen.

The older "New Sarum" still divides itself naturally into the religious and secular areas planned by Bishop Poore; into the cathedral with its close, and the "Chequers", the built-up squares between the streets. The working town once had fifteen guilds; of their halls, the finely-timbered *Joiners' Hall* is in St Ann Street, *Crewe's Hall* in Salt Lane, home of the Company of Shoemakers and in Penny Farthing Street, fragments of the *Tailors' Hall* can all be seen. the corner of Silver Street by the Market Place is the 15th-century *Poultry Cross*, the survivor of four similar structures; the Cheese Cross, Wool Cross and Barnewell Cross have long been demolished. Of this same period, and now behind the fake-Tudor facade of a cinema, is the *Hall of* John Halle, a wool merchant who bought the land for his great house in 1467. Restored by Pugin in the 19th century, Halle's House retains its original scrolled glazing and other original features. Built at the same time was *John à Port's House*, off Queen Street, timber-framed again, and standing close to the former *Plume of Feathers Inn*, another medieval building. An even earlier structure, possibly 14th-century, is the charming three-gabled house in High Street, now *Beach's Bookshop*.

The town possessed a very large number of inns. Of the great medieval period are the *Pheasant Inn*, in front of Crewe's Hall, the *Old George* and the *Crown Hotel* in High Street, and the *New Inn*,

a low timbered building in New Street. Later came the Georgian *White Hart Hotel* in St John Street and the *King's Arms* nearby.

Salisbury is now administered from comparatively modern buildings, but the older civic headquarters are to be found in the 18th-century *Guildhall*, by the Market Place and the handsome *Council House*, next to St Edmunds church on Bourne Hill. After the Elizabethan Guildhall was destroyed by fire in 1780, funds were provided by the second Earl of Radnor and the new building, designed by Sir Robert Taylor, was completed in fine classical style within the next few years. Inside it has a banqueting room and collection of portraits. *The Council House*, formerly a Jacobean mansion of the Wyndham family, was Georgianized in the 18th century and bought by the town in 1925. It stands on the site of the College of St Edmund, a canonry founded in 1269. Within the gardens is the medieval porch of the north transept of the cathedral, brought here and re-erected in 1791 after "Destroyer Wyatt's" restoration. Not far away in Bedwyn Street can be seen the elegant little block of *Edward Frowd's Almshouses* 1750) and a little further along, *Taylor's Almshouses* of 1698, a Dutch-gabled building restored in the 19th century. Salisbury is rich in "hospitals" and charitable foundations. In addition to *Blechynden's Almshouses* (1683) and the rebuilt Tudor *Hussey's Almshouses*, there is the charming *Trinity Hospital*, begun in 1379: its present buildings of 1702 are arranged round a courtyard. The Hospital of *St Nicholas*, originated by Bishop

SALISBURY
p. 144: *St Thomas of Canterbury wall painting on east wall of nave, 16th century*
p. 145: 1, *Market Place with St Thomas' church.*
2, *The North Gate from The Close with High Street and St Thomas' beyond*

SALISBURY:
The classical silhouette

Poore at the time of the building of the cathedral, was planned, with its infirmary and twin chapels, for the accommodation of "a master, eight poor men and four poor women". Its work still continues. St Nicholas' Hospital, near Harnham Bridge, was the "Hiram's Hospital" of Trollope's book *The Warden*. In the cathedral close, the *Matron's College*, in a Wren style, is still another charitable house.

There are several ancient churches. The finest is *St Thomas of Canterbury*, a building of the early 15th century, tall, light and airy with a dark, busy Doom painting above the chancel arch. The lead roof is attractive outside, and the church is an ornament of the city. *St Edmund's* is also Perpendicular, though much restored by Sir Gilbert Scott in 1865. Parts of *St Martin's* are older than the cathedral; there are traces of Norman work in the tower and the chancel dates from 1230. In Exeter Street, Pugin built the Gothic–Revival *St Osmund* in 1848 and *St Francis* Anglican church was built in the 1930s in Castle Road; a pleasing building, this. Busy T. H. Wyatt did a 14th-century style church, *St Paul's*, in Fisherton Street (1851) and the Almshouses there are of the same name, completed in 1860 in the Tudor style. In the North Bemerton district, the big new church of *St Michael* was built in 1957 (Cachemaille Day, architect).

The *Close* is the incomparable setting for one of the great churches of Christendom. It is lined on all sides by houses and buildings of charm and variety, low in scale compared with the cathedral, and spaced as an excellent background array, in varied brick and stone colours, in form sometimes flat and Georgian in character, sometimes picturesquely gabled. This is a perfect example of architectural polyphony, many voices speaking

The Audley Chantry,
SALISBURY Cathedral

individually but producing a single harmonious entity. *Mompesson House*, built in 1701, is now owned by the National Trust (open to visitors). It has a high wrought-iron gate and railings, and a brick pediment with carved garland. *Malmesbury House*, at the end of the North Walk, is of about the same date and has a beautifully proportioned facade. Inside are mid-18th-century features, Gothic but in Classical order. Also in North Walk, the much older house, numbered 21, was one of the original canons' residences: it contains medieval work and the oldest parts are contemporary with the Cathedral. The Close

SALISBURY, the west front

also contains the *Bishop's Palace, Theological College, Cathedral School, Deanery* and many minor buildings all concerned with the affairs of the Diocese. *The Deanery* is behind a modern building, and has been restored to something like its original 13th-

The cloisters against the south wall, SALISBURY Cathedral

OLD SARUM

century form since the last war. It has a remarkable timber trussed roof, and a central opening for the smoke in the gable apex.

The *Cathedral* in its original form was finished in 1258, thirty-eight years after the laying of the foundation stones. No other medieval cathedral in England was so conceived as a whole and built in a continuous operation. Later additions were to come, but Salisbury remains a remarkably pure expression of the Early English style. The Cloisters and Chapter House, begun in 1264 and completed about thirty years later, were the work of Bishop Walter de la Wyle and their design already shows how Early English was merging into Decorated. In 1334, a building contract was signed for the heightening of the tower and the erection of the spire. More than 400 feet high, it took nearly thirty years to complete. Towards the end of the 15th century, the sumptuous Beauchamp and Hungerford Chapels were added. These, together with a late-13th-century campanile which had been erected to the north-west of the main structure, completed the building history of the Cathedral.

Alteration and destruction began with the Georgians. The spiritual father of the later Victorian "restorers", James Wyatt, was called in by Bishop Barrington to carry out "alterations and repairs". Between 1782 and 1791, he dealt so brutally and unfeelingly with the cathedral that he earned for himself during his own lifetime the name of "The Destroyer". Wyatt tore out much of the ancient stained glass, swept away screens and porches, drastically altered the Lady Chapel, demolished the two Perpendicular chapels after claiming that they were too dilapidated to repair and pulled down the Early English campanile with its fine spire. It is difficult to comprehend how all this destruction was undertaken with the sanction of the church authorities and to a general chorus of approval from the world at large, who considered Wyatt's work "tasteful, effective and judicious".

Further restorations have followed. In 1863, Sir George Gilbert Scott attempted to re-interpret what Wyatt had misinterpreted, and other artists and architects have been busy since Scott's day. Salisbury Cathedral somehow survives. Its symmetry, based on the double cruciform plan, carries through the whole structure and seems to defy even drastic change. The interior is indeed somewhat cold and colourless, and too uninterrupted in the extensive vistas. The recent removal of the fine Victorian metal screen, designed by Skidmore, does nothing to improve matters. It is in itself a sad loss. The proposed removal of the whole of the Victorian glass by Ward in the Chapter House is a new chapter in the same lightening and sterilizing process to which there seems no end in Salisbury. This was abandoned (1967), for the wrong reasons – i.e., because it was jeopardizing the restoration appeal, but after the glass in two windows had been removed. Some original stained glass remains, in spite of Wyatt's clearance. A good deal of the original grisaille – elaborate patterns painted on greenish or greyish white glass – is intact in the west window and elsewhere, and has been much studied and copied by Victorian and later glass painters. In the south aisle are figures of the 14th century. Fragments and small panels of the original Early English glass are found in neighbouring churches, and there is a whole panel of the stoning of St Stephen in Grateley church, between Salisbury and Andover. The most patronized 19th-century glass designers were Clayton and Bell and Holliday. Burne-Jones is also represented.

The monuments and chantry chapels make a fine show, medieval Georgian and Victorian ones combining well together visually, and sustaining the tourist's need for the tempering of mere "interest" with beauty and quality of design. Among the finest are early bishops, and there is also an extraordinary brass of a 14th-century bishop framed in a towered fortress. Sir Thomas Gorges, builder of Longford Castle, has a monument worth finding, erected in 1635.   15

Sarum – Old Sarum, the original Salisbury, began as a prehistoric site and an Iron Age hill fort. After the Romans came, the hill was taken over by the invaders and became Sorviodunum, an important town at this crossing of main roads. The Saxons came here during the Dark Ages; they called the place Sarobyrig and left traces of their occupation in the form of jewellery and ornaments. The huge circular earthwork, 56 acres in enclosed area, then passed into the guardianship of Osmund, kinsman of William the Conqueror. The episcopal see having been transferred from Sherborne to Sarum in 1072, Osmund, its first bishop, later made a saint, spent fifteen years building a cathedral within the earthwork enclosure. He also built the castle, and about these two main buildings a little town grew up. Over the years, however, there was bickering between the priesthood of the cathedral and the military occupying the castle. The growing population did not help matters, a general shortage of water causing dispute. After enlarging the cathedral and building the castle keep in the early 12th century, the famous Bishop Roger was in trouble with King Stephen, and the quarrels between castle and clergy grew. The castle was closed against clerics and, it was written: "the cleargie and people missing their belly-cheere ...conceived forthwithe a deadlye hatred against the Castellans." In 1220, the ecclesiastics removed themselves two miles downhill to the site of New Sarum and began to build a new cathedral. The church was demolished and used as a stone quarry for the neighbourhood. The castle lasted longer, but by the end of the 14th century was going to ruin. Now all that can be seen are its fragments and the neatly excavated plan of the cathedral, indicated by the lines of its foundations in the turf. Old Sarum remains impressive. One of the "rotten boroughs", its ten voters sent two members of Parliament until the passing of the Reform Bill in 1832. Samuel Pepys, coming to visit this "prodigious fortification", was awed by its size and atmosphere and frightened at the mere thought of having to spend a night alone here.   15

Sandy Lane is a pretty hamlet. A thatchers' heaven, with many stone cottages and picture-postcard straw roofs. The *Strict Baptist Chapel* has character, and the *George Inn* has a curly porch.   8

Savernake is a district and a forest rather than a place. It is the most French of English forests, with its straight, rectilinear avenues across undulations and intersections. With a circumference of 16 miles, 4000 acres of woodland and rides through great avenues of oaks and beeches, this estate has been a royal forest since the Norman Conquest. Let at a peppercorn rental by the Crown to Lord Ailesbury, the area is open to all; a fine place in which to wander, with long cathedral-like vistas of lofty trees. *Eight Walks*, from Cadley, and the *Grand Avenue*,

Bath Road toll house, SAVERNAKE

from Forest Hill on the Newbury road, are particularly recommended. *Tottenham House*, at the end of the Grand Avenue, was built in 1670 to replace Wolf Hall as the family home of the Seymours and Bruces (see *Burbage*). The present huge classical mansion, now Hawtrey's School, was completed in 1825 for the Marquess of Ailesbury at a cost of £250,000. The architect was Thomas Cundy. The park had been laid out by Capability Brown. On a west-north-western axis from the house, down an immense ride, is a column crowned with an urn erected in 1781. *St Katherine's church*, by Wyatt, 1861, is in a clearing, half-a-mile to the north, and looks across fields to the Deer Park. Much of the attractive contemporary glass has been removed (Clayton and Bell or O'Connor), and the windows re-glazed with rectangular leading which spoils Wyatt's effect. It must have been fine in its heyday with its stone screens and arcade, now blocked. With a churchyard ha-ha and big firs and cypresses, it was lavishly built with a stone spire for the second Marchioness. Wyatt also did the estate church at *Cadley*. Nearby are a few neat and tidy estate houses. To the south-west *Brimslade Farm* is a red-brick and tile-hung house on the Kennet and Avon Canal, which preservationists, who have formed a Trust, are saving from dereliction. 9

Seagry had in Seagry House a fine and stately Georgian mansion which was gutted by fire in 1949; now nothing remains but the elegant iron gates on the roadside. In the village, the house known as *The Chestnuts* is a mid-18th-century building. *Manor Farmhouse* with its dovecote is Jacobean. The church was rebuilt in 1849. It has Norman font, 15th-century screen, two medieval effigies and one good memorial tablet to Charles Bayliffe (died 1735). 5

Sedgehill. A scattered parish. The church stands on a small plateau with views over lush country. The church tower looks good Perpendicular work, but may belong to the end of the 17th century; brass candelabra and candles on pulpit, lectern and readers desk. Otherwise, dainty glass lampshades; infra-red heaters and electricity meters. A restoration here in 1844. 13

Seend. The main Trowbridge–Devizes road winds through a pleasant collection of houses, one group of which is Georgian and built by prosperous wool men. *Seend House*, with lodges, is a mansion in golden stone; the *Manor* next door is somewhat older and less impressive, although the big stable block along the road is excellent. The two flank the pathway to the church, providing it with an almost monumental approach. Seend was once a busy weaving centre; some of the smaller houses were occupied by the home-industry weavers and the church owes some of its lavishness to John Stokes, a rich clothier who built the north aisle in the 15th century and has his tomb here. At the end of the 17th century, there was another Wiltshire spa in the area. The well still exists and was described by Aubrey as "attracting much company". 7

Semington, is a main road village of 17th- and 18th-century houses; the mullioned *Manor House* is small and dated 1698, and in the lane beyond the church are two excellent farmhouses of the same late-Jacobean period. *St George's Hospital* used to be one of the "new" Victorian Poor Law Workhouses and is grimly classical. The simple bellcoted church, almost entirely of 1860, has a large and vari-coloured marble monument to the Blagden and Bisse families, and another wall monument. A new organ dominates the nave. There is colourful glass in east and west windows by Gibbs (1860). There is an excellent collection of carved churchyard table-tombs. 7

SHAW church, by C. E. Ponting, 1905

SHERSTON: In the stony landscape of north-west Wiltshire

Semly has houses and cottages scattered about a big green. *Church Farmhouse* is mullion-windowed and 17th century. T. H. Wyatt built the Victorian church here for the Marchioness of Westminster. It has a good tall tower with a little spire over the stair turret. The stair enclosure sticks into the nave and is carried on giant stone corbels. A lady chapel has recently been furnished in the south aisle. 16

Sevenhampton, near Highworth, has a Victorian church with a big west tower; a little gaunt, perhaps, but in a pretty setting with a 17th-century house alongside; parkland and woods in the background. A few thatched cottages and what is left of *Warneford Place* – one wing, called the Ballroom – a big Georgian mansion and once the seat of that family, many of whom have monuments in Highworth parish church. 3

Sevington. A stone-built hamlet on the fringe of the old Neeld estate (see Grittleton). There are 17th-century houses and early Victorian cottages. Next to one of the entrance lodges, the curious school building has a huge medieval bell turret and Gothic arched entrance; easy to mistake it for a quaint church, and no wonder, since these genuine bits and pieces came from the demolished church at Leigh Delamere. 4

Shalbourne is a village in a hollow of the Downs, with many thatched cottages and barns and a pretty Gothic Revival school. The church, outside the village, is of Norman origin but was rebuilt in 1873 with many of the old parts re-used. The battlemented tower displays weathercock, an 18th-century flagpole and a double-ended red flue-pipe. The elaborate chancel screen was made by a Victorian vicar. In the chancel, ceiling by Bodley. Glass in east window by Kempe. Impressive Elizabethan monument to Sir Francis Choke: "Praye Ye Al For the Sole of Francis Choke – Desessed in The Yere Of Oure Lord A. 1562." Reclining effigy in recess. Also striking 18th-century standing figure in niche. 9

Shaw, is dotted with "desirable residences". Near it is a remarkable forest of pylons and transformer equipment. Overhead wires run in many directions. Set back from the road is *Shaw House*, a pedimented stone Georgian house. The early 20th-century church by C. E. Ponting is a rebuilding of an earlier church by T. H. Wyatt; tall, with a somewhat "over-designed" tower and shingled spire, and a flèche over the crossing. Half-timbered clerestory and much timbering inside, even the columns being big wooden posts. The whole is in a late Perpendicular style. There is some pale greyish and "restrained" stained glass (contemporary) with a W monogram between the horns of a stag's antlers. 7

Sherrington is very good to look at. The approaches run between large stretches of clear water in which cress is grown. The village has pretty cottages and a thick-thatched vicarage, all of the later 1600s. A high mound near the church was the castle of the Giffords; the crusading Sir Alexander is buried at Boyton and his overseas activities may have been responsible for the unusual dedication of Sherrington church to the Middle Eastern saints,

Cosmos and Damian. A small building, originally dating from the 14th century and partly rebuilt in 1624. The Jacobean furnishings, pews, altar rails and pulpit, are complete; candle holders on the pews. Victorian stained glass and some other tidying have removed a lot of the 17th-century atmosphere however. 14

Sherston. A large stone village standing above the Avon with its wide High Street having some of the atmosphere of a country town. 17th- and 18th-century houses, and several long-established inns, including the gabled and mullioned *Angel* (1648). Most of the buildings are mellow stone; a few colour-washed, the favoured shocking pink not excluded. *Court House*, Queen Anne, has a shell porch and some excellent late 17th-century work inside. The church is splendid; the interior Norman and Early English with grand arcades of the earlier period in the nave. The crossing tower is of 1730; a rare example of Gothic Survival. It was built by Thomas Sumsion of Colerne, one of the last master masons to work in the medieval tradition. For the design he received £1 15s 0d. There are monuments, and built into the big porch outside is the carved figure of "Rattlebones"; probably Romanesque. Pale greys in stained glass of east window, but glass mostly clear. Victorian over-furnished atmosphere. Well carved churchyard tombs, including table-tombs. 4

Shrewton in the middle of Salisbury Plain has a badly modernized row of cottages built in 1842 out of funds

> Subscribed to Repair the Losses sustained by The Poor of This and Five Neighbouring Parishes in the Great Flood of 1841.

The fund also provided for *Fuel and Clothing . . . to be distributed among The Poor on the 16th January For Ever . . . That being the Anniversary of That Awful Visitation.* Near the bridge over the Till that brought such great disaster is the *Blindhouse*, a big bee-hive lockup in sombre stone. The *Catherine Wheel* is an L-shaped inn with iron verandah and there are several houses of the 17th and 18th centuries. The church was heavily restored by T. H. Wyatt, but retains its strong-looking exterior and sturdy tower; inside, the trans-Norman arcades survive, but the general feeling is Victorian. The new vestibule and the timber screen filling the tower arch are somewhat institutional. A winding village with many small bridges over the streams and some magnificent copper beeches. 11

Silbury Hill *see* AVEBURY.

Slaughterford is in a wooded valley with a bridge and discreet paper mills. The simple church, derelict for two centuries, was rebuilt in 1883. Hidden in the woods are the ruins of a 17th-century Quaker meeting house. 4

Sopworth. This small village has a delightful group of 17th-century houses and cottages before a handsome Georgian *Manor House*. The tower of the church is Perpendicular, but the rest was violently restored – almost rebuilt – in 1871. There are traces of Early English and Decorated work, Jacobean pulpit and a memorial window by Burne-Jones, executed by William Morris's firm. Carved churchyard tombs and table-tombs. Cotswold stone barns, some unfortunately re-roofed in corrugated sheeting. 4

South Marston has a variety of council houses on its outskirts, but the old village is pleasing. The church retains its solid square tower, but the queer turret above the roof of the nave dates from the over-restoration by John Belcher in 1886. It has an agreeable interior. There are two Norman doorways, an Early English chancel and memorials set against plain whitewashed walls. Nearby is the Victorian school, and across the fields a late-Georgian house. The countryside is flat and watery. 11

South Newton. The valley setting with the River Wylye running through lush fields is better than the place itself. A main road village. The church is a Wyatt rebuilding, 1862. Perpendicular tower and original 13th- and 14th-century work in the arches of the nave. A re-set Norman doorway is sheltered by a Victorian timber porch. The pinks and blues of the east window, contemporary with the rebuilding, are attractive. In the churchyard, a fine cedar tree. 14

Southwick. Development, with many new bungalows. A *fin-de-siècle* church with a spiky spirelet was completed in 1904 by C. E. Ponting, typical of his final church-building phase. Among the nondescript is stuffed a handful of better buildings. The *Baptist Chapel* of 1815 has an outdoor tank for total immersion. *The Poplars* is a late-Victorian name for the late-17th-century house by the school. Outside the village is *Southwick Court* farmhouse, dated 1567. 10

South Wraxall has a great deal of modern housing. Near the church is a good group of older buildings, among them the 17th-century *Longs Arms*, *Church Farmhouse*, of the same period, and a pretty Gothic school of 1841, with stone-tiled roofs. The church has a tower dating from the end of the 13th century, with a quaint pack-saddle roof with 17th- or 18th-century capping, and a big stair turret, and looks much older outside than the over-restored interior suggests. Half the inside walls are in fine ashlar, and half scraped, and too-neatly pointed. There is a thin iron screen and poor stained glass. In the Long Chapel are monuments to this family, beginning with a medieval tomb chest and the latest a memorial to the second Viscount Long, killed in action in Holland during 1944. The big architectural piece of Thomas Long (died 1759) with its columns and massive urn is a splendid design. *South Wraxall Manor* is a superb mansion, whose oldest parts are as early as 15th century. These include the gatehouse and Great Hall. Ranged round three sides

SHERSTON tower, 1730

of a courtyard, this composite Medieval–Elizabethan–Jacobean house is a building to remember (p. 27). The farmhouse nearby was a 14th-century hospice for travellers. The hall and Chapel of St Audeon survive. The Manor was begun by Robert Long about 1430 and the family have had the ownership of the property ever since. 7

Standlynch. There is no village, this being a farming area along the Avon below Salisbury. The name is notable for Trafalgar House, once called Standlynch. See *Trafalgar House*. 18

Stanton Fitzwarren. In the country, still, but dangerously near Swindon. Suburban houses and council houses already, and Vickers' factory near. The church of St Leonard has a Norman-proportioned nave, with chancel arch of that date. The chancel is Perpendicular, and the tower 17th-century. Gothic fireplace, an *art nouveau* screen carved by a past rector, linenfold panels from a cottage as part of the organ case, a door from Winchester Cathedral and a Bavarian carving of the Adoration of the Magi. In fact, there are so many bits and pieces, and red and patterned tiles, that it is difficult to "see" as a whole at all. There is also a fine Norman font carved with the virtues and vices under arches. *Stanton House* is a Cotswold-style manor built in 1935 for an American business man, and has a fine lakeside setting. Its stone walls and roofs are already weathered to a semblance of an old Cotswold house. 3

Stanton St Bernard in the Vale of Pewsey has big farmhouses and bright red council houses. There is a much-altered 17th-century *manor house* with a pretty doorway dated 1677. The house is of sarsen stone, which looks as blue as the blue lias of Bridgwater district. Perpendicular tower excepted, the church dates entirely from 1833. It has a little character of that period, but is overwhelmed by later, poor, glass in the chancel. Round the chancel arch is a wall painting in bluebell-wood colours, with cherubs and angel choirs: vaguely *art nouveau*. The unused vestry is boarded off from the chancel and has a squint through to the congregation. 8

Stanton St Quintin. Dull housing on the fringes (R.A.F. Married Quarters). In contrast, some of the newer bungalows nearby are decently designed. *Stanton Court* is a late-Georgian manor house. The remains of a Roman villa were discovered in the park some years ago. The church has a Norman tower (the upper, Norman-looking part is Victorian) and rebuilt door, and some fine arches of the period. Ponting built the elaborate chancel in the 1880s. There are one or two very well-carved table-tombs in the churchyard. 4

Stapleford. In the Wylye valley, and clear of the main road. In spite of a growing number of new houses it remains a charming place, with thatched cottages and several small, attractive houses some chequered in flint and stone near the church, Norman drum pillars are built in alternate bands of white and green stone; sturdy round arches descend onto massive capitals. The power and tall proportion of the period remains, although there has been much later work and restoration. Handsome medieval sedilia. Agreeable early 19th-century coloured and frosted glazing in south transept window. A stone bench inside the two-storey porch is marked out with the squares of Nine Men's Morris, an early form of draughts or chequers. The big earthwork above the village is the site of Stapleford Castle, once owned by Waleran, William the Conqueror's huntsman. 14

Startley. A nondescript farming village with some old and some newer cottages, more recent speculative-type houses and bungalows – and an overhead mess of telephone and electricity lines. 5

Staverton, like several of the villages near Bradford-on-Avon, was once a minor weaving centre; the three-storeyed weavers' cottages here are not dissimilar to those found in Yorkshire. All is dominated by the big red Nestlé's factory, by the Bristol Avon. The plain church dates from 1826, and is wide and chapel-like, with a brownish east window. 7

Steeple Ashton has its main approaches guarded by bungalows and flanked with terraces of dull council houses, but these are quickly forgotten at the first unforgettable sight of the church, "like a great silver ship sailing over the flat meadows..." *St Mary's* is a splendid Perpendicular church. The spire was struck down by lightning in 1670. The interior is light, with intricate vaulting. Roofs of chancel and aisles are in stone, that to the nave in wood, the timber ribs being carved and fitted in exactly the same way, with intricate bosses at the intersections. The north and south aisles were built at the expense of Robert Long of South Wraxall and Walter Lucas, both clothiers. Good 18th-century wall tablets. The enormous lock on the entrance door is even bigger than the giant one at Marden. The east end is somewhat marred by the badly fired, though not unattractive, stained glass in the east window, of 1862, and paintings in the panels of the reredos. There is a lot of 15th-century glass, mostly tracery fillings and border pieces, but enough to show the original glazing scheme. The high street of the village moves at obtuse angles through a variety of houses and features of interest. On the triangular Green is the lockup, octagonal and be-knobbed, with the cross beside it; *Ashton House*, well proportioned and impressive, dates from 1724. The half-timber *post office*, infilled with herringbone brickwork, is good also. Gabled 17th-century *Manor*; half-timbered *Market House* and the *Vicarage*, a building which began in the 14th century, has additions of many subsequent periods. 10

Steeple Langford. The village is

STEEPLE ASHTON

well-disposed about the water-meadows. Chequered flint and stone cottages combine well with brick and thatch. The whole is like a village in northern France, or in one of the open valleys towards Troyes. Willows, and the lead-covered pyramid of the church, accentuate the likeness. On the Warminster road is the façade of *Bathampton House*, built in 1694 with this handsome front added in the 18th century. The much-altered *Yarnbury Grange*, nearer to the village, dates from 1580. *All Saints*, a flint and stone church, has indications of every architectural style from the Norman period onwards, but is mainly 14th-century. The tall tower arch of that date is fine. Norman font is Purbeck marble, Jacobean pulpit and reader's desk, and some impressive coats of arms from Elizabethan tomb chests. The vicarage across the road is a chequerboard house of the late 1600s. From the church gates a willow-shaded path leads to *Hanging Langford*; a pretty walk across the many streams that feed the River Wylye. A peep over the hedge by the churchyard is rewarding: here is a delightful garden with the river flowing beneath the well-modernized mill house. During the Civil War, the rector of Steeple Langford, the Rev. Joseph Collier, was turned out of his church and home by the Puritans on the grounds that he was "ignorant, scandalous and inefficient". With his wife and eleven children he was ejected one winter's night and they were left to wander about in deep snow. Two of his sons were later sold as slaves in Jamaica after taking part in the ill-fated Penruddocke Rebellion against the Commonwealth. 14

Stert has pretty thatched cottages and stands high. The small and simple church clings to the brink of a rural precipice. The architect, J. H. Hakewill, practically rebuilt it in 1846, although he retained the original Perpendicular pillars and arches of the nave. The gabled *Manor Farmhouse* close by has a large and well-used duck pond. On the main road at the foot of Etchilhampton Hill a memorial pillar of 1786 is surmounted by a battered lion and commemorates the *Publick Spirit and Benevolence* of James Long who promoted the new road, *so avoiding the former tedious and dangerous way over the adjoining hill....* 8

Stockton. The main street, lined with many thatched estate cottages of stone and half timber has at one end the triple-gabled *Stockton House*, built by John

Topp, Elizabethan cloth merchant who also founded the charming *Topp Almshouses*. A side turning leads to a group of buildings round the church. Here are *Long Hall*, part half-timbered with an elegant Georgian front; then some cottages and a Victorian school all set about with flowering shrubs and climbing plants. The church is impressive. It has Norman work in the nave arcades; nave and chancel are separated by a thick wall pierced by a very small archway, and two little side openings like unglazed windows; all Early English and undisturbed; but the 1910 rood screen here is big and ornate. But it is a well-kept interior with several fine recumbent effigies and other monuments. There is an early 14th-century effigy of a lady lying on her side; a big tomb of John Topp with wife and children (1640), and another big monument of 1708 to Henry Greenhill, a sailor of brave deeds who became Governor of the Gold Coast and ended his days building the Royal Dockyard at Devonport. His memorial is surrounded by a bevy of cherubs, alternatively sad, talkative and weeping; below them a skull crowned with a laurel wreath and a collection of marble sextants, pistols, telescopes and an assortment of more fearsome weapons. There are inventive wall tablets also. There is too much brownish, middle-way late Victorian glass and wrought iron lighting fittings. There is deeply cut carving on a stone table-tomb in the churchyard, with skulls in a shroud. *Manor Farmhouse*, in the village, was the home of Jerome Poticary, another clothier whose tomb is also here (died 1596). 14

Stonehenge. Approached across the plain the broken circle of Stonehenge looks from far off rather small and unassuming. Nearer there is a Ministry of Works wire fence, green notices, a ticket office and several flat hats. Nothing seems to suggest the once grass-choked romance of its tumbled stones or to foster

STEEPLE ASHTON *church*

the magic aura created by centuries of inspired or absurd guess-work as to its origin. This is the bleak reality that first faces every visitor, well-informed or ignorant. Those who know nothing about it except its fame feel a sense of anti-climax and those who know it from Inigo Jones's or Camden's or Stukeley's writings and engravings, or from Geller's sensational painting "The Druids' Sacrifice", or Turner's or Constable's marvellous watercolours, want to go back to their books and pictures. But of course the monument is stronger than its circumstances. Once inside the fence and within the sacred ground a sense of wonder is more than restored. The immense size of the tallest stones compared with the little people looking round, the shadow of stone on grass and stone on stone, stone and sky seen past stone and under lintel, the curves of those lintels, the batter on the uprights, the grey, red and gold gleam of the sarsens and the cold glint of the smaller, mysterious bluestones all proclaim the importance and purposefulness of the place. Once felt, this immenseness stays in the mind. The car-park and officialdom no longer destroy the scale and cut it off from the silent barrows of the surrounding hills. These barrows, long, or round or disc, were the burial places of the men and women of the scattered agricultural and hunting population who built it, and for whom it was probably a ceremonial meeting place for worship or legislation, or both.

The most persistent legends about it, – that it was a temple to the Sun, that worship was organized by Druid priests who indulged in human sacrifice, that no one knows how it was built, that the blue stones were whistled there by Merlin, with or without the aid of the Devil from Ireland or from the Prescelly mountains, – die hard. It was not until the beginning of this century that the systematic archaeological exploration of the site began, and at first it seemed that dry facts and cautious conclusions only combined to destroy the glamour

without putting anything significant in its place. But recently archaeologists have become at once more relaxed and more daring and the possible interpretation of facts already established and still being discovered by no means close the subject to imaginative speculation.

It was built about a thousand years after the pyramids and a few hundred years before the fall of Troy, in three stages, the third stage being itself divided into three phases, during the three hundred years between 1800 and 1500 B.C. During the years of its building the Stone Age in Britain came to an end and the first Bronze Age was flourishing in what no archaeologist can resist calling "the brilliant Wessex Culture". Stonehenge I was a circular earth work, two banks with a ditch between, about 100 feet outside the present circle. It had an opening on the north-east aligned to the midsummer sunrise. *This alignment has persisted throughout all the stages.* The entrance is marked by the stone, originally one of a pair, now known as the Slaughter Stone. 100 feet outside the entrance is the large sarsen known as the Heel Stone. South and west of the Heel Stone towards the circle entrance are four wooden post holes. Inside the inner bank is a circle of fifty-six holes first noticed by John Aubrey, the 17th-century antiquarian, and so called the Aubrey holes. They never held stones and were filled with chalk, rubble and bones. Four other positions (two still have stones, two are empty) belong to this period or just after; they are on the circumference of the Aubrey holes and lines joining them form a rectangle with the long side perpendicular to the Heel Stone axis; the diagonals cross almost at the centre. The layout of this first phase, as well as the later ones, was remarkably accurate, the intervals between stones or holes varying only by a few inches. It was built by early farming colonists.

In Stonehenge II the bluestones, now proved to have been brought from Carn Ingli on the Prescelly

STONEHENGE

Mountains, no doubt already a sacred place, by sea from Milford Haven to the Wiltshire Avon, first made their appearance. Eighty-two were placed in two small concentric circles (never in fact quite completed) 6 feet apart and 35 feet from the original centre and arranged so that, had the lines of stones been continued to the centre, they would have formed the spokes of a wheel. There was an entrance to the north-east and the Heel Stone was untouched. To this time also belongs the stone avenue, which continues north-east beyond the Heel Stone and then turns towards the Avon, indicating the route overland taken by the stones at the end of their journey from Wales. The vestiges were first discovered in the 17th century by Stukeley and have now been extended and clarified by air-photography. This stage was built after the arrival of the Beaker Folk (so called from the type of earthenware bowls they made), agricultural invaders from Europe who settled alongside the inhabitants peaceably and ultimately produced with them the Wessex culture that developed its riches and skills by being on the great trade route from Ireland to the Mediterranean. For the first phase of Stonehenge III the bluestones were removed entirely and big sarsen stones, brought overland from the Marlborough downs, were arranged in an inner horseshoe of five trilithons (two uprights and a cap stone) open to the north-east and graded in height to the centre of the curve and an outer circle of 30 uprights joined right round with lintels. In the second phase an oval of bluestones was introduced within the horseshoe containing two miniature bluestone trilithons; the so-called Altar Stone was placed in the centre. Outside the sarsen circle two circles of holes were dug, presumably to receive the remaining sixty-two bluestones. This stage was interrupted or abandoned and the holes were never filled. Finally, in the third phase the bluestones were arranged in a horse-shoe within the horse-shoe of sarsens and in a circle between it and the outer sarsen circle. The Altar Stone, now fallen, remained in the centre. During the whole three hundred years of its development the building of Stonehenge must have depended upon the mobilization and discipline of enormous man-power.

Modern experiments have shown that the physical work could have been done with primitive bone tools (almost as fast as with our ordinary pick and shovel) with enough energy, man-power and organization; but the conception and the architectural details suggest a certain sophistication. The trilithons are unique to Stonehenge, the stones are worked, the lintels are grooved and kept in place with a shallow mortice and tenon (a method adapted from wooden building), the uprights have a slight and elegant entasis; these and the extraordinary geometrical accuracy of the positioning made archaeologists wonder if the Mediterranean influence on the Wessex culture could have extended further than the mere exchange of objects and jewels (such as those found in the surrounding graves). Homer said: "Who, pray, of himself ever seeks out and bids a stranger from abroad unless it be one of those who are masters of some public craft, a prophet or a healer of ills or a builder, aye, or a divine minstrel, for these men are bidden all over the boundless earth." In 1953 Professor Atkinson made a triumphant discovery; thirty shallow carvings of axe-heads and one bronze dagger on the sarsen stones. The axes were of the type made in Ireland and exported to the Mediterranean between 1200 and 1400 B.C., but the nearest prototype to the dagger comes from the shaft graves of Mycenae. So a surmise became a probability.

Modern archaeological methods have yielded an enormous number of facts about the time, method and order of building. What they have not been able to establish is the reason for the growth from the first ditch, banks and monoliths to the elaborate pattern of trilithons and circles of the final state. What *has* been dryly and finally refuted is the part played by the Druids, the most cherished illusion of amateurs of Stonehenge for centuries. The Druids were a Celtic priesthood and could not have appeared or operated in Britain before the arrival of the Celts about 500 B.C. By this time Stonehenge had been completed a thousand years and was probably already in ruins. The Druids were described by Pliny and subsequent Roman and Roman–British historians rightly as sun-worshippers, doubtfully as indulgers in human sacrifice. Stonehenge was not mentioned before the 6th century but subsequently its mystery and its alignment to the mid-summer sunrise made the association with the notorious priesthood natural. The names Altar Stone and Slaughter Stone were bestowed by romantic historians and the whole conception was given an almost indestructible build-up in the 17th century, first by Aubrey and then Stukeley (who added his theory of serpent worship into the bargain). In 1781 the association was exaggerated by the formation of "the most ancient order of Druids", whose members still perform invented rituals there on mid-summer eve and were, until a short time ago, allowed to bury the ashes of their most important dead within the circle.

Archaeologists have always thought that the alignments from the centre part of the Heel Stone to the mid-summer sunrise and through the large trilithon to the mid-winter sunrise were, at their simplest, a method of fixing a day from which to calculate the year and the seasons – a primitive calendar, essential to an agricultural community. Recently Dr Hawkins, an Englishman living in the United States, has, with the help of a computer to do astronomical calculations that would otherwise have taken years, discovered an enormous number of alignments on the varying seasonal positions of the sun *and* the moon from varying positions between and over the stones of the circle. The most significant and the most convincing thing about his first set of results was that they took into account every single hole and stone from Stonehenge I to Stonehenge IIIc except the Aubrey holes. In correspondence after the first publication of these findings, the archaeologist Professor Newall drew his attention to the first century historian Diodorus who said that there was a famous temple of Apollo in the land of the Hyperboreans (people from the north – probably here the inhabitants of Britain) and that the people were also interested in the moon; "the god visits the island every nineteen years, the period in which the return of the stars to the same place in the heavens is accomplished". He was led, through this and other hints, to go back to his computer, this time to find out the relative dates and times of eclipses of both sun and moon. The nineteen year cycle of the moon is in fact a triple cycle, roughly two periods of nineteen and one of eighteen years. Calculating therefore over three cycles he suddenly realized that 19.19.18 add up to fifty-six. There are fifty-six Aubrey holes – the last elements to be absorbed into the Hawkins astronomical system. These are the facts; he has modestly said that it is for archaeologists to tell us why the builders of Stonehenge went to so much trouble, consistently, but more and more elaborately, for three hundred years.

His own suggestions (much simplified) are these: that it was essential for primitive man to mark the seasons and essential for rulers and priests to keep their power through knowledge and divination. Their power would have been greater if they not only kept an accurate calender of the seasons but could also predict and let the people observe in dramatic circumstances celestial events that were exciting and frightening, especially total eclipses. All this could have been achieved by observation over long periods plus the use of the fifty-six Aubrey holes as a primitive computer. Several spaced and related stones or posts would be moved round once a year to keep track of the moon and the sun.

It became, he suggests, from the first simple beginning to the final complex, an ingenious (if necessary) game, architects and priests contriving more and more astonishing observation posts through the stones for more and more surprising views of the sun and moon – the god and goddess – in relation to the sacred temple and the lives of their devotees. 15

Stourhead. Palladian mansion, home of the Hoares, the banking family. House and park are part of *Stourton*, which at first sight seems to end at the entrance to the park, but actually drifts through the gateway and ends in a charming group of buildings. Here are the village inn, the Arts-and-Crafts style Stourton Club, some 18th-century cottages in silvery stone, a larger dwelling of the same period and St Peter's church. Beyond stands the old Bristol High Cross, medieval, brought to Stourhead in 1780; beyond that the lake, with the house hidden over the slope to the right. The church is Perpendicular, and with its fretted parapets and background of fine beeches, highly picturesque; the interior walls are, unfortunately, scraped of their plaster. The monuments to the Hoare family are fine, by Harris and others, with urns, cherubs, and other decorations. The park and house were given to the National Trust in 1946 by Sir Henry Hoare, along with 2000 acres of farmland, the income from which helps to pay for the upkeep. Stourhead, and its gardens, are open to visitors. The grounds, laid out in the middle of the 18th century, are planned as an entity that can be taken in by a walk round the lake; one that changes with the weather and the seasons, but can essentially be appreciated on a single pedestrian "tour". This starts with the *High Cross* and the *church*, which are the picturesque point of departure, and form a desirable picture also from the other side of the lake. The *Bridge*, the *Temple of Flora* (1755), the

STONEHENGE

Grotto (1740, by the water-side, with Cheere's nymph), the *Pantheon* (1753) and the *Temple of the Sun* (1767, Flitcroft) are the chief buildings on the route. But the planting, which is of great ingenuity and variety of colour and texture, and is now at full maturity, is the greatest attraction. The undulating flanks of the lake with its dells and declivities, and the use of trees with dark-coloured foliage, have resulted in a natural-looking but highly organized landscape that is totally English and totally original. The house was designed by Colin Campbell and completed in its original form during the 1720s. The two wings and portico are later. Inside are paintings by Angelica Kauffman, fireplaces by Grinling Gibbons and sculpture by Rysbrack, who also did many of the statues in the park. On *Kingsettle Hill*, two miles to the west but within the estate, is *Alfred's Tower*, triangular, of brick, 160 feet high, erected in 1772 to commemorate the place where King Alfred raised his standard before his victory over the Danes in 879. From the top (950 feet) are vistas over Wiltshire, Dorset and Somerset. 13

Stratford-Sub-Castle. Named from its position below the great green ramparts of Old Sarum, for which rotten borough the Elder Pitt once sat as M.P.; he lived for a time at Mawarden Court, a much altered Jacobean house near the church, now known as the *Old Vicarage*. His grandfather, Thomas Pitt, modernized the Court in 1710 and paid for a lot of improvement work at the church in the following year. Chancel Early English, all else Perpendicular except the tower of 1711, St Lawrence's has good bossed wagon roofs, high Jacobean pulpit with elegant stairs and hour glass, panelled Georgian reredos and choir stalls and a west gallery of 1800. The doors have been removed from the box pews, but this is one of the most attractive interiors in the country. A copy of Donatello's St Lawrence was presented to the church in 1957. There is a fine carved Royal Arms of 1713. *Prebendal House* is very early 18th-century. *Parsonage Farm* of about 1800. The *Manor House* to the north has flint and stone gables of the 17th century. 15

Stratford Tony. There was – and still is – a "Strete-ford" here; a crossing of the Roman road to Salisbury. Ralph Toni, William the Conqueror's standard bearer at the Battle of Hastings, was given a grant of land here. The village is pretty. The River Ebble runs free along the fronts of cottages, with a ford. The church on the hill slope, has a Perpendicular tower and a Decorated body. The late 17th-century furnishings are most attractive, with delicate colonnaded cresting, but the effect of them in the interior is spoiled by a poor modern east window and the jig-saw cementing of the chancel window splays. *Stratford Tony House*, Georgian front, brick with stone dressings 17

Stratton St Margaret was once a separate village, but expanding Swindon reached out years ago and made it a suburb. Along the Cirencester road (Ermine Street) is untidy development, but the old church is away down a dead-end lane in a beech and cypress-planted churchyard, and has stone tiles. The tower is 19th-century, so is the general atmosphere inside, with poor stained glass and dark furnishings. But the walls are plastered and the tall nave with clean pointed arches springing from big round pillars; Early English. There are wall monuments, memorials, and a painted board over the south door to "William Lacy *alias* Hedges" is decorated with rabbit-like skulls (1645). 6

Sutton Benger. A main road village. Church violently dealt with by J. H. Hakewill, 1851. The surviving medieval parts are the 14th-century south aisle and chapel, and the Perpendicular tower and south porch. The interior has been recently coated (1966) with whitewash; stonework and all. Norman font. Among the gargoyles outside pigs' heads figure prominently. Colourful glass by Gibbs and others. There is a Gothic *rectory*, and the *Wellesley Arms* is 18th-century, with a well-painted coat of arms on its signboard. 4

Sutton Mandeville. The regimental badges were cut into the chalk of the Downs by First World War soldiers. The village has a pretty approach through a deep wooded glade. At the bottom is a sprinkling of old stone cottages and a farm or two. The church stands high; easily seen, yet hard to reach. In the churchyard, are table tombs and a 17th-century column sundial. With the usual exception of the tower, the church was rebuilt in 1862, and has been suffering much from damp. It has a simple and uneventful interior. A clumped hill towers to the west. 14

Sutton Veny has one or two pretty cottages and a *Manor House* of many periods with a restored hall of the 14th century. *Sutton Veny House*, outside the village, is a handsome late-Georgian building with a semicircular portico. There are two churches, one ruined, one in use. *St Leonard's*, down a side lane, was a cruciform structure, partly Norman and partly 13th century. When J. L. Pearson was called in for advice on the old building in 1860, he suggested that a new church would be better than an attempt at restoration of the dilapidated old one. *St John's*, in the main street, is the result: an impressive Victorian church. It has a big, lofty interior in the Early English style; rib-vaulting over the crossing and chancel; transepts, the north one with a rose window. Good Clayton and Bell glass in several windows, including the rose; Kempe glass in two. West window (correctly, and with splendid results as to lighting of the building) left clear. 13

Swallowcliffe. Standing above the lane that drops into this quiet village is a 17th-century *Manor House*. An unexciting place, the village, and a little dilapidated, with a few stone cottages. The setting in a small wooded valley is pretty. The church is Norman Revival, designed by the young G. G. Scott while he was still in partnership with Moffatt and before his days of Gothic eminence as Sir Gilbert. Round arches, and everything quite exuberant; even the stone pulpit has an arcade of miniature Norman columns. Attractive, bright glass in chancel, with a lot of jewel-like silver whites among the rich colours. In the porch is the very well-preserved effigy of a crusader knight. 17

Swindon is made up of the pre-Railway Age *Old Town*, with a personality all its own, and the *New Town* that sprawls increasingly and looks much the same as many another industrial place. New Swindon may expand even more rapidly in the future than it has done in the past: it has been recently mentioned as an important area for full-scale regional development. Architecturally, the Old Town is quite distinct. It possesses its own high street, market place and church, and retains something of the village atmosphere. In the main street, a big gateway leads to the ruined church of *Holy Rood*, in what were the grounds of *The Lawn*, the vanished mansion of the Goddards, a family of much cultural, archaeological and ecclesiastical influence in 19th-century Wiltshire. A pleasant stretch of woodland here overlooks the main town. The new parish church, by Scott, replaced Holy Rood in 1851. It is in the Decorated style and big, but fails to impress. In the small market place is the *Old Town Hall*, adjoining the Victorian Market House. A 19th-century inscription over the entrance begins:
BLESSED BE THE LORD WHO DAILY LOADETH US WITH BENEFITS
and goes on (more recently)
DANCING, BINGO, SKATING AND WRESTLING.
Across the square is a handsome Georgian house, and more good 18th-century work is to be seen in the High Street, where the *Bell Hotel* and the *Goddard Arms* are reminders of coaches and pre-railways transport. In contrast, the *New Town* is superficially ugly, with its centre messy with pre-war and post-war "developments" of various kinds. The place grew at a great pace after the Great Western Railway Company decided to run its main line close to Swindon and to set up locomotive workshops here. A model village of three hundred workmen's houses was built in Bath stone brought from the enormous excavations of the Box tunnel. These still exist, outside the mighty walls of the railway works, as if under the protection of this grim castle. The later housing was not so well done and became "the red brick rash which stretches up the hill to Old Swindon and strangles it...". Nevertheless, the newer town has some commendable buildings. The railway church of *St Mark*, also by Scott, has a clean exterior of the 1840s, Decorated. The *Railway Museum*, built at the same time as a lodging house for Irish labourers, has a pointed Victorian frontage not spoiled by recent re-glazing. *Apsley House*, now the Museum, is a Greek Revival building to which has been added a successful modern annexe – picture gallery above and shops below. On the industrial estates towards the edges of the town, well-designed modern factories have been built since 1960. The finest example of modern architecture in Swindon, however, is undoubtedly the new *Princess Margaret Hospital*. On a superb site, overlooking a great stretch of countryside, this group of buildings by Powell and Moya is one of the best new hospital buildings in the country. 6

Teffont Evias is a charming place, almost every house having its own bridge over the clear waters of the stream. There is a Victorian-Tudor rectory, and a noticeable tall, wide-eaved house in a Swiss style among the old stone cottages. The church is an interesting earlyish exercise in the Gothic Revival, being a rebuilding in a Perpendicular

STOURHEAD:
The Temple of the Sun, 1767

style, using some old materials, of 1824–6 (Architect, Charles Fowler). The tall steeple is impressive and the whole church, on the lawn of the manor house, is a real eye-catcher. The interior is lofty, light and airy, with 1824 furnishings. There is a great deal of foreign glass in roundels and fragments leaded into all windows, with very pretty glass of 1824 still filling the west window. Some features of the old church were well re-used; there is a triple tomb chest of Henry Ley (died 1574) and two of his sons. The father, in black armour, lies alongside them. The original dedication of this church has been forgotten, and in 1965 it was re-dedicated to St Michael and All Angels. The *Manor* is a 17th-century stone house with considerable 19th-century additions, including towers, behind. The whole group is picturesque. 14

Teffont Magna, as charming as Evias, if somewhat smaller, has humpy thatched cottages round the church and along the road between the two places; again there is the clear stream and numerous miniature bridges. The church is old and very simple, Early English. 14th-century chancel screen, Georgian plaster ceiling and a few box pews. Fragments of Saxon interlace carving on inside wall. *Fitz House*, along the road towards Evias, is a gabled and mullioned farm of the 17th century with a pretty courtyard. 14

Tidcombe. Attractive hamlet on a gentle north slope from sweeping downland. Well-grown beech trees abound here and the slope from church to small brick, stone-dressed, pedimented manor has many daffodils in the grass. The 13th-century church has aisles and a pleasing plastered interior. Tower Elizabethan; furniture Victorian, except for Norman font and Jacobean pulpit. Well-coloured and original east window with central, small Cruci-

TEFFONT EVIAS:
Manor house and church

fixion and flanking scenes, perhaps by O'Connor. The scraping of the window splays is a pity. An early 19th-century group of wall monuments is agreeable. 9

Tidworth, *see* NORTH TIDWORTH. 12

Tilshead has an austere appearance and the cold beauty of the plain around it. The church shares this character. The village is in the slightest of hollows and bounded by majestic horizons. The wide main street has pleasant houses and cottages, some thatched, with the local flint and stone chequerwork much in evidence. The church is of ancient origin with a massive low tower. It was restored in 1846, but the work was judiciously carried out and most of the earlier features survive. The stonework has been plastered and painted over and the round arches of the Norman nave lose strength thereby. The building is cruciform with a delightful Early English chancel; there is an original 14th-century shutter to one of the windows in the south wall, also the yoke-shaped wooden lintels over the rere-arches of the windows next to it. All cream-washed. Most of the 19th-century glass has been renewed. Wall tablets. Old stone floors. 11

Tisbury. A big village – quite a town; the road through it climbs a hill between many buildings. *Old House* and *Gaston House* are both of the 17th century; *Tisbury House* is of about 1800, a simple classical building. At *Place Farm*, on the easterly fringe, is a fine group of medieval buildings, once a grange of Shaftesbury Abbey: 14th- and 15th-century, with inner and outer gatehouses and the largest barn in England. This building is nearly 200 feet long and needs 1450 square yards of thatch for renewal. Near the church are some pleasant houses and *Vicar's Cottages*, a row of 17th-century almshouses with an ungainly top storey, in red brick bearing a pious inscription and dating from the Victoria Jubilee of 1887. The dominating feature of Tisbury is St John's church, cruciform, happily unscathed by Victorian restoration. Some Norman work, but more of the Decorated and Perpendicular periods. Lofty nave with fine waggon roof with angels (15th century) and aisles with 16th-century panelled ceilings, all beautifully done; the crossing is finely managed and at the end of each aisle a big, spacious arch gives a wonderful depth. The tower top was renewed when a spire fell in 1762 and the design was by "Mr Bennett of Pytt House". The elaborate pink alabaster reredos by Ewan Christian is true High Victorian, and unfortunately fades into cheaper wall tiling on each side. There are pretty bits in the Victorian east window, but it is badly fired. A one-time window in the chancel now forms part of the organ front; a neat trick. The low, wide timbered porch at the west end is a good feature. In the churchyard Rudyard Kipling's parents are buried; here too is the famous Tisbury Yew, supposedly 1000 years old and gripping between the thews of its split trunk a vast boulder. *Pyt House* (open to visitors) and *Hatch House* are in this area, (see *Newtown*). 14

Tockenham, has a pretty church, long and low with leaning walls and a spiked bell turret supported from inside on massive timber uprights. It is over-restored, but the late 13th-century nave is pleasing and has some wall tablets including a fine portrait bust of Mrs Mary Goddard Smith, 1726, with an obelisk on each side. A carved Roman figure of Aesculapius is built into the wall of the porch. Raw new bungalows; also *Tockenham Court Farm*, a good group of early 18th-century buildings with a moat-like pool in front. 5

Flint and stone cottages: STEEPLE LANGFORD

Tockenham Wick has some thatched cottages, and beyond them is *Tockenham Manor*, a fine L-shaped house, gabled and mullion-windowed, dated 1608. It is in silver-grey stone with 18th-century and modern additions well done in brick and other materials. 5

Tollard Royal. From the north, the road to the village goes over Cranborne Chase by way of *Win Green Hill* (National Trust) and from here are views in all directions. The village lies in a hollow, with the church at the top of a steep lane. Much restoration work here, but a pleasing interior with some of the Early English features remaining. The cross-legged effigy of a 14th-century knight is set between two pillars of the nave. A marble tablet of 1900 commemorates the archaeologist General Pitt-Rivers who lived down the valley at *Rushmore*, a late-Georgian house which is now a school. He restored the remarkable *King John's House*. This is a delightfully irregular, tall house, where old stone and wood combine to provide a medieval atmosphere inside. Some of it is 13th-century. The gardens were laid out by the General, and are splendidly developed and tended today. So are the *Larmer Grounds*, which the General laid out for the local populace and visitors. There is a *theatre* of wood, and temples in an Indian style diversify the boskage. The ancient "larmer tree" – a wych elm – which used to be here was the site of meetings of the old Court Leet and, by much longer tradition, the spot at which King John met his huntsmen. Tollard is in romantic country on the Dorset border and at Farnham, over the border, is the excellent *Pitt-Rivers museum*. 17

Trafalgar House, near Downton, is in a park and can be seen from the winding country lane that fringes Barford Park. Of old called Standlynch, this handsome Georgian brick and stone house was begun in 1733 and designed by Roger Morris, "Carpenter, Engineer to the Board of Ordnance and Architect". He was also the brother-in-law of Sir Peter Vandeput, the city banker for whom the house was built. There was later work by John Wood the Younger of Bath and by Nicholas Revett, and in 1814 the whole place with its estate was presented by the nation to Nelson's heirs and its name changed to Trafalgar House. The Admiral's descendants lived here until recent years; the one nautical touch is the so-called Ganges Room, panelled with

TILSHEAD

timbers from the old ship-o'-the-line *Ganges*. The house overlooks from its eminence a long stretch of the Avon; close to the river is the church, a pretty building of flint and stone with a date stone in the gable, 1677. It has some older elements. It is disused. The dark interior (there is some pleasant grisaille glass of c. 1890) has a big Gothic monument and a delicate marble tablet. 18

Trowbridge, though not the county town, is the administrative capital of Wiltshire, taking over that function from Salisbury many years ago. A busy, working place with much traffic in its streets; a variety of industries from light engineering to brewing and bedding manufacture has been added to the weaving on which the town's prosperity was built. And what prosperity it was! The streets are rich in good buildings, particularly those of the 18th century, and the elegant Georgian houses of the clothiers are not easily forgotten. The group in *The Parade*, creamy stone and owned and maintained by Ushers Brewery, must be one of the finest collections of 18th-century town mansions in England. Such houses have been largely taken over by commercial enterprises; most of the banks in the centre of the town are accommodated in equally elegant buildings, once lived in by the cloth merchants. *St James's* church, where the poet George Crabbe was rector from 1814 until his death in 1832, was heavily rebuilt in Victorian times but is still quite a magnificent Perpendicular-style building; it is possible to take exception to such features as the brightly-coloured roofs of the chancel and lofty wide-arched nave, but the whole must be accounted as a fine piece of architecture, light and cool as it was in the historian Leland's day, when he described it as "lightsum and fair". There is a profusion of monuments, some of them climbing the sides of the tall tower arch. That to Crabbe, by E. H. Baily, a tender deathbed scene, is in the chancel. There is much Victorian and Edwardian stained glass. The west window is the best, and most highly coloured. Another biggish stone church is *Holy Trinity*, 1838. Trowbridge possesses a surprising number of 19th-century churches and chapels, mostly rather dull; but some of its other Victorian buildings are beginning to be recognized as fair examples of the architecture of this period. There are good early-Industrial Revolution mills, too. It was to a cloth mill at Lyttleton, not far away, that the youth Thomas Helliker led a mob of workman to smash the new power looms invented by the Rev. Edmund Cartwright. He was arrested and tried at Salisbury in 1803 and later executed on his nineteenth birthday, exchanging, as the memorial in St James's churchyard states, "mortality for immortality". 7

Turleigh is pretty and relatively unspoiled. The road twists and turns above Bradford-on-Avon among a collection of mellow stone houses. Here is a charming William-and-Mary *Manor House* with a neat Gothic chapel next door (100 years later) now used as private garages. *Turleigh Farmhouse* and *Uplands* are two of the many 17th- and 18th-century houses poised above the Avon. 7

Tytherington. At the north end of the village are two unusual farm buildings, half-dovecote, half-barn; brick. The church of St James is old and small. Together with "a dwelling for two chaplains" it was founded in 1083 by Queen Maud, mother of Henry II. It is narrow and barnlike, and has a tiny 12th-century window on the north side. No stained glass. Old open benches. Yellow-washed. The village has a few cottages and one unassuming Georgian house down the lane to Heytesbury. 13

Tytherton Lucas has a few cottages and one or two farms. The small church lies across a field and is much restored, although 13th century with Norman font and a 12th-century bell. Flat plastered ceilings and classical cornices go strangely with the more ancient exterior. Here is a Norman tub font with geo-metrical decoration, and some Georgian woodwork. Across the lane, *Manor Farm* with its long low 17th-century front is marred by a gaunt conservatory of recent date. 5

Upavon. There is now a permanent caravan site on the outskirts. Pleasant village street. The *Antelope Hotel* has an early-Georgian front and the straw birds of the district peck their way along the ridges of a number of pretty thatched cottages. The church has a sturdy tower of the 13th century and walls strong with black flints laid alternately with bands of grey stone. Norman chancel arch. Restorations by Wyatt and Seddon, and the interior is brown and dull, with poor "cathedral" glass. An east window by Henry Holliday is not much of an addition. 12

Upper Woodford. Here are a few cottages and mounted on the roof of a stable building a George V Silver Jubilee Clock in the most dashing neo-Georgian style. *Heale House* is 17th century and was very well modernized by Detmar Blow in the 1890s; it has a Japanese garden with bridge brought from Japan. 14

Upton Lovell. The church has a 13th-century chancel. The nave and pews are of 1633. But all is much renewed. There is 20th-century glass of the Beatitudes and a 14th-century effigy – a knight in armour, well preserved and fresh. 14

Upton Scudamore. Half-timber and thatch. Too many overhead wires for beauty in this open, sweeping country. The *Angel* is an old inn with a 17th-century cottage next door. In the church there are signs of building of all sorts of dates. The Scudamore chantry – disfigured again by electrical apparatus – is early 14th-century but much of the rest was rebuilt in 1855, though "long-and-short" work shows the building's early origin and there is

TISBURY: Zion Hill Congregational Church, 1842

Norman work, too. The tower is of 1750. General effect mid-Victorian. *Manor Farmhouse* is 15th century, and was modernized in the 1600s. *Temple Farmhouse*, near the inn, was built in the 17th century and dressed up with tile hanging in Georgian times. 10

Urchfont is an attractive place. The focal point is a large duckpond with Georgian houses and thatched cottages around, and, to one side the *Manor Farmhouse*, 18th century with a Chinoiserie iron porch. The large and impressive church is cruciform, with a stone-vaulted chancel beautifully framed in a very wide Early English arch. Externally it is buttressed and crested in a very individual way, and internally it is highly effective, though almost invisible owing to poor Victorian glass. Vaulted stone porch; Perpendicular. There are good monuments; elaborate wall tablets and a "set-piece" to Robert Tothill (died 1753) by Scheemakers with two busts and two weeping *putti*. Another big memorial to Thomas Ernle is elegant. Two patterned windows in Powell's impressed glass are attractive. *Urchfont Manor*, on the edge of the village, is a classical mansion of 1688, with later Georgian work; all in warm brick and mellow stone. It was purchased by Wiltshire County Council some years ago and is used as a residential college. 11

Wanborough. Widely scattered housing developments everywhere. The church, at the highest point of the higher village, on a site that looks like a pagan-sacred site from the south has good views over the countryside with Swindon romantically distant. *St Andrew's* is a symmetrically aisled, 14th-century building, unusual in possessing both a western tower and, at the opposite end of the nave, a hexagonal spire which is hollow and open to the church inside. One looks upwards through a plate glass "picture window" at lichened stone and fernery high above. It is thought that the windowed lower portion of this spire was once fitted with lamps and acted as a lighthouse for travellers on the Downs. There is a lovely north doorway from the original 14th-century building with quatrefoils in a running trellis pattern. But the interior is scraped and cold, and there is poor "cathedral" and other stained glass, though the east window has a genuine Victorian drama. Monuments. Brass. 13

Wardour has no village or church but possesses three well-known buildings. *Old Wardour Castle* is a noble ruin, hexagonal, built as a military stronghold in the 14th century, made into a Renaissance house in Elizabethan times and now in the hands of the Ministry of Public Buildings and Works. (Open to visitors all the year round.) These ruins stand high above a wood-fringed lake, and the beautiful approach is by a winding drive through wild parkland. (All the lanes are well signposted.) Here the aged Lady Arundell, with a handful of servants, held out for five days during the Civil War against 1300 of Cromwell's soldiers. She surrendered on honourable terms, afterwards shamefully broken by the Roundheads. *Old Wardour House*, late 17th-century, can be seen "round the corner" from the old castle and shares the view of the lake. (Not open to visitors.) About a mile away is *New Wardour Castle*, a Georgian mansion, designed by James Paine for the eighth Lord Arundell – the largest 18th-century house in Wiltshire. The huge central block has a circular stair-

Medieval tithe barns:
below, *at BRADFORD-ON-AVON.* opposite, *at TISBURY*

WESTBURY: Cement works in the landscape below the White Horse

case nearly 50 feet in diameter. In one of the flanking pavilions is a Roman Catholic chapel enlarged and decorated by Sir John Soane in 1788. It has recently been well re-decorated (1966). After being empty for several years, Wardour is again occupied, as the home of Cranborne Chase School, and is sometimes open to visitors. 16

Warminster is set against a background of wooded downs. The approaches are modern, but these give way to pleasing small houses of the Georgian period and mullion-windowed cottages. Lord Weymouth's Grammar School was built in 1707 but is in the style of the previous century. Dr Arnold of Rugby was once a pupil here. The *Bath Arms* and the *Old Bell* are two nice 18th-century inns in contrasting materials. In Vicarage Street and Silver Street are several excellent houses of the same period and *Portway House*, sternly handsome, has wrought ironwork in its gates and railings. So far, the activities of commercial shop and office developers seem to be minimal; the newest buildings in Warminster, such as the recent *Fire Station*, are mostly local-authority work. The parish *church* of St Denys is large and cruciform, with a Perpendicular tower over the crossing. Sir Arthur Blomfield did a drastic restoration in the 1880s, but some of the 14th-century work survives. The beautiful organ case came from Salisbury Cathedral, and is of 1792. But the big-boned interior is brownish, the textures unattractive and the coloured glass singularly uncolourful. In the High Street, *St Lawrence's church* has a 15th-century tower. The rest is Victorian. There is a church (*St John Evangelist*) by Street, 1865, at Boreham. Nave and chancel, with a bellcote on the east end of the nave. Stone. 10

Wedhampton, near Devizes. A pretty curving lane leads to a group of cottages, mostly thatched. Early Georgian *Manor House*, its entrance doorway with a nice curly pediment. 11

West Ashton. An early Victorian church, built for Walter Long by Wyatt and Brandon, stands in the grounds of Rood Ashton. There is pretty, colourful glass of the date of the church, but the interior is dominated by a Post-Pre-Raphaelite east window, by H. Wilson, of 1919. *Rood Ashton* is a vast house designed by Sir Jeffrey Wyatville in 1808, altered in 1836 and now gutted. Seen from the church in a wooded setting, it is still quite a staggering ruin. Further demolitions are in progress and modern houses are appearing in the jungled gardens (1968). On the Steeple Ashton road, a towered and castellated lodge is decorative enough. 10

Westbury has a charming little Georgian market place, with small town houses, three pleasant inns, a number of shops and the *Town Hall*, Classical and in stone. There are also Georgian houses and cottages round the churchyard, giving it (as at Mere) quite a small cathedral close atmosphere. The *Cloth Mills* nearby, late Georgian, of brick, are also one of the town's good features. The parish church is Perpendicular, but was much restored in 1847. The interior has good scale, and is given colour by much stained glass of the 1840s and later. The window, half hidden by the organ enclosure, is very good of its brash early Victorian kind. A big 17th-century monument with lying effigies is eclipsed in beauty by the much more modest tomb with a bust to William Phipps by Sir Robert Taylor, 1748. There is quite a Poet's Corner of monuments here, with other wall tombs of merit. 10

Westbury Leigh, now a suburb of Westbury, has a church and some individuality. St Saviour's was not completed until 1890, but is a good essay in Perpendicular. The so-called High Street is more of a main road, but has a few decent Georgian houses; there are also some Victorian ones. 10

West Dean focusses itself on a large green. What at first appears to be a duckpond is a slow flowing river. A pretty place, with thatched cottages, a small railway station and two churches, one disused. Flint and red brick St. Mary's was built in 1866 and incorporates medieval bits and pieces from the old church. The "old church" was, in fact, a chantry, which stood a short distance south-west of the vanished medieval church – also St Mary's. This is approached by a lane to the south of the new rectory garden, which ends beside the remains of a motte and bailey castle in a copse on the one hand and a new bungalow called "Tanglewood" on the other. The medieval fragment, flint and stone built, contains monuments, one of them among the most remarkable in the country. That in the position where an altar would be in a church is a splendid composition within brass-lined folding doors, with a kneeling figure of Robert Pierrepont, 1669, attended by a fluttering cherub. He is praying. This, says Margaret Whinney (*Sculpture in Britain, 1530–1830*) is almost certainly by John Bushnell, and it has his "deeply undercut, tossing draperies" (though she doesn't like it very much, and calls it "fleshy and exaggerated in modelling") that he had learned to do during a long spell abroad. He worked in Venice and elsewhere, and brought Baroque ideas to England. The other monuments here – all pretty grand – are of the 17th century also, and to members of the Evelyn family. *Church Farmhouse* nearby has a brick tithe barn of the early 1500s. 18

West Grafton is no more than a few thatched cottages and some newer houses down a lane that peters out among fields. The railway runs nearby and there is an ugly Southern Electricity Board transformer station. 9

West Grimstead. A few old houses and cottages – even some thatch – among the new, somewhat suburban, houses in this near-Salisbury upland, coppice country. The church is mostly 19th century, wide-gabled, dull and plain, with a brick tower. 13th-century remains inside. 18

West Harnham. The *Old Mill* and the *Mill House* stand away from the main road. The place is very close to the spot at which Constable did the sketches for his famous picture of Salisbury Cathedral. It is a matter for great regret that the view is now partly obscured by a block of modern brick buildings. The mill house is plain and 19th century, but the old mill belongs to medieval times, its race waters foaming underfoot. The church has a Norman nave and chancel and some Early English work, but a restoration by Butterfield gave the exterior an entirely Victorian look. 15

West Kennett. *West Kennett House* is an 18th-century urban

WARDOUR CASTLE, by James Paine, begun 1769

house quite at home in the country. 8

West Kington. A pretty place near the Gloucestershire border with thatched cottages grouped by an ancient bridge in a deep wooded dell. The church stands above, approached by a steep ferny cutting; on the way up is a derelict Gothick cottage. The church is plain and dates mainly from the rebuilding of 1856; the Perpendicular west tower, as usual, survives. It has well-panelled upper stages. Bright, chaste glass inside. The fine 15th-century pulpit is the one from which the martyred Bishop Latimer preached. He spoke of West Kington as "my little bishoprick". 4

West Knoyle. Twisting lanes make a way through the finest countryside to this hamlet with its old cottages and farms. The church is on a small hill, its 14th-century tower a landmark. Much rebuilt in the 1870s, but the external stonework has become so well weathered and lichened that it is not easily distinguished from the medieval tower. The inside has cemented walls and greenish glass. But what a landscape around! 13

West Lavington is a straggle of a place in its newer parts, but the old village has some interesting buildings. *Dial House*, the *Parsonage* and parts of the *Old Manor* are all 17th-century. *Hunts*, the *Vicarage* and *Pyt House* are all Georgian. The present *West Lavington Manor* was built in the Cotswold style sixty years ago. The church shows work of all periods from Transitional–Norman onwards; the simple unadorned interior is surprisingly impressive, although the chancel is very short for so large a nave. It is somewhat bleak, in spite of some acceptable Victorian glass. There are two side chapels and many monuments to members of the Danvers and Dauntsey families. Elizabeth Dauntsey (died 1636), in alabaster, smiles and reads a book in a comfortable tomb recess, reclining elegantly: much more sophisticated than the medieval lady next to her. There

WEST DEAN church; monuments

are several beautifully designed table-tombs in the churchyard, forming a good group. A small brass in the church remembers John Dauntsey, who in 1543 founded *Dauntseys*, the public school near by. After being closed down for many years, it came into existence again in 1895 and now occupies many large buildings and a number of houses in the village. 11

West Overton is a small village with thatched cottages. The church has a slender neo-Perpendicular tower and dates from 1878; a good essay in that style by Ponting. One wonders why the rebuilding was necessary: a drawing of the previous church shows a pleasant and substantial medieval building. The churchyard is thick with fine yew trees. The *Manor House* has its origins in the 16th century. 8

Westwood. On the outskirts it is all rural suburbia, but there are old and new stone houses near the church. *St Mary's* is entered under its Perpendicular tower and there is an immediate and dramatic view of the strange-roofed chancel and beautiful east window; a rich composition of 15th-century stained glass of Christ crucified on a lily with angels and Passion emblems against a background of deep crimson. The nave is tall and narrow with clustered columns, also 15th-century. There are good monuments including a charming tablet to Charles Francklin with a laudatory verse, each line of which begins with a letter of his name. Close to the church is *Westwood Manor*,

opposite:
WEST DEAN: Detail of the Pierrepont monument, 1669

p. 178: *WESTWOOD church east window: Christ crucified on a lily, late 15th century*

p. 179: *WESTWOOD tower*

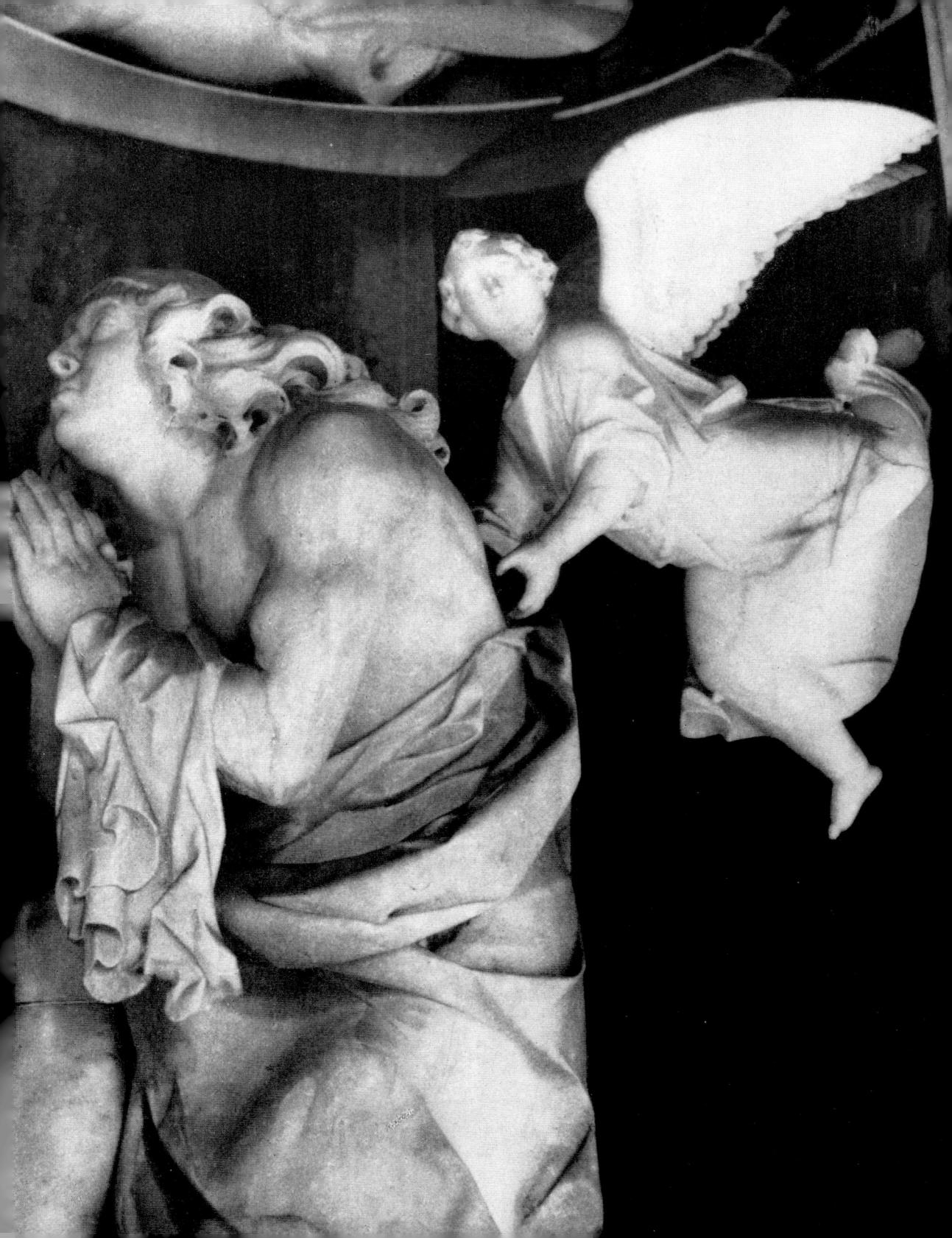

178

whose earliest parts date from about 1400. Once the home of the clothier Thomas Horton who built the church tower, this delightful house was altered and extended, the last major works being Jacobean. There is a medieval great hall with a great chamber above and the so-called King's Room has panels painted with portraits of twenty-two English sovereigns up to Charles I. The house has formal gardens with well-kept topiary; one huge bush is trimmed into the shape of a cottage and has a doorway to walk through. The manor is now National Trust property. At *Upper Westwood* is *Greenhill*, a handsome early Georgian house with older wings and a pleasant formal garden. 7

Whaddon. A narrow lane winds across fields and, humping itself over the Kennet and Avon Canal, arrives in this hamlet of scattered cottages and farm buildings. The lane peters out and the church stands bleak and isolated on the edge of a bare common. There is a Norman doorway with a Tree of Life tympanum and a battered medieval door, but otherwise it is a rebuilding of the 1870s. On the north side is the Long family vault, of the late 18th century. An enormous white marble monument for Walter Long, 1807, has very little in its favour. There is a Westmacott relief of 1814 also. 18

WILTON House: The Double Cube Room

Whiteparish has a church with late-Norman arcades and other medieval fragments. But it was rebuilt by William Butterfield in 1870 on this centre-of-the-village site and is a picturesque feature with a stocky shingled spire – looking like Surrey rather than Wiltshire, maybe – and with flint and stone walling. Inside it is light and decent and has a colourful (not inspired) east window of 1853. A pleasant village street with some old houses; up a side lane is *Lynches*, once a handsome 17th-century house, now split into three makeshift cottages and sadly dilapi-

below and opposite: *Ladies' Bridge on the Kennet and Avon canal at WILCOT*

dated. *Abbotston House* is a gabled building 1627. *New House*, south of the village, was built in 1619 and a most unusual house it is, the plan being like a three-bladed propeller with a hexagonal central hall and three projecting wings. It was built as a hunting lodge for the eccentric Sir Thomas Gorges of Longford Castle, itself built in the form of an equilateral triangle. Sir Thomas was always fascinated by the niceties of geometry and science, as his tomb in Salisbury Cathedral indicates. 18

Wilcot. Thatched inn and well-designed cottages, all quite formal. The centre of the village is pretty, with the church flanked by the long mellow tile roofs of the manor house and a pleasant late-Georgian building across the way. But it will be some years before the self-conscious modern residence round the corner begins to lose its rawness. The chancel arch of Holy Cross is late Norman, but the church was much restored after a fire in 1876; pine pews and 19th-century finishings, heating grilles and tiles in the floor, cemented walls (where they are not scraped) give it a remarkable absence of personality. *Wilcot Manor* and its vineyards were mentioned in Domesday Book; the present house originated in the early 17th century but was and is now a rather attractive congeries of 18th- and 19th-century remodellings. *Stowell Park*, to the north, is a big classical mansion completed in 1813. The road here from Wilcot passes some delightful brick and thatch cottages on the Kennet and Avon Canal; and nearly a mile west of the church down an unmetalled track, on a deserted and picturesque section of the canal, is an elaborate bridge, known as the *Ladies' Bridge*. It was designed by Rennie and is dated 1808. 9

Wilsford (near Amesbury). No more than a hamlet, with the church standing among trees and a small group of good houses above the Avon. Norman tower, square and solid. The rest was rebuilt by T. H. Wyatt in 1851 and it has a strong and pleasing Victorian atmosphere. There are some repulsively fascinating Renaissance-style carved and coloured panels in the chancel, early 20th century, and two splendid Arts-and-Crafts style brass candlesticks of much the same date. In the nave is a carved slate memorial tablet by Eric Gill; well done, although the inscription is sentimental. *Wilsford House* is good neo-Jacobean, done in 1905 by Detmar Blow. The same architect was responsible for the excellent rebuilding of Lake House, further down the Avon in the hamlet of *Lake*. 15

Wilsford (near Upavon). Thatched and timber-framed cottages, a small Georgian house and St Nicholas' church; an unpretentious and largely unrestored building; simple 15th-century tower and Early English nave and chancel whose plainness and innocence are impressive. Some windows in clear glass; others would be better so. Small wall tablets, but no other decorative features, except some corbels. 11

Wilton (near Pewsey) is a pretty little place between Great Bedwyn and the Graftons. Some nice thatched barns on the outskirts, a pleasing group of thatched cottages by the village duckpond, and a nonconformist chapel. 9

Wilton, one of the oldest boroughs in Wiltshire and once the county town, had a nunnery founded by Alfred the Great and throughout the Middle Ages was famous for the large number of its religious houses. Benedictines, Knights Hospitallers of various orders, Magdalenes and several others were all here from the 12th century onwards. Leland said that in his time, Wilton had twelve parish churches. Coming from Salisbury one passes first the impressive entrance to Wilton House. Across the road, seen through a thin screen of trees, the Georgian brick *Island House* stands on a small stream-girt peninsula with a very new and correct neo-Georgian town residence which has been well done. Nearer the centre, *Kingsbury Square* has modest 18th-century houses ranged around a smal green; the formerly very pleasing lime trees have now been savaged by the local authority and will take some time to recover. The Market Place, now full of parked cars, should be a pleasant space. Here is the big plain *Market House* of 1738, its long roof line relieved by a large clock turret. Across the square, *St Mary's church* was the old parish church and is now a ruin with only the chancel remaining intact. This was restored at the instigation of Robert Bingham, American Ambassador to the United Kingdom from 1933 to 1947. Bishop Robert Bingham, his ancestor, was consecrated in this church in the year 1229. The Georgian *Old Rectory* nearby incorporates fragments of the hospice of the Priors of St John, whose main buildings were at Ansty. The chancel of their medieval chapel survives in the remains of *St John's Hospital* in West Street, the rest of their church having been absorbed into the cottages adjoining. The "new" parish church of Wilton (*Saint Mary and Saint Nicholas*) was built by T. H. Wyatt for Sidney Herbert and his Russian mother. Completed in 1843 at a cost of £20,000, it is a *tour-de-force* in Italianate Romanesque. At Wilton, Wyatt was given the chance to do something especially splendid and he took advantage of it. Here is no approved 19th-century church, but an Italian basilica full of mosaics, stone barley-sugar columns, coloured marbles and magnificent medieval glass that was acquired in France and Germany. There is also fine Victorian glass, by Wailes, Gibbs, O'Connor and other artists and firms.

The English carpet industry began in Wilton, being started here in the 17th century. The *Royal Wilton Factory*, which may be visited, has a good range of buildings from Georgian through to modern times. Also Georgian is the pleasant *Bulbridge House*, in South Street. Beyond the park, and late 17th-century, is *Washern Grange*, which also possesses a medieval barn. Near the railway station at the other end of the town, *Kingsway House*, now a

WINTERBOURNE STOKE

furniture repository, was once the district workhouse.

Wilton House, the family seat of the Earls of Pembroke, is open to visitors. (Tuesdays to Saturdays, April to September and on certain Sundays during August and September.) Built on the site of the old nunnery, the estate was given by Henry VIII after the Dissolution of the Monasteries to William Herbert, first Earl of Pembroke. The first house was started about 1545 and its beautiful porch – traditionally designed by Holbein – remains as a garden feature. The second Earl married Mary, the sister of Sir Philip Sidney, in 1577. "And in her time," says Aubrey, "Wilton House was like a college, there were so many learned and ingeniose persons." Ben Jonson, Edmund Spenser and Christopher Marlowe came here; Shakespeare may have done, appearing with Burbage's company. Charles I followed Queen Elizabeth as a royal visitor and subsequent literary celebrities were George Herbert and Izaak Walton. This first mansion stood for a hundred years, but in 1647 was gutted by fire. The fourth Earl called in Inigo Jones for the rebuilding, which was eventually completed by Inigo's son-in-law, John Webb. Much of their work remains in the south and east fronts and the state rooms behind; the splendid *Double Cube Room* is as good as anything of its kind in Europe. During the 18th century, Sir William Chambers built the *Triumphal Arch* with equestrian statue of Marcus Aurelius; this was later brought down from its original site in the grounds to its present position in the entrance forecourt. In the same period, the building called the *Riding School* was designed by Roger Morris. He was also responsible for the *Palladian Bridge*. Little was done to the main building, until James Wyatt did much remodelling, rebuilding the north front, building a theatrical two-storey cloister in the Gothic manner, ripping out a good deal of Inigo Jones's work and generally re-organizing the layout. Further alterations have been made in the present century, but Wilton remains splendid. 14

Wingfield is at the end of a dead-end lane. *Church Farmhouse* is a gabled building of 1636. Plain rectory. Pretty Victorian school. The tower of the church is 15th-century. Restoration in Georgian and Victorian times; the interior is simple with curved plaster ceilings decorated with brightly painted rosettes in the chancel; plain in the nave. The whole effect is of an early Victorian church, about 1840. Poppyhead pews. The north aisle is later (1861). An impressive monument with barley-sugar columns to John Bayley (died 1665). At *Midway Manor*, the home of General Shrapnel, the gateposts carry representations of shrapnel shells and the names of battles at which they were used. In the nearby hamlet of *Stowford* is an old mill and a gabled

WOOTTON BASSET

farmhouse of the 16th century. 7

Winsley has many new bungalows and houses, carefully built with stone facings in an attempt "to preserve the amenities of the district". It is a pity that the design of most of them does not live up to the material. The old village is of stone, with winding streets. The church is a rebuilding of 1841. As at Atworth, there is a detached Perpendicular tower – all that remains of the old church – connected at ringing-loft level by a little stone bridge that gives access to the gallery. *Winsley Manor House*, now a school, dates from 1612, although its arched windows may be of the previous century. 7

The Winterbournes. The county has six Winterbournes: *Earls*, *Dauntsey* and *Gunner* run into one another in the Bourne valley above Salisbury. *Bassett* and *Monkton* are north of Avebury. *Winterbourne Stoke* is on Salisbury Plain, to the west of Stonehenge.

Winterbourne Bassett. The church looks down a wide stretch of grass and gravel, flanked by a (now) concrete-tiled farm on one

side and an early-Victorian rectory on the other. The row of big trees that lined the approach until quite recently has been replaced by a row of stone staddles. The church is mainly Decorated, and rather beautiful. Some windows and a tall nave, good tracery and there is a west tower. Pulpit, reader's desk and other woodwork are Jacobean. The reredos has been made up of bits of 17th-century panelling on which a painted angelic sextet play instruments. Wall tablets, and a 13th-century coffin lid carved with a couple holding hands. This could be better displayed. 5

Winterbourne Dauntsey. The old church was pulled down in 1867, but there is a Georgian *Manor House* in brick and stone. *The Grange,* another 18th-century house, is bold and pedimented, with two-tone brick, and stone dressings and arched windows. A few pleasant cottages lead on to: 15

Winterbourne Earls. The church, St Michael, was built by T. H. Wyatt to replace the two destroyed churches of St Michael and St Edward Confessor at Winterbourne Dauntsey. He re-used material from these medieval buildings. It is dull inside, but has two small panels of 13th-century glass, one with two angels fluttering beside a corpse, like a Blake. They are badly placed for visibility. 15

Winterbourne Gunner. A large Army camp nearby. The name comes from Gunnora, wife of Henry de la Mere, who was lord of the manor in the reign of Henry III. The small church stands in a field near the river. Largely 13th century, its short tower is Norman and has been recently whitewashed, giving the building quite a continental look against its bright red-tiled roofs. It has lost its south aisle, but not the arcade. Interior simple, attractive; chairs. Aubrey writes: "St Thomas à Becket was sometime a cure priest at Winterbourn and did use to go . . . up to a chapell in Clarendon Parke to say Masse." There is no record of which Winterbourne was intended, but certainly St Mary's church could have been here when the Saint was alive. 15

Winterbourne Monkton is a scattered handful of farms and cottages. Along the main road, *Middle Farm* is built of sarsen stones, a strong grey house of the 18th century whose big barns are in the same enduring material. The church, rebuilt by Butterfield in 1878, is down a short lane. Church and small graveyard are almost encircled by the corrugated iron roofs of farm buildings. Norman font; Early English lancet windows, Jacobean pulpit. Great circular posts support the western turret. A conventional church for Butterfield, but appropriate. 8

Winterbourne Stoke. A village of pretty cottages; thatch and stone dotted about the bends of a winding lane and a little river gently moving weeds under the bridge. The church is easily missed, down a dead-end road southwards. There are two Norman doorways and much original work of the 13th century, with little sign of savage restoration by the Victorians. Plain interior with box pews that have lost their doors, and Jacobean pulpit. Fragmentary attractive coloured glass dated 1835. The 17th-century *Manor House* is in the flint and stone chequerwork of the district, and is viewed from the bridge. 14

Winterslow. A name shared by the three hamlets of *East*, *Middle* and *West Winterslow* as well as the main village of Winterslow itself. They have for long been celebrated for racehorse training and truffle-gathering. The name is a corruption of the Old English *wunters hloew*, meaning "burial mound". This may well refer to a group of prehistoric barrows in the neighbourhood; in addition, there are two cemeteries of the Saxon period on *Roche Court Down*. The main village is visually unremarkable and much of its hilltop church is rebuilt. T. H. Wyatt was here in 1866; he removed the old "music gallery" but left a reasonable amount of Norman and Early English work in the nave. But the church looks undistinguishedly Victorian, inside and out. On the main road near Middle Winterslow is the *Pheasant Inn*, otherwise known as the "Winterslow Hut", to which the poet Hazlitt moved after living in a cottage nearby. Charles and Mary Lamb visited him here. In 1816, a lioness escaped from a travelling circus, attacked and killed the leading horse of the Exeter mail coach outside. *Roche Court* is a plain stone house built in 1804; *Old Court Farm* nearby is 17th-century and has a medieval barn. On *Easton Down* are the shafts of many flint mines, worked in the New Stone and the Bronze Ages. 15

Wishford, *see* GREAT WISHFORD. 14

Woodborough, near Pewsey, has a fierce Station Hotel in red brick, some mellow cottages, and some less mellow, and an entirely Victorian–Gothic church by T. H. Wyatt, in a pretty churchyard. 8

Woodlands Manor on the outskirts of Mere and almost in Dorset is a half-medieval, half-Elizabethan house with well-kept lawns enclosed by thick yew hedges and old roofs that sag and lean in the most romantic way. It seems a pity that so many big drain pipes descend the main frontage. The lane leading to Woodlands makes its winding way across rich meadowland; the journey is well worth the effort. 13

Wootton Bassett is a charming little town in the north of the county, on a hill. In the wide main street, the trees have been chopped to stumps, but on both sides the pleasant blending of styles, colours and materials in shops and houses remains. Here are brick, plaster, colourwash, concrete, timber, stone, all cheek by jowl and very happy together. In the middle, a pretty half-timbered *Town Hall* is set up on stone pillars, and splits passing traffic into two streams. Built by the first Earl of Rochester in 1700 and heavily restored in 1889, it is now a branch library. Under the colonnade below, iron railings guard the town stocks and an ancient fire engine. The good and mainly Victorian *church* was designed by G. E. Street; with its tall and slender pillars, the nave is particularly elegant and successful; strangely the south aisle is the nave of the original 13th-century church. There is an 18th-century brass chandelier in the chancel; poor lighting fittings in the rest of the building. Good Hardman glass in both east windows: a Jesse Tree in the south aisle. Some of the Victorian shops in the main street are really pleasing: *Maslins*, the drapers, has a fine big front; on a smaller scale, *Wallis & Co.*, Plumbers & Decorators, is equally successful. One or two new small-shop developments are excellent; entirely modern, but their scale and colour (dark brick and slate hanging, white paint) fit in beautifully with the older stuff. 5

Wootton Rivers straddles the Kennet and Avon Canal to the east of Pewsey. A small place with some brick, half-timbered

A farm in north-west Wiltshire, West Yatton, YATTON KEYNELL

and thatched cottages, and a larger Georgian house near the church. The church, St Andrew, is mainly Decorated, and was restored by Street in the 1860s. The Victorian broach spire is supported inside the church on a complicated arrangement of timber trusses resting on iron columns. It has many characteristic Street features: pulpit of stone, very florid ironwork on the doors. No stained glass. Big sarsens in the outside walling. The church clock, with the letters of G.L.O.R.Y. B.E. T.O. G.O.D., used as hour marks, was made out of old prams and bedsteads by Mr Jack Spratt; it commemorates the Coronation of King George V. There is a row of well-carved headstones outside the east wall, and some excellent table-tombs. 9

Worton has an early Victorian church, among trees overlooking rich grasslands. Tall windows with ogee arches and box pews in the plain interior. Along the road is *The Grange*, a modernized brick and half-timber house. *Worton House* is Georgian. A quiet and unremarkable farming area which shares its church with nearby *Marston*. 11

Wroughton and **North Wroughton** are now almost a part of Swindon and there is a great deal of pre-war and post-war housing. The church, on a hill and with fine views, has two Norman doorways and a Decorated chancel. More than usual survives from an early Victorian restoration, including the Perpendicular tower. Many memorial tablets to members of the Benet family. There are several good Georgian houses in the neighbourhood. On *Hackpen Hill* to the south is a White Horse cut in 1838. 6

Wylye. River valley village with a fine background of wooded hillside. There is flint and stone chequerwork in mullion-windowed houses of the 17th century, and there are Georgian houses too, with touches of late 18th-century Gothick here and there. The main road winds, and passes the *Bell Inn*, with Jacobean mullions above and Georgian sashes below. The church, as so often, retains its Perpendicular tower, but was otherwise rebuilt in 1846 and has a typical Victorian interior. Splendid wooden pulpit of 1628 with tester, a vigorously carved three-decker brought from the parish church at Wilton when it was demolished. Colourful pattern glass of c. 1850 in east window. A *collage* of bits, mostly 19th century, in another window. The fine brass chandeliers in the nave also came from Wilton and have been electrified. In the river below the bridge is the stone figure of a man blowing a horn, said to commemorate the guard of a mail coach drowned here in the 18th century. 14

Yatesbury. There is a disused R.A.F airfield here; but it is being slowly cleared. There are sites for desirable bungalow residences, with red brick houses already staring across the lanes at thatched cottages. The church was rebuilt in the 19th century, but has a Norman doorway and traces of Early English work inside. The tower is 15th century. Stained glass fragments. 8

Yatton Keynell. At the junction of several country roads; the place at which John Aubrey learned his grammar. The gabled *Manor House* is of 1659 and can be seen across fields from the churchyard. The original church was built in 1250 by Sir William Keynell as a thank offering for his safe return from the Crusades – hence the uncommon but appropriate dedication to St Margaret of Antioch. The present building, with its thin Perpendicular tower, retains his 13th-century chancel, but was otherwise heavily restored in 1868 by G. E. Street. There is an elaborate little interior with a screen in stone. Carved headstones and many table-tombs in churchyard. There are some excellent Georgian farmhouses in the vicinity and in the hamlet of *Long Dean*, a pleasing group of cottages in a deep combe. 4

Zeals. This place of thatched cottages still bears some of the scars of wartime occupation by the services, but has fine views. The church was built by the young Mr Scott before the days of his eminence and has some strangely youthful features: for instance, the spire sits on an octagonal pedestal which in turn seats itself on a square tower. The rest is in a more serious Decorated vein, with hammer beam roof and tall arches to tower and chancel. On the roadside is a block of Victorian-Tudor almshouses, now nicely lichened. *Zeals House* has traces of medieval work but is a mixed composition, much of it 19th-century. A pair of derelict lodges now make a poor job of guarding the big chestnut avenue. Nearby is an 18th-century farm with grand old barns and outbuildings. The views from Zeals over the plain towards Shaftesbury are superb. 13

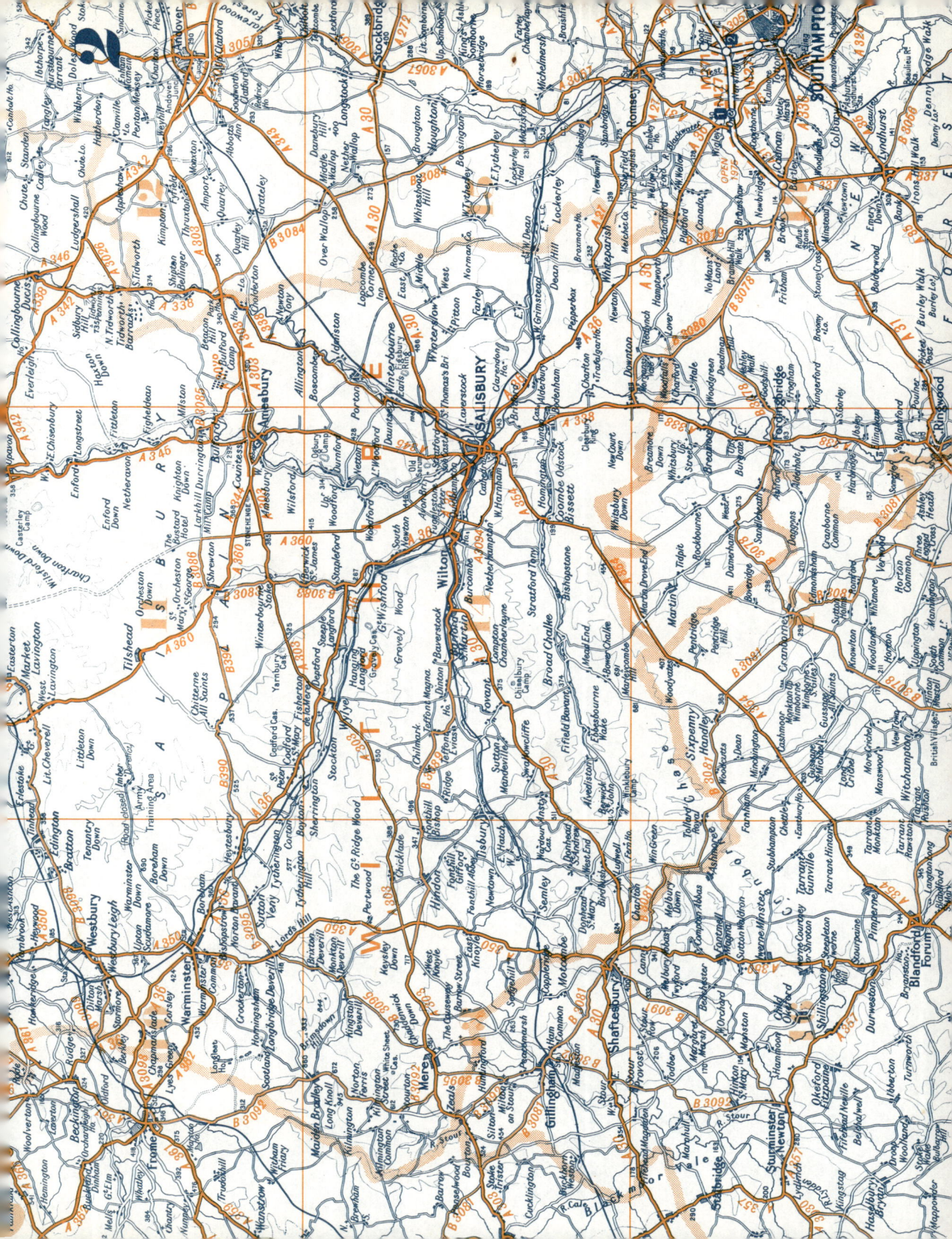

INDEX

Abbotson House, *see* Whiteparish
Ablington, *see* Figheldean
Abraham, Robert, *see* Mildenhall
Adam, Robert, *see* p. 32 and Bowood
Adam's Grave, *see* p. 42 and Alton Priors
Addison, Joseph, *see* Milston
Aesculapius, *see* Tockenham
Ailesbury, Lord and Lady, *see* Broad Town and Savernake
Alexander, David, *see* Longford Castle
Alfred, King, *see* Bishopstrow, Brixton Deverill, Chippenham, Cricklade, Pewsey and Wilton
Alfred's Tower, *see* p. 15 and Stourhead
All Cannings Cross, *see* p. 47 and Allington (nr Devizes)
Amesbury, *see* p. 20
Antrobus House, *see* Amesbury
Apsley House, *see* Swindon
Archer, Thomas, *see* Clarendon
Arnold, Dr, *see* Warminster
Arundell, Lord and Lady, *see* Wardour
Arts and Crafts style, *see* p. 24, Corsley, Ford (nr Chippenham), Redlynch, Stourhead, and Wilsford (nr Amesbury)
Ashbee, C. R., *see* Calne
Ashton House, *see* Steeple Ashton
Athelstan, King, *see* Malmesbury
Atkinson, Professor, *see* Stonehenge
Aubrey, John, *see* p. 30, Avebury, Bradford-on-Avon, Broad Chalke, Crudwell, Kingston St Michael, Lydiard Tregoze, Orcheston St Mary, Seend, Stonehenge, Wilton, Winterbourne Gunner, Yatton Keynell
Augustinians, *see* Bradenstoke-cum-Clack, Lacock, Longleat and Maiden Bradley
Avebury, *see* pp. 15, 42 and 43
Avon rivers, *see* pp. 10, 34, 41, 42, Alderbury, Amesbury, Avoncliff, Bodenham, Bradenstoke-cum-Clack, Britford, Brokenborough, Christian Malford, Dauntsey, Downton, Durrington, Easton Grey, Great Somerford, Limpley Stoke, Longford Castle, Milston, Netheravon, North Newnton, Salisbury, Sherston, Standlynch, Staverton, Stonehenge, Trafalgar House, Turleigh, Wilsbury (nr Amesbury)
Ayliffe, George, *see* Foxley

Bacon, Quartus, *see* Ansty
Baily, E. H., *see* Trowbridge
Bannings, *see* Avebury
Barbury Castle, *see* pp. 47, 51
Barford Park, *see* Trafalgar House
Barnes, William, *see* Mere
Barnett of Newcastle, *see* Little Bedwyn
Barrington, Bishop, *see* Salisbury
Barry, Sir Charles, *see* Alderbury, Bowood and Derry Hill
Bates Mechanical Organ, *see* Norton
Bath Academy of Art, *see* Corsham
Bath, Marquess of, *see* Longleat
Bath stone quarries, *see* Box
Bathampton House, *see* Steeple Langford
Battlesbury Fort, *see* p. 46 and Bishopstrow
Bayley, John, *see* Wingfield
Bayley, William, *see* Bishop's Cannings
Bayliffe, Charles, *see* Seagry
Baynton Chapel, *see* p. 20
Baynton House, *see* East Coulston
Baynton, Sir Edward, *see* Bromham
Beach, Ann, *see* Keevil
Beacon Hill, *see* p. 51
Beaker folk, *see* Stonehenge
Beauchamp Chapel, *see* Salisbury
Beauties of England and Wales, *see* Kington St Michael
Becket, Thomas à, *see* Clarendon and Winterbourne Gunner
Beckford, William, *see* Fonthill Gifford
Beggar's Opera, The, *see* Amesbury
Belcher, John, *see* South Marston
Belcombe Court, *see* p. 34
Bemerton, *see* p. 34
Benedictine nunnery, *see* Kington St Michael
Benet family, *see* Wroughton
Bennet family vault, *see* Norton Bavant

Bennett family, *see* Tisbury
Beran Byrig, Battle of, *see* Barbury Camp
Berreshorne, Sir John, *see* Mere
Bewley Common, *see* Bowden Hill
Bewley Court, *see* Bowden Hill
Bibury Rings, *see* p. 47
Biddesden, *see* p. 32
Bingham family, *see* Wilton
Bingham's Farmhouses, *see* Bower Chalke
Bishop Ken's Library, *see* Longleat
Bishop's Cannings, *see* p. 20 and All Cannings
Bisse family, *see* Semington
Black Field, Mildenhall, *see* p. 49
Blagden family, *see* Semington
Blechynden's Almshouses, *see* Salisbury
Blomfield, Sir Arthur, *see* Grittleton, Hullavington, Luckington, Marlborough and Warminster
Blore, *see* Marlborough
Blow, Detmar, *see* p. 30, Berwick St Leonard, Fonthill Gifford, Lacock, Newtown, Upper Woodford and Wilsford
Bodley, *see* Shalbourne
Bodley and Garner, *see* Marlborough
Bohune Common, *see* Manningford Bohun
Bokerly Dyke, *see* p. 50
Bolehyde Manor, *see* Allington (nr Chippenham)
Boleyn, Ann, *see* Great Bedwyn
Bolingbroke family, *see* Lydiard Tregoze
Bonham, Sir Thomas, *see* Great Wishford
Boreham, *see* Warminster
Borenius, Professor, *see* Clarendon
Boulton and Watt, *see* Crofton
Bourne, J. C., *see* pp. 34, 37
Bourne river, *see* Allington (nr Salisbury), Cholderton, Ford (nr Salisbury), Idmiston, Milford, Newton Toney and The Winterbournes
Bouverie, Canon Pleydell, *see* Pewsey
Bowden Hill, *see* Bromham
Bowles, William, *see* Bremhill
Bowood, *see* p. 32

191

Box tunnel, *see* p. 37 and Swindon
Bradfield Farm, *see* Hullavington
Bradford-on-Avon, *see* pp. 24, 34
Bradford Workhouse, *see* Avoncliff
Bradley House, *see* Maiden Bradley
Bratton Down, *see* p. 46 and Brixton Deverill
Bray Street, *see* Avebury
Brettingham, Matthew, *see* Charlton (nr Malmesbury)
Brick, Mr, *see* Draycot Cerne
Bridgman, Sir Orlando, *see* Bowood
Brimslade Farm, *see* Savernake
Britford, *see* p. 16
Britton, John, *see* Kington St Michael
Bromham, *see* p. 20
Bromham House, *see* Bowden Hill
Brooks, James, *see* Marston Meysey
Brown, Capability, *see* Bowood, Corsham, Longford Castle, Longleat and Savernake
Bruce family, *see* Savernake
Brunel, I. K., *see* p. 34 and Box
Brunton, *see* Collingbourne Kingston
Brydges, Sir Richard, *see* Ludgershall
Buckhurst, Lord, *see* Charlton (nr Malmesbury)
Bulbridge House, *see* Wilton
Bulidge Manor, *see* Allington (nr Chippenham)
Bupton, *see* p. 51
Burbage, *see* Great Bedwyn and Wilton
Burcombe, *see* p. 16
Burderop Park, *see* Chiseldon
Burne Jones, E., *see* Bromham, Salisbury and Sopworth
Bush Barrow, *see* p. 44
Bushnell, John, *see* West Dean
Butterfield, *see* p. 24, Amesbury, Ashton Keynes, Baverstock, Blunsdon St Andrew, Bremhill, Broad Blunsdon, Castle Eaton, Chirton, Clyffe Pypard, Foxham, Heytesbury, Highway, Knook, Landford, Latton, Lyneham, Netherhampton, West Harnham, Whiteparish, Winterbourne Monkton
Button, Mr, *see* Avebury
Byron, Robert, *see* p. 24 and Cadley

Cadenham Manor, *see* Foxham
Cadley, *see* Savernake

Calstone Wellington, *see* p. 50
Camden, *see* p. 9 and Stonehenge
Campbell, Colin, *see* Stourhead
Campden Guild, *see* Calne
Caroline, Queen, *see* Charlton (nr Upavon)
Cartwright, *see* Longford Castle
Cartwright, Rev. Edmund, *see* Trowbridge
Castle Hill, *see* Broad Blunsdon
Chalcot House, *see* Dilton
Chambers, Sir William, *see* Wilton
Chancey, William, *see* Charlton (nr Upavon)
Chantrey, *see* Longbridge Deverill
Chapel Plaster, *see* Box
Charles I, *see* p. 30, Maiden Bradley, Marlborough, Westwood and Wilton
Charles II, *see* p. 30, Manningford Bruce, Marlborough, Mere and Ramsbury
Charlton Park, *see* p. 30
Cheere, *see* Longford Castle and Stourhead
Chelsea Hospital, *see* p. 24 and Farley
Cheshire Foundation, *see* Kington Langley
Cheyney Court, *see* Ditteridge
Chilmark stone, *see* p. 20
Chilver Combe Bottom, *see* Donhead St Mary
Chippenham, *see* p. 41
Chisbury, *see* Little Bedwyn
Chiselbury, *see* p. 49
Chisenbury Priory, *see* Enford
Choke, Sir Francis, *see* Shalbourne
Cholderton, *see* p. 24
Christian, Ewan, *see* Market Lavington and Tisbury
Church End Ring, *see* p. 47
Chute, *see* p. 15 and 24
Chute Forest, *see* p. 24
Civil War, *see* Bromham, Devizes, Highworth, Marlborough, Steeple Langford and Wardour
Clacy, J. B., *see* Manningford Bohun
Clarendon, Earl of, *see* Dinton
Clarendon Forest, *see* Alderbury
Clarendon House, *see* p. 24 and Alderbury
Clayton and Bell glass, *see* Aldbourne, Alderbury, Chute, Chute Forest, Manningford Bruce, Marston Meysey, Salisbury, Savernake and Sutton Veny
Clearbury Ring, *see* p. 49
Clouds, *see* East Knoyle

Cluniac priory, *see* Monkton Farleigh
Clutterbuck glass, *see* Cholderton
Clyffe Hall, *see* Market Lavington
Clyffe Pypard, *see* p. 24
Cobbett, William, *see* Norton Bavant
Cockerell, C. R., *see* Bowood
Codford St Peter, *see* p. 16
Cold Kitchen Hill, *see* p. 49
Coleridge, Samuel, *see* All Cannings
Colerne, *see* pp. 16 and 20
Collier, Rev. Joseph, *see* Steeple Langford
Conock, *see* Chirton
Constable, *see* Stonehenge
Cook, Capt., *see* Bishop's Cannings
Coombe Bissett, *see* p. 50
Corsham Court, *see* pp. 29 and 34
Cottingham, Lord, *see* Bishop's Fonthill
Cotswold Bruderhof, *see* Ashton Keynes
Court Leet, *see* Tollard Royal
Coventry, Sir John, *see* Mere
Cowage Farm, *see* Foxley
Cowley, Adelaide, *see* Draycot Cerne
Crabbe, George, *see* Trowbridge
Crace, *see* Longleat
Cranborne Chase, *see* p. 15, Broad Chalke, and Tollard Royal
Cranborne Chase School, *see* Wardour
Crockford memorial, *see* Fonthill Gifford
Cromwell, Oliver, *see* Bishopstrow, Devizes, Littlecote, Marlborough, Odstock and Wardour
Cundy, Thomas, *see* Savernake
Cunetio, *see* p. 50 and Mildenhall

Danby Chapel, *see* Dauntsey
Danvers, Ann, *see* Dauntsey
Danvers family, *see* West Lavington
Darell, William, *see* Littlecote
Daubeny, Charles, *see* North Bradley
Dauntsey family, *see* West Lavington
Dauntsey's School, *see* Little Cheverell, Littleton Pannell, and West Lavington
David of Scotland, *see* Alderbury
Day, Cachemaille, *see* Salisbury
Day House Farm, *see* p. 42
de la Mere, Henry, *see* Winterbourne Gunner

de la Wyle, Bishop Walter, *see* Salisbury
Dean Farm, *see* Oaksey
Devall, John, *see* Clyffe Pypard
Devizes, *see* p. 19
Dial House, *see* West Lavington
Dickens, Charles, *see* Pickwick
"Diocletian" wing, *see* Bowood
Diodorus, *see* Stonehenge
Domesday Book, *see* Chippenham, Luckington and Wilcot
Donatello, *see* Stratford-sub-Castle
Druids, *see* Stonehenge
Dryden, John, *see* Charlton (nr Malmesbury)
Dryden's Warehouse, *see* p. 34
Duck, Stephen, *see* Charlton (nr Upavon)
Dundas aqueduct, *see* p. 34 and Limpley Stoke
Durrington Walls, *see* p. 43

Earle, Miles, *see* Hankerton
Eastcott Manor House, *see* Easterton
Easton Down, *see* Winterslow
Easton Piercy, *see* Kington St Michael
Ebble river, *see* pp. 10, 47, 49, Bishopstone (nr Salisbury), Broad Chalke, Ebbesbourne Wake, Odstock, Stratford Tony
Ecclesiastical Politie, *see* Boscombe
Eden, F. C., *see* Great Somerford
Edington, *see* p. 20
Edward I, *see* Chippenham and Great Bedwyn
Edward III, *see* p. 34 and Alderbury
Edward VII, *see* Hindon
Eliot mill, *see* p. 34
Eliot, T. S., *see* Bemerton
Elizabeth, Queen, *see* p. 30 and Wilton
Ermine Street, *see* Stratton St Margaret
Ernle family, *see* Bishop's Cannings
Ernle, Thomas, *see* Urchfont
Ernle, William, *see* All Cannings
Essay of Dramatic Poetry, see Charlton (nr Malmesbury)
Etchilhampton Hill, *see* Stert
Ethandane, Battle of, *see* Monkton Deverill
Evelyn family, *see* West Dean
Evelyn, John, *see* Durnford
Eyre family, *see* Landford
Eyre's folly, *see* Alderbury

Faerie Queene, see p. 29 and Longford Castle
Farley, *see* p. 24
Farquhar, John, *see* Fonthill Gifford
Faulstone House, *see* Bishopstone (nr Salisbury)
Ferne House, *see* Berwick St John
Ferraby, Parson, *see* Bishop's Cannings
Ferrar, Nicholas, *see* Bemerton
Ferrey, Benjamin, *see* Chilton Foliat and Great Grafton
Fifield Down, *see* p. 45
Finche's farm, *see* Baydon
Fitz House, *see* Teffont Magna
Flaxman, *see* Ashton Keynes and Market Lavington
Flitcroft, *see* Stourhead
Fonthill Park, *see* p. 29 and Bishop's Fonthill
Fort, Alexander, *see* Farley
Fosse Way, *see* Nettleton
Four Quartets, see Bemerton
Fovant, *see* p. 41
Fowler, Charles, *see* Swindon
Fox almshouses, *see* Farley
Fox family, *see* p. 24
Fox, Sir Stephen, *see* Farley
Francis, Rev. Charles, *see* Mildenhall
Francklin, Charles, *see* Westwood
Fraser, Rev. James, *see* Cholderton

Gane, Rev. John, *see* Berwick St John
Ganges, see Trafalgar House
Gaston House, *see* Tisbury
Gawen, Sir John, *see* Alvediston
Gay, John, *see* Amesbury
George, Sir Ernest, *see* Iford
Gibbons, Grinling, *see* Compton Chamberlayne and Stourhead
Gibbs glass, *see* Box, Boyton, Castle Eaton, Heytesbury, Knook, Latton, Lydiard Tregoze, Lyneham, Netherhampton, Semington, Sutton Benger and Wilton
Giffard tombs, *see* Boyton
Gifford family, *see* Sherrington
Gifford Hall, *see* Broughton Gifford
Gilbert, *see* Longbridge Deverill
Girouard, Mark, *see* Longford Castle and Longleat
Gladstone, family, *see* Bowden Hill
Glanville, Colonel, *see* Broad Hinton
Goddard family, *see* Aldbourne, Aldborne Chase and Swindon

Goodridge, H. E., *see* Devizes
Gore Copse, *see* p. 50
Gorge, Sir Thomas, *see* p. 29, Longford Castle, Salisbury and Whiteparish
Greenhill, *see* Westwood
Greenhill, Henry, *see* Stockton
Great Chalfield, *see* p. 24
Great Exhibition, *see* Bradenstoke-cum-Clack
Great Yews Plantation, *see* Odstock
"Grey Wethers", *see* p. 15
Grey, William, *see* Allington (nr Salisbury)
Grims Ditch, *see* Odstock
Grittleton House, *see* Norton
Grobham almshouses, *see* Great Wishford
Grobham, Sir Richard, *see* Great Wishford
Grovely woods, *see* Baverstock and Great Wishford
Gunnora, *see* Winterbourne Gunner
Gwynn, Nell, *see* Salisbury

Hackpen Hill, *see* p. 15, Barbury Camp, Berwick Bassett and Wroughton
Hakewill, J. H., *see* Stert and Sutton Benger
Hall, John, *see* Bradford-on-Avon
Halle, John, *see* Salisbury
Hallstatt period, *see* Allington (nr Devizes)
Ham Hill, *see* p. 51
Hamilton, Lady, *see* Fonthill Gifford
Hanging Langford, *see* p. 47 and Steeple Langford
Hansom, *see* Bradenstoke-cum-Clack
Hardenhuish, *see* p. 24
Hardman glass, *see* Berwick St John, Compton Bassett and Wootton Bassett
Hardwick, P. C., *see* Hartham Park
Hardy, Thomas, *see* p. 46
Harnham Bridge, *see* Salisbury
Harnham Hill, *see* p. 51
Harold, King, *see* Luckington, Monkton Deverill
Harris, *see* Stourhead
Harris, Rev., *see* Mildenhall
Harris's Bacon Factory, *see* p. 37 and Calne
Hartham Park, *see* Corsham
Hastings, Battle of, *see* Stratford Tony
Hatch House, *see* Newtown and Tisbury

Hawkeswell, *see* Little Cheverell
Hawkins, Dr, *see* Stonehenge
Hawtrey's School, *see* Savernake
Hazlebury manor, *see* Box
Hazlitt, *see* Winterslow
Heale House, *see* Upper Woodford
Hearst, *see* Bradenstoke-cum-Clack
Helliker, Thomas, *see* Trowbridge
Henry Esmond, *see* Biddesden
Henry II, *see* Clarendon and Tytherington
Henry III, *see* p. 24, Clarendon, Salisbury and Winterbourne Gunner
Henry VIII, *see* Clarendon, Great Bedwyn and Wilton
Herbert family, *see* p. 30
Herbert, George, *see* Bemerton, Dauntsey and Wilton
Herbert, Sidney, *see* Wilton
Herbert, William, *see* Wilton
Hertford, Earl of, *see* Easton Royal
Heytesbury, *see* p. 42
Hillcot Manor Farmhouse, *see* North Newnton
History and Description of the Great Western Railway, *see* p. 37
Hoare family, *see* Stourhead
Hodson, *see* Chiseldon
Holbein, *see* Wilton
Holiday glass, *see* Salisbury
Holliday, Henry, *see* Upavon
Homer, *see* Stonehenge
Honey Street, *see* p. 34 and Alton Barnes
Hooker, Richard, *see* Boscombe
Horton, Thomas, *see* Westwood
Howard, Robert, *see* Charlton (nr Malmesbury)
Howe, George, *see* Berwick St Leonard
Howe School, *see* Great Wishford
Howe, Sir Richard, *see* Great Wishford
Hugall, J. W., *see* Figheldean
Hughes, H., *see* Bishopstrow
Hungerford Almshouses and School, *see* Corsham
Hungerford Chapel, *see* Chippenham and Salisbury
Hungerford, George, *see* Bremhill
Hungerford, Lords, *see* Heytesbury
Hurdcott House, *see* Barford St Martin
Hussey's Almshouses, *see* Salisbury
Hyde House, *see* Dinton

Iford Manor, *see* p. 34
Inglesham, *see* pp. 16 and 20
Island House, *see* Wilton
Ivychurch, *see* Alderbury

James I, *see* Bishop's Cannings
Jane Seymour, *see* Burbage
Jefferies, Richard, *see* Barbury Camp and Coate
Jenner's School, Robert, *see* Cricklade
Jervoise, G. P., *see* Britford
John, King, *see* Aldborne Chase, Clatford, Preshute and Tollard Royal
John of France, *see* Alderbury
John of Gaunt, *see* Aldborne Chase
Jones, Inigo, *see* pp. 29, 30, Amesbury, Bishop's Fonthill, Bradford-on-Avon, Fonthill Gifford, Stonehenge and Wilton
Jones, Sir William, *see* Ramsbury
Jonson, Ben, *see* p. 30 and Wilton

Kauffman, Angelica, *see* Stourhead
Keene, Henry, *see* Bowood
Keevil, *see* p. 30
Keiller, Alexander, *see* Avebury
Kelmscott, *see* p. 24
Kempe glass, *see* Baydon, Erlestoke, Latton, Little Hinton, Lydiard Millicent, Marston Meysey, Pitton, Shalbourne and Sutton Veny
Kennet and Avon Canal, *see* p. 34, Alton Barnes, Avoncliff, Crofton, Horton, Limpley Stoke, Savernake, Whaddon, Wilcot and Wootton Rivers
Kennet Avenue, *see* Avebury
Kennet river, *see* p. 10, Axford, Chilton Foliat, Fyfield (nr Marlborough) and Ramsbury
Kettlewell, J. and M., *see* Marden
Keynell family, *see* Yatton Keynell
Kilvert, Francis, *see* Hardenhuish and Langley Burrell
King John's House, *see* p. 24 and Tollard Royal
Kingsbury Square, *see* Wilton
Kingsettle Hill, *see* Stourhead
Kingsway House, *see* Wilton
Kipling, Rudyard, *see* Tisbury
Knap Hill, *see* p. 42 and Alton Priors
Knights Hospitallers, *see* Ansty
Knook, *see* pp. 16 and 45
Knowle Farm, *see* p. 41

Knyvett, Sir Henry, *see* Charlton (nr Malmesbury)

Lacock, *see* pp. 20, 24
Lacock Abbey, *see* p. 24
Lake, *see* Wilsford (nr Amesbury)
Lake House, *see* p. 30 and Wilsford (nr Amesbury)
Lake Downs, *see* pp. 42 and 45
Lamb, Charles and Mary, *see* Bremhill and Winterslow
Lanhill, *see* p. 42
Lansdowne, Marquis of, *see* Bowood and Kellaways
Lansdowne memorial, *see* Cherhill
Larmer Grounds, *see* Tollard Royal
Latimer, Bishop, *see* West Kington
Lavers and Barraud glass, *see* Great Somerford and All Cannings
Lawes, William, *see* Dinton
Leigh Delamere, *see* p. 24
Leland, *see* Malmesbury and Trowbridge
Leonardo's *Last Supper*, *see* All Cannings
Lewisham Castle, *see* Aldbourne
Ley, Henry, *see* Swindon
Lisle, Lady, *see* Holt
Little Gidding, *see* Bemerton
Littlecote, *see* p. 29
Long Dean, *see* Yatton Keynell
Long family, *see* North Bradley, South Wraxall and Whaddon
Long, James, *see* Stert
Long, Robert, *see* Steeple Ashton
Long, Walter, *see* West Ashton
Longbridge Deverill, *see* p. 47
Longford Castle, *see* p. 29, Alderbury, Salisbury and Whiteparish
Longford Park, *see* Bodenham
Longleat House, *see* p. 29 and Longbridge Deverill
Longleat Park, *see* Hornsingham
Louis the Dauphin, *see* Aldbourne
Lucas, Walter, *see* Steeple Ashton
Ludgershall, *see* p. 24
Ludlow, Edmund, *see* Maiden Bradley
Ludlow family, *see* Hill Deverill
Lugbury, *see* p. 42 and Nettleton
Lydiard Tregoze, *see* p. 24
Lynches, *see* Whiteparish
Lyte almshouses, *see* Kington St Michael
Lyttleton, *see* Trowbridge

Malmesbury, *see* pp. 16–19

194

Malmesbury House, *see* Salisbury
Mancombe Down, *see* p. 47
Manners and Gill, *see* Kingston Deverill
Manningford Bruce, *see* p. 19
Mansells House, *see* Minety
Marcus Aurelius, *see* Wilton
Marden Circle, *see* p. 43 and Marden
Marlborough Castle, *see* Preshute
Marlborough College, *see* Marlborough
Marlborough, Duke of, *see* Biddesden
Marlborough Downs, *see* pp. 10, 42, 45, Alton Barnes, Beckhampton, Berwick Bassett, Bower Chalke, Charlton (nr Upavon), Cherhill, Easterton, Edington, Fovant, Fyfield (nr Marlborough), Heddington, Homington, Huish, Kingston Deverill, The Ogbournes, Rockley, Shalbourne, Stonehenge, Sutton Mandeville and Wanborough
Marlborough Museum, *see* Barbury Camp
Marlowe, Christopher, *see* Wilton
Marshwood House, *see* Dinton
Martin, A. C., *see* Little Cheverell
Martin Chuzzlewit, *see* Alderbury
Massinger, *see* p. 30
Maud Heath's Causeway, *see* Kellaways
Maud, Queen, *see* Tytherington
Maurice, Miss, *see* Great Chalfield
Mawarden Court, *see* Stratford-sub-Castle
Methuen Chapel, *see* North Wraxall
Methuen family, *see* pp. 29, 34, All Cannings and Corsham
Methuen, Paul, *see* North Wraxall
Middle Ages, *see* p. 19
Middle Hill, *see* pp. 46, 50 and Ditteridge
Midway Manor, *see* Wingfield
Mildenhall, *see* p. 24
Mill House, *see* West Harnham
Miller, Sanderson, *see* Lacock
Milton, John, *see* Dinton
Mison, John and Elizabeth, *see* Lower Wraxall
Moffatt, *see* Swallowcliffe
Mompesson House, *see* p. 32 and Salisbury
Mompesson, John, *see* Codford St Mary
Monasteries, Dissolution of, *see* Amesbury

Monks Conduit, *see* Monkton Farleigh
Monkton House, *see* Broughton Gifford
Montgomery, Rev. G. A., *see* Bishopstone (nr Salisbury)
Moor Green, *see* Corsham
Moore, J. F., *see* Ramsbury
Moore, Tom, *see* Bremhill and Bromham
Moravian brethren, *see* East Tytherton
Morgan's Hill, *see* p. 50
Morris, Roger, *see* Trafalgar House and Wilton
Morris, William, *see* p. 24, Allington (nr Salisbury), Inglesham, Rodbourne and Sopworth
Morrison, Hugh, M.P., *see* Berwick St Leonard
Mozley, T., *see* Allington (nr Salisbury) and Cholderton
Mycenae, *see* p. 44 and Stonehenge

Nadder river, *see* pp. 10, 49, Baverstock, Burcombe, Donhead St Mary and Quidhampton
Nash, John, *see* Corsham
National Trust, *see* Alderbury, Avebury, Bowden Hill, Dinton, Great Chalfield, Holt, Lacock, Salisbury, Stourhead, Tollard Royal and Westwood
Neale Chapel, *see* Great Chalfield
Neeld estate, *see* Sevington
Neeld, Joseph, *see* Alderton, Grittleton and Leigh Delamere
Nelson, Lord, *see* Fonthill Gifford and Trafalgar House
Neston, *see* Corsham
Newall, Professor, *see* Stonehenge
Newman, *see* p. 24
Newton, Sir Isaac, *see* Baydon
Newton, W. G., *see* Marlborough
New College, Oxford, *see* Berwick St John and Edington
Nicholas, Charlotte, *see* Ashton Keynes
Nicholas, Mary, *see* Manningford Bruce
Nollekens, *see* Hankerton
Nonsuch House, *see* Bromham
Normanton Down, *see* p. 44
Norrington Manor, *see* Alvediston
Northumberland, Duke of, *see* Cricklade
Norwood Castle, *see* Oaksey

O'Connor glass, *see* Alderton,
Cholderton, Savernake, Tidcombe, and Wilton
Og valley, *see* The Ogbournes
Ogbury, *see* p. 46
Old Basing, *see* Cholderton
Old Court, *see* Avoncliff
Old Ditton, *see* p. 24
Oldbury Castle, *see* p. 47
Oliver's Castle, *see* p. 46
Orcheston St Mary, *see* p. 24
Overton Down, *see* Barbury Camp
Ox Drove ridgeway, *see* p. 49

Paine, James, *see* Amesbury and Wardour
Paine and Soane, *see* p. 24
Palmer, Samuel, *see* Potterne
Pearson, J. L., *see* pp. 19, 24, Charlton (nr Upavon), Chute, Chute Forest, Manningford Bruce, Milton Lilbourne, Porton, Sutton Veny
Pembroke family, *see* Bemerton and Wilton
Penruddocke family, *see* Compton Chamberlayne
Penruddocke Rebellion, *see* Steeple Langford
Pepper Box, the, *see* Alderbury
Pepys, Samuel, *see* Salisbury
Pertwood Down, *see* p. 45
Petersfinger, *see* p. 51
Peto, Harold, *see* Iford
Petty, Sir William, *see* Cherhill
Pewsey, *see* Alderbury
Pewsey, Vale of, *see* pp. 11, 43, Alton Barnes, Beechingstoke, Chirton, Patney, Rushall, Stanton St Bernard
Pevsner, Dr, *see* Edington
Philipps House, *see* Dinton
Phipps, William, *see* Westbury
Pickwick, *see* Corsham
Pierrepont, Robert, *see* West Dean
Pile family, *see* Collingbourne Kingston
Pitt family, *see* Stratford-sub-Castle
Pitt-Rivers, General, *see* Berwick St John and Tollard Royal
Pliny, *see* Stonehenge
Ponting, E. C., *see* p. 24, Bemerton, Ford (nr Chippenham), Holt, Leigh, Redlynch, Shaw, Southwick, Stanton St Quintin and West Overton
Pontle, *see* Ramsbury
Poore, Bishop, *see* Salisbury
Pop art, *see* Bushton
Popham memorials, *see* Chilton Foliat

195

Portmeirion, *see* Oare
Portway House, *see* Warminster
Poulton House, *see* Marlborough
Powell glass, *see* Burbage, Figheldean, Fosbury and Urchfont
Poticary, Jerome, *see* Stockton
Potterne, *see* p. 20
Poynder Estate, *see* Hilmarton
prehistoric remains, *see* p. 41 et seq., Allington (nr Devizes), Alton Priors, Avebury, Barbury Camp, Berwick St John, Bishopstrow, Bratton, Broad Blunsdon, East Kennett, Liddington, Marden, Nettleton, Sarum – Old Sarum, Stonehenge and Winterslow
Prescelly mountains, *see* p. 43 and Stonehenge
Prynne, Sir Gilbert, *see* Allington (nr Chippenham)
Pugin, *see* Alderbury, Bishopstone (nr Salisbury) and Salisbury
Pyt House, *see* Newtown and Tisbury

Queensberry, Duchess of, *see* Amesbury

Radnor, Earl of, *see* Longford Castle and Salisbury
Rainscombe House, *see* Oare
Ramsbury, *see* pp. 16, 30–2
Reddish House, *see* Broad Chalke
Reminiscences Chiefly of Oriel College and the Oxford Movement, *see* Cholderton
Reminiscences of Towns, Villages and Schools, *see* Allington (nr Salisbury)
Rennie, John, *see* p. 34, Avoncliff, Limpley Stoke and Wilcot
Repton, Humphrey, *see* Bowood, Corsham and Longleat
Return of the Native, *see* p. 46
Revett, Nicholas, *see* Trafalgar House
Ricardo, David, *see* Hardenhuish
Richmond, George, *see* Potterne
Ridgeway, Great, *see* p. 49
Riding School, *see* Wilton
Rivar Hill, *see* p. 51
Robin Hood's Ball, *see* p. 42
Robinson, P. F., *see* Little Langford
Roche Court Down, *see* Winterslow
Rochester, Earl of, *see* Wootton Bassett
Roger, Bishop, *see* Sarum – Old Sarum
Roman remains, *see* pp. 45, 46, 47, 49, 50, Amesbury, Atworth, Cricklade, Great Bedwyn, Mere, Mildenhall, Nettleton, Sarum – Old Sarum, Stanton St Quintin and Stonehenge
Rood Ashton, *see* West Ashton
"rotten boroughs", *see* Great Bedwyn, Heytesbury, Hindon, Sarum – Old Sarum
Roundway Down, *see* p. 50
Rowdeford House, *see* Rowde
Royal Dockyard, Devonport, *see* Stockton
Royal Wilton Factory, *see* Wilton
Rybury Hill, *see* p. 42 and Allington (nr Devizes)
Rysbrack, *see* Alvediston, Longford Castle, Lydiard Tregoze, Maiden Bradley and Stourhead
Rudloe Manor, *see* Box
Rushmore, *see* Tollard Royal
Rutter, *see* p. 29

Saintsbury, Thomas, *see* Market Lavington
Salisbury Canal, *see* p. 34
Salisbury Cathedral, *see* pp. 20, 29, Alderbury, Ansty, Chilmark, Laverstock, Malmesbury, Warminster and Whiteparish
Salisbury Plain, *see* p. 11, Amesbury, Berwick St James, Bishopstrow, Rollestone, Winterbourne Stoke
Salvin, Anthony, *see* Longford Castle
Sarobyrig, *see* Sarum – Old Sarum
Sarsen stones, *see* pp. 15, 42
Sarum, Old, *see* p. 47
Savernake Forest, *see* Cadley
Saxon remains, *see* p. 47, Cricklade, Downton, Great Bedwyn, Sarum – Old Sarum, and Winterslow
Scheemakers, Peter, *see* Broad Blunsdon, Downton and Urchfont
Scott, Sir Gilbert, *see* Mere, Salisbury, Swallowcliffe, Swindon and Zeals
Scratchbury Fort, *see* p. 46 and Bishopstrow
Scudamore Chantry, *see* Upton Scudamore
Sculpture in Britain 1530–1830, *see* West Dean
Seddon, *see* Upavon
Sederbach, *see* Lacock
Sedley, Sir Charles, *see* Charlton (nr Malmesbury)

Seymour, Edward, *see* Amesbury and Maiden Bradley
Seymour, Jane and family, *see* Burbage, Great Bedwyn and Savernake
Shaftesbury Abbey, *see* Tisbury
Shakespeare, *see* p. 30 and Wilton
Shambles, The, *see* Chippenham
Sharington, Sir William, *see* Bowden Hill and Lacock
Shelburne, Earl of, *see* Bowood
Shrapnel, General, *see* Wingfield
Sidney, Sir Philip, *see* p. 30 and Wilton
Silbury Hill, *see* p. 44, Avebury and Beckhampton
Skidmore, *see* Salisbury
Skull House, *see* p. 16
Slater and Carpenter, *see* Devizes and Hannington
Sloperton Cottage, *see* Bromham
Smith, Campbell, *see* Atworth
Smith, Joshua, *see* Erlestoke
Smith, Mrs Mary Goddard, *see* Tockenham
Smith, Sidney, *see* Netheravon
Smythson, Robert, *see* Bradford-on-Avon and Longleat
Soane, Sir John, *see* Wardour
Somerset, Duchess of, *see* Froxfield
Somerset, Duke of, *see* Amesbury and Marlborough
Somerset Hospital, *see* Froxfield
Sorviodunum, *see* Sarum – Old Sarum
South Wraxhall, *see* p. 24
Spackman, Thomas, *see* Clyffe Pypard
Spenser, Edmund, *see* pp. 29, 30, Longford Castle and Wilton
Spratt, Jack, *see* Wootton Rivers
Spye Park, *see* Bowden Hill, Bromham and Chittoe
St Aldhelm, *see* p. 15 and Bishopstrow
St John family, *see* Lydiard Tregoze
St Marie's Grange, *see* Alderbury
Stael, Mme de, *see* Bremhill
Stafford, Emma, *see* North Bradley
Stafford, John, *see* North Bradley
Standen House, *see* Chute
Standlynch, *see* Trafalgar House
Stanley, W. H., *see* Corsley
Steeple Ashton, *see* p. 20
Stephen, King, *see* Alderbury, Sarum – Old Sarum
Stokes, John, *see* Seend
Stone, John, *see* Aldbourne

Stonehenge, *see* pp. 11, 15, 42, 43 and 44
Stonor Park, *see* p. 29
Stourhead, *see* pp. 15 and 34
Stourton, *see* Stourhead
Stowell Park, *see* Wilcot
Stowford, *see* p. 34 and Wingfield
Street, G. E., *see* p. 24, Chapmanslade, Corsham, Erlestoke, Great Bedwyn, Hilmarton, Marlborough, Pewsey, Warminster, Wootton Bassett, Wootton Rivers, Yatton Keynell
Stukeley, *see* p. 43, Amesbury and Stonehenge
Suffolk memorials, *see* Charlton (nr Malmesbury)
Suger, Abbot, *see* p. 20
Summerson, Sir John, *see* Bradford-on-Avon
Sumsion, Thomas, *see* Sherston
Sutton Veny, *see* p. 24
Swindon Corporation, *see* Lydiard Tregoze
Syrencot House, *see* Figheldean

Talbot family, *see* Lacock
Talbot, W. H. Fox, *see* Lacock
Tallboys, *see* Keevil
Tan Hill, *see* pp. 10 and 50
Tapley, Mark, *see* Alderbury
Taylor, Sir Robert, *see* Chute Forest, Salisbury and Westbury
Tellisford, *see* p. 34
Teulon, S. S., *see* Alderbury, Fosbury and Oare
Thackeray, W. M., *see* Biddesden and Rodbourne
Thames, the, *see* p. 11, Ashton Keynes and Latton
Thames and Severn Canal, *see* p. 34, Latton, Marston Meysey
Thompson, James, *see* Leigh Delamere
Thorn Hill, *see* p. 42
Thorpe, John, *see* p. 29
Throope Manor, *see* Bishopstone (nr Salisbury)
Thynne almshouses, *see* Longbridge Deverill
Thynne family, *see* Corsham, Horsingham, Longbridge Deverill and Longleat
Tidcombe, *see* p. 15
Till river, *see* Shrewton
Tilshead, *see* pp. 42 and 45
Tisbury, *see* p. 24
Tocotes, Sir Roger, *see* Bromham
Tollard Royal, *see* p. 24
Toni, Ralph, *see* Stratford Tony
Tooker family, *see* East Kennett

Topp Almshouses, *see* Stockton
Topp, John, *see* Stockton
Tosny family, *see* Newton Toney
Tothill, Robert, *see* Urchfont
Tottenham House, *see* Savernake
Townsend, James, *see* Great Cheverell
Townson's Dr Almshouses, *see* Calne
Trafalgar House, *see* p. 34 and Standlynch
Travers, Martin, *see* Cricklade
Trenchard family, *see* North Bradley
Tresham, Sir Thomas, *see* Longford Castle
Trollope, Anthony, *see* East Harnham and Salisbury
Tropenell, Thomas, *see* Great Chalfield
Trusloe Manor, *see* Avebury
Turner, *see* Stonehenge
Tytherington, *see* Heytesbury

Upham House, *see* Aldborne Chase
Uplands, *see* Turleigh
Upper Upham, *see* Aldborne Chase
Upper Westwood, *see* Westwood
Usher's Brewery, *see* Trowbridge

van Gelder, *see* Ramsbury
Vathek, *see* Fonthill Gifford
Verey, David, *see* North Tidworth
Verlucio, *see* p. 50
Vespasian, *see* p. 50
Vespasian's Camp, *see* Amesbury
Vicar's Cottages, *see* Tisbury
Vicar's Poorhouse, *see* North Bradley

Wailes glass, *see* Wilton
Waleran, *see* Stapleford
Walker's Hill, *see* p. 42 and Alton Barnes
Walker, William, *see* Charlton (nr Shaftesbury)
Walrond, William and Edward, *see* Aldbourne
Walton family, *see* Boscombe
Walton, Izaak, *see* Boscombe and Wilton
Wansdyke, *see* pp. 47 and 50
Ward glass, *see* p. 20
Warden, The, *see* East Harnham and Salisbury
Wardour Castle, *see* p. 24 and 34
Warneford Place, *see* Sevenhampton
Warneford, Sub. Lieut., *see* Highworth

Water Dean Bottom, *see* p. 45
Warrington, William, *see* Oaksey
Watts, G. F., *see* Foxley
Washern Grange, *see* Wilton
Washington family, *see* Garsdon
Washington, George, *see* Garsdon
Webb, *see* p. 30
Webb, Christopher, *see* Nunton
Webb, General, *see* Biddesden
Webb, John, *see* Amesbury, Ramsbury and Wilton
Webb, Philip, *see* East Knoyle
Webb, Sir Aston, *see* Marlborough
Weeks, John, *see* Brinkworth
West Dean, *see* pp. 15 and 24
West Kennet, *see* p. 42
Westbrook Farmhouse, *see* Avebury
Westbury White Horse, *see* Bratton and North Bradley
Westinghouse Brake Co., *see* p. 37 and Chippenham
Westmacott, *see* North Wraxall, Nunton and Whaddon
Westminster family, *see* Fonthill Gifford, Hindon and Semly
Westwood, *see* p. 24
Weymouth, Lord, *see* Warminster
Whinney, Margaret, *see* West Dean
Whitesheet Hill, *see* pp. 42 and 49
Wilbury House, *see* Newton Toney
William I, *see* Stapleford and Stratford Tony
William III, *see* Berwick St Leonard
William of Malmesbury, *see* pp. 15–16
Williams, Alfred, *see* Barbury Camp
Williams-Ellis, Clough, *see* Oare
Wilton, *see* pp. 20, 30, Netherhampton and Wylye
Wilton carpets, *see* p. 37
Wilton Estate, *see* Quidhampton
Wiltshire and Berkshire Canal, *see* p. 34
Wiltshire Moonrakers, *see* Bishop's Cannings
Wilson, H., *see* West Ashton
Win Green Hill, *see* p. 49 and Tollard Royal
Winchester, Bishop of, *see* Edington
Winchester Cathedral, *see* Bishopstone (nr Salisbury)
Windmill Hill, *see* pp. 41, 42
Winklebury Hill, *see* p. 47 and Berwick St John

Winterbourne Bassett, *see* pp. 15 and 42
Winterbourne Stoke, *see* pp. 42 and 45
Woden's Dyke, *see* Wansdyke
Wolf Hall, *see* Burbage and Savernake
Wolsey, Cardinal, *see* Marlborough
Wood, Christopher, *see* Broad Chalke
Woodhenge, *see* p. 43 and Durrington
Woods, the John, *see* pp. 24, 34, Hardenhuish and Trafalgar House
Woodyer, Henry, *see* Berwick St John and Compton Bassett
Woolstore, *see* Codford St Peter
Worcester, Battle of, *see* Mere
Wordsworth, *see* Bremhill
Works, Ministry of, *see* p. 42, Stonehenge and Wardour
Wren family, *see* p. 24, Bishop's Fonthill, East Knoyle and Farley
Wroughton, Sir Thomas, *see* Broad Chalke
Wyatt, Benjamin, *see* Devizes
Wyatt, James, *see* Alderbury, Bowden Hill, Corsham, Hartham Park, Salisbury and Wilton
Wyatt, Sir Matthew Digby, *see* Rowde
Wyatt, T. H., *see* p. 24, Alvediston, Bemerton, Berwick Bassett, Bishop's Fonthill, Bower Chalke, Boyton, Burbage, Burcombe, Cadley, Charlton (nr Salisbury), Chitterne, Chittoe, Cholderton, Codford St Mary, Codford St Peter, Crockerton, Dilton Marsh, East Harnham, Fonthill Gifford, Fovant, Great Wishford, Hilperton, Hindon, Laverstock, Little Langford, Littleton Drew, Marlborough, Melksham, Middle Woodford, Monkton Deverill, Monkton Farleigh, North Bradley, Nunton, Preshute, Salisbury, Savernake, Semly, Shaw, Shrewton, South Newton, Upavon, Wilsford (nr Amesbury), Wilton and Winterbourne Earls
Wyatt and Brandon, *see* p. 24, Newton Toney and West Ashton
Wyatville, Sir Jeffrey, *see* Dinton, Longleat and West Ashton
Wyndham family, *see* Alvediston, East Knoyle and Salisbury
Wylye river, *see* p. 10, Corton, Knook, Longbridge Deverill, Monkton Deverill, South Newton and Steeple Longford

Yarnbury hill fort, *see* p. 46
Yarnbury Grange, *see* Steeple Langford
Young, John, *see* Draycot Cerne

To Mr. M. J. Moriarty
For you to select
the book of your choice

From the Justices'
Clerks' Society

September 1978